KALECKI AND UNEMPLOYMENT EQUILIBRIUM

Also by Mario Sebastiani

KALECKI'S RELEVANCE TODAY (*editor*)

THE NOTION OF EQUILIBRIUM IN THE KEYNESIAN THEORY (*editor*)

Kalecki and Unemployment Equilibrium

Mario Sebastiani
Professor of Economics
University of Rome 'Tor Vergata', Italy

M

St. Martin's Press

First published in Great Britain 1994 by
THE MACMILLAN PRESS LTD
Houndmills, Basingstoke, Hampshire RG21 2XS
and London
Companies and representatives
throughout the world

A catalogue record for this book is available
from the British Library.

ISBN 0–333–53464–6

Printed in Great Britain by
Antony Rowe Ltd
Chippenham, Wiltshire

First published in the United States of America 1994 by
Scholarly and Reference Division,
ST. MARTIN'S PRESS, INC.,
175 Fifth Avenue,
New York, N.Y. 10010

ISBN 0–312–10585–1

Library of Congress Cataloging-in-Publication Data
Sebastiani, Mario.
Kalecki and unemployment equilibrium / Mario Sebastiani.
p. cm.
Includes bibliographical references and index.
ISBN 0–312–10585–1
1. Employment (Economic theory) 2. Equilibrium (Economics)
3. Kalecki, Michał. 4. Keynesian economics. I. Title.
HD5701.5.S43 1994
331. 12'5—dc20 93–5865
CIP

Contents

Introduction

Michal Kalecki's *oeuvre* evinces a rare versatility, ranging from analysis of capitalist economies to analysis of socialist societies, from problems of development of backward areas to questions arising from the war economy. Its notoriety within western circles, however, derives chiefly from studies concerning mature capitalism.

This may be explained by the particular field of interest of western economic theory and the fact that it is precisely on these themes that Kalecki attained the most important and definite results. However, knowledge of Kalecki's work, in relation to the capitalist economy also, is far from being satisfactory as it is largely neglected by most scholars, while is often approached by others with rather tiresome apologetic emphasis, or with regard to specific aspects only.

In recent years, increasing interest in Kalecki's work has been evidenced by a number of comprehensive studies (from Feiwel, 1975, to Sawyer, 1985) and by the publication in English of the collected works (Kalecki, 1991). Unfortunately, the rediscovery came too late (or too early), at the height of the success of the so-called 'mainstream economics', once again confining the debate to a narrow circle of 'heretics'.

Yet, the persisting supremacy of 'mainstream economics' in economic theory and policy makes a return to the great tradition of the 'high theory', from Marx to Schumpeter, and then to Keynes, of which Kalecki can be regarded as an exponent, even more necessary.

Against this backround, this book (which is a revised version of a earlier volume published in Italy (Sebastiani, 1985)) aims at systematising Kalecki's thought, with special focus on unemployment equilibrium. Not all of Kalecki's reflections on capitalism (which focus for an important and perhaps better-known part on dynamics) are covered, but the book traces what appears as the most innovative core of his theory and its most controversial aspects.

The emphasis on the notion of unemployment equilibrium, far from underlining static aspects as compared with dynamics, is bound to single out the building blocks of the author's work. The distinction between equilibrium analysis and dynamics is a methodological device allowing Kalecki to consider the short and the long period separately, while nothing static is involved in his notion of equilibrium.

For too long Kalecki has been regarded as primarily concerned with business cycles, or as an author of a theory of capitalist development. This view is strongly reductive and prevents a proper appraisal of Kalecki's contribution; indeed, while his theory of the business cycle is 'rather mechanistic' (by the author's own admission), his theory of capitalist development does not appear really innovative as regards vision (drawn from Marx), and it is seriously unsatisfactory as regards analytical structure. As we shall argue, a fair evaluation of Kalecki's thought is that he conceived a very interesting *theory* of unemployment equilibrium, within a *vision* of the dynamics of capitalist economy which he failed to convert into a fully developed theoretical scheme.

Many reasons account for the scant attention given to Kalecki's analysis of unemployment equilibria. Among these, the first is Kalecki's treatment of unemployment equilibrium *together with* the business cycle, which has led many interpreters to focus on the latter alone. A second is that when Kalecki's work began to be known, the theory of unemployment equilibrium was indisputably associated with Keynes and Kalecki's contribution was consequently considered lacking in innovation.

Our purpose here is to demonstrate that the above appraisals are based on unfair or hasty interpretation. It will be argued that the notion of unemployment equilibrium is the core of Kalecki's thought about capitalism and the synthesis in which the theory of effective demand and investment, the theory of prices and money, and the theory of economic policy find their proper standing. We will try to argue that this aspect more than any other permits us to trace the relationships and divergences between Kaleckian theory and other approaches of economic thought.

With this premise in mind, we will systematically analyse the maturation of Kalecki's thought over forty years on questions relating to the concept of unemployment equilibrium, the theoretical roots and the relationships with other contemporary approaches, the controversies it raised, and the developments it underwent or those it promoted. The book is structured to satisfy these multiple purposes, so that the reconstruction of the evolution of Kalecki's work is mingled with considerations regarding other economic theories, first and foremost the Keynesian theory, which represents the most obvious, but also the most valid, reference for analysing Kaleckian thought.

Part I is accordingly devoted to an analysis of Kalecki's thought on unemployment equilibrium, its theoretical roots and its development over time, its shortcomings and its insight as regards contemporary capitalism. To avoid interrupting the main thread of reflection, several specific topics related to the history of economic thought, which call for closer investigation on account of their relevance in interpreting the origin of Kalecki's theory or the room they received within the economic debate, are considered separately in Part II.

The author is greatly indebted to F. Caffé and A. Vercelli for reading earlier versions of the book, and to G. Calzoni, O. Capponi, G. Caravale, A. Chilosi, J. Kregel, M. Matteuzzi and A. Rosselli for comments on specific aspects. Gratitude is especially due to M.D'Antonio, whose comments helped me to focus my understanding of several points.

Part I

The Theory of Unemployment Equilibrium

1 General Aspects

1.1 INTRODUCTORY REMARKS

The great economic and social problems of the 1930s were accompanied by equally great ferments in economic theory and policy. This is hardly surprising considering that circumstances have always played a dominant role throughout history in stimulating the progress of knowledge.

Unlike logical linear schemes – where careful interpretation of the problems leads to the setting up of policy devices – in the thirties the *policy* anticipated the *theory* owing to pressing economic difficulties and the impatience of public opinion. Although the measures undertaken in the thirties by countries with democratic regimes were influenced by liberal English thought (*in primis*, by Keynes), they were nevertheless implemented in a substantially theoretical vacuum, spurred on by 'the flair and the instinct' which Keynes himself hastened to yield[1] in the absence of sounder arguments.[2]

Keynes was the best known author but not the only one to advocate this line, emphasising the search for rigorous explanations but also relying on good sense in the face of the urgency of the problems and the manifest inadequacy of the orthodox solutions. At the same time other economists were also developing approaches to effective demand, namely Kalecki and those adhering to the Stockholm School. Although they were inspired by theoretical traditions based on quite separate ideologies and historical realities, they nevertheless shared scepticism about the automatisms of the market and the search for theoretical foundations of public intervention.

The purpose of this chapter is to outline the distinctive features of these three approaches to the theory of effective demand and how they inspired economic policy proposals that are usually related but are only superficially similar, i.e., similar with respect to the realities of those years, but different in their interpretation of unemployment and their basic outlooks.

The ground for comparing these approaches is not the conviction that unemployment is a problem that has to be actively faced. This conviction, common to all three,[3] was also accepted by conservative circles, notably by Pigou who supported it as early as 1912;[4] not even the 'Treasury view', which considered measures for favouring employment ephemeral, led to any concrete opposition, recognising at least their immediate efficacy as well as their opportunity from the political and social angle.

However, a motive for discord, then as now, concerned the nature of unemployment, and precisely whether it represented a phenomenon of crisis – i.e., related to contingent, though recurring factors – or a permanent, chronic phenomenon prompted by general, systematic and persistent causes; and, again, whether these causes derived from the failure to comply with the rules of the free market, or whether these very rules were at the root of the problem. From the interpretation of this phenomenon came the need to set up a *general* theory of unemployment or a theory of cyclical depressions and, consequently, the need to devise political economy proposals for intervening systematically and continually or just for making recovery easier.

It is along these lines that it is worth comparing the innovative import of the Keynesian, Kaleckian and Swedish approaches to the theory of employment through an analysis of the following aspects: (a) the interpretation of unemployment as a permanent condition or, alternatively, as a crisis phenomenon, and its causes; (b) the elaboration of general or, alternatively, cycle theories; (c) the statement of political economy proposals in agreement with the above, designed to correct or, on the contrary, to restore the *natural* working of market forces.

This introductory chapter concerns an analysis of the theories of Keynes and Kalecki, and only incidentally of the Stockholm School. By treating Keynes and Kalecki together for the general part, some current aspects of the debate on Keynes, which are also important in relation to Kalecki, can be reviewed. The Stockholm School, which dealt less directly with the theory of aggregate income and which, until not long ago, was kept out of the Keynesian controversy, will be discussed in Part II. Finally, we will be primarily concerned here with Keynesian thought; our concern for Kalecki will be limited to anticipating the aspects necessary for developing a comparison with Keynes.

Another important point that should be considered now is why Keynes's ideas were so much more widespread and debated than those of his 'competitors'.

It has been emphasised that in Keynes's favour were his vast celebrity, his academic status inside the citadel and relations with the outstanding circles of the time, and his brilliance in spreading his ideas. Taken together these circumstances would have provided Keynes with a formidable sounding board which effectively covered voices coming from other directions.

There are, however, additional reasons explaining the muted response, at least in the beginning, to Kalecki's work and to that of the Swedish economists. In the first place, the fact that Kalecki approached underemployment equilibrium together with economic fluctuations certainly weakened perception of the innovative input of his ideas;[5] similar considerations apply to the Swedish economists who were interested in studying the fluctuations of prices and quantities jointly.[6] To this should be added the fact that the organic arrangement of Kaleckian thought was worked out twenty years after his early works on employment, so that the *Theory of Economic Dynamics* (1954) appeared at the height of the Keynesian era; similarly the contributions from Sweden became known in Anglo–Saxon circles by virtue of the controversy between Ohlin and Keynes over the *General Theory*. It was therefore natural to place these contributions among those intended to develop variants in Keynes's original themes.

Some further brief considerations stem from the observation that the interest raised by new ideas depends on the perception of their novelty together with their pervasiveness; this in turn is directly proportionate to the capacity of these ideas – while reforming or even revolutionising the way of looking at certain problems – to maintain solid ties with the *milieu*, using a common language and being grounded in a common vision of reality. In other words, the innovation must be visible but must not challenge convictions and affinities that go beyond the strict scope of the theory. Since one's view represents an element which is prior to economic analysis, the debate arises mostly over approaches finding ground for convergence in a common view; indeed, among the many reasons for embarking on a debate, the most important ones – competition between ideas, the search for affinities, the effort to come to an integration – often presuppose uniform premises of value.

Throughout the *General Theory*, Keynes more or less consciously combined continuity and struggle with neoclassical orthodoxy; accordingly, he joined the rebuttal of Say's law with an otherwise reassuring theoretical framework, the belief in the allocative efficiency of the market and, above all, the acceptance of the capitalistic organisation as such. Probably not by chance, this work marked a regression in the conservative sense compared to previous writings, but it was for this very reason that Keynes's ideas perhaps gained the maximum pervasiveness together with the maximum break with tradition he could achieve subject to the constraints imposed by the first objective.[7] Indeed, even if the missing solution of important aspects left him open to attempts to reabsorb his thought in the traditional theory, the immediate effect was to facilitate the spreading of his ideas. In substance, Keynes was one of the 'family', an economist with whom it was worth debating (given the common ideological ground) and with whom, obviously, one had to confront.

These conditions do not apply to Kalecki, whose research was marked by the criticism of capitalism as such. By ascribing the main cause of unemployment and instability to the relative misery of the masses, the anarchy of production and the policy of public powers, Kalecki placed himself in the archipelago of neo-Marxist exponents (probably alongside Rosa Luxemburg), with whom his contemporaries had little to discuss since there was so little in common. Over and above differences in character and perhaps a certain diffidence due to their claimed paternity of the 'Keynesian' economics, the main reason of the lack of familiarity between the two authors may have been Keynes's reluctance to enter into a dialectical relationship with an economist whose cultural background he felt foreign and whom he had perhaps classified among the exponents of that obscure underworld of heretics where he had placed Marx.

It is also probable that among the reasons why even today Kalecki's contribution is completely neglected on the right-wing side of the Keynesian debate[8] is the conviction that it belongs to a line of thought substantially foreign to Keynesian culture.

Finally, the *General Theory* was not born in the space of a night but was the fruit of an immense effort in preparation[9] and an enormously vast work in which Keynes demonstrated his ability to range over the most disparate fields with an intuition, fantasy and originality hard to find in the history of economic thought. Keynesian theory comprises all this, and claiming to confine its significance and the reasons for its success to the *General Theory* alone would be greatly and unjustifiably reductive.

For several decades 'non-Keynesian' theories of employment were practically clandestine within the world of economists. Kalecki's position was long relegated among the left-wing variants of Keynesian theory; its revaluation was mainly due first to Joan Robinson, and later to the post-Keynesians (especially to their American components) which made it the flag of a theoretical design where Keynes too would have to converge.[10]

The existence of a Swedish approach to effective demand became known in the thirties within Anglo–Saxon circles mostly by virtue of the debate between Ohlin and Keynes in the *Economic Journal.*[11] For a long period the debate then remained within Swedish circles, set off by an essay by Landgren (1960) questioning the existence of an independent Swedish approach to effective demand; the discussion that followed finally led to a series of debates and articles in English.[12]

The controversy that came after these rediscoveries not only concerned *if* and *how* theories of effective demand were born as alternatives to that of

Keynes, but also (with a marked and boring emphasis) *who first* conceived them. We shall not enter this aspect here for it appears of little interest (except from the authors' personal perspective), once it has been recognised that their views were acquired independently.

A final preliminary aspect concerns the obstacles and problems the various approaches met along the way to maturity, and how such difficulties in the end made the authors further aware of the novelty of their ideas.

As we know, Keynes's research was dominated by the effort to get away from ideas and schemes of thought inherited from theories of the past. In what would seem to be his intellectual manifesto Keynes wrote:

> We have to invent new wisdom for a new age. And in the meantime we must, if we are to do any good, appear unorthodox, troublesome, dangerous, disobedient to them that begat us (1925a, p. 306).

This preoccupation is manifest in the *General Theory*, where (in the Preface) Keynes states that the work is 'a struggle to escape from habitual modes of thought and expression' (1936a, p. xxiii). Independently of his success in really breaking with the past,[13] Keynes had a precise target to fight and oppose, and this made the elements of a break, however true or boasted they were, immediately evident.

The situation with Kalecki and the Swedish economists, who conversely sought to emphasise aspects reflecting continuity with their own traditions, is quite different. The problem of effective demand is strongly rooted in Marxist culture, even though its origins were not fully clarified; this made Kalecki's approach less troubled, but at the same time probably led him to minimise the innovative scope of his theory. From this came the propensity to emphasise economic fluctuations, which he considered (as according to Marx) the emblematic representation of the contradictions inherent in the accumulation of capital.

Similar considerations apply to the Stockholm School, whose economists endeavoured to see their own theories as the natural extension of the Wicksellian framework:

> In Sweden, where we grew up in the tradition of Knut Wicksell, Keynes's works were read as interesting and important contributions along a familiar line of thought, but not in any sense as a revolutionary breakthrough (Myrdal, 1972, p. 5).

1.2 THE THEORY OF EFFECTIVE DEMAND

1.2.1 Savings–Investments Adjustment and Unemployment

Opening the *General Theory,* Keynes puts forward the purpose to present a *general* theory of employment, i.e., general with respect to the 'classical' theory which would only represent a *special* case – full-employment equilibrium. The cornerstones of this general theory, as Keynes saw them, are: (a) the plurality of possible underemployment equilibria; (b) the lack of *a priori* reasons for believing in spontaneous forces able to bring the economy to full-employment equilibrium.[14]

These two plans of analysis can be more generally examined and verified in the theories we are concerned with as: (a) the existence of unemployment as a phenomenon of equilibrium *in a given moment*, because of the lack of effective demand; (b) the *persistency* or otherwise of unemployment (i.e., the stability of the equilibrium) because of the preceding factor. In the following analysis we will verify these two aspects separately since, on the one hand, they are logically separable – the first concerning (if we wish) the role of income in balancing savings to given investments, the second concerning the long-period dynamics of investments and of the propensity to consume – and since, on the other, part of the Keynesian controversy appears to some extent vitiated by the mixing of these two points.

The controversy which arose over the second aspect, the long-run tendencies, led to a broad consensus in identifying the core of the Keynesian theory of effective demand in the sole principle of adjustment of income, a minimal recognition which does not preclude widely different interpretations of the rest of the theory. In this regard, the consensus ranges from the supporters of the neoclassical synthesis (see Patinkin, 1982) – as this principle does not in itself exclude convergence towards positions of full employment in the long run – to those adhering to the classic approach to Keynes (for example Garegnani, 1979) since, on the one hand, its validity is not limited to the short period and, on the other, the principle does not necessarily require accepting Keynes's own criticism against tendencies towards full employment. In other words, the principle of adjustment of income has been widely accepted throughout economic thought for its neutrality with respect to long-run tendencies, that is to say, for the very reason that it has been viewed as a tool distinct (or separable) from the theory.

The same principle appears in all the approaches to effective demand conceived in the 1930s, to the extent that it implies the existence of a regular, stable and systematic dependence of savings on income.

Long before the *General Theory* was published, this relationship was anticipated by Keynes in a draft as early as 1932:

> Provided that changes in savings and changes in income have the same sign, and that investment does not change, any level of output is a position of stable equilibrium ... there is no presumption whatever that the equilibrium output will be anywhere near the optimum output. The essence of the above process is that the real income of the community has to be forced down to a level at which the rate of saving is not so excessive relatively to investment (*CW*, XIII, p. 387).[15]

This principle does not appear in immediately preceding works, where savings appear *substantially* independent of income, except for particular cases such as 'marked poverty', when the possibility for a 'spurious equilibrium' of underemployment is taken into consideration.[16] On the one hand Keynes is still far from attributing to income the role of balancing savings and investments *in general*; on the other, the possibility of an equilibrium at particularly low levels of income does not necessarily seem to imply the abandonment of Say's law as the general case.[17]

After the parenthesis of the *General Theory* (where it appears over-shadowed) this way of stating the principle of effective demand returned to the fore in 1937 (Keynes, 1937a), claimed as the author's 'initial novelty'.

The savings–investments adjustment mechanism is analysed by Kalecki starting with *Proba Teorii Koniunkturi* (1933a, 1933b), though framed within the context of a theory of cyclical fluctuations. Here Kalecki argues that overall profits depend on capitalists' real expenditure for consumption and investments, while their share in the national income depends on the firms' price policy.[18] From these premises it ensues that the national income will be pushed up to the level at which – given the profit share – it brings about a volume of profits equal to capitalists' spending decisions:

> When production of investment goods rises the aggregate production increases directly *pro tanto*, but in addition there is an increase due to the demand for consumer goods on the part of the workers newly engaged in the investment goods industries. The consequent increase in employment in the consumer-goods industries leads to a further rise in the demand for consumer goods...
>
> The account of the process is not yet complete because changes in capitalists' consumption have not been taken into consideration ... *The aggregate production and the profit per unit of output will ultimately rise to such an extent as to assure an increment in the real profits*

equal to that of production of investment goods and capitalists' consumption.[19]

While lacking formalisation, the above passage is a clear description of the process of the multiplier and of the adjustment between savings and investments; it is worth noting that there is no evidence that Kalecki was acquainted with Kahn's article (1931) on the multiplier of employment. It must be added that in (1934b) Kalecki outlined the concept of 'quasi-equilibrium', associated with unemployment of labour and determined by the rate of interest in conjunction with the expected profitability of investments and the capitalists' spending habits.[20]

1.2.2 Main Causes of Unemployment

Comparing Keynes and Kalecki is made complex and often ambiguous by the fact that important affinities in theory and methodology are matched by strong differences over the underlying conception of the nature of the capitalist economy – Keynes adhering to the liberal view, Kalecki to the Marxist – although neither of them rigidly adhered to ideological schemes.

Kalecki's Marxism is more philosophical than theoretical; it is founded on historical materialism, on the idea that production relationships deeply condition economic and social life, as well as people's behaviour and way of thinking, and on the conviction of the contradictory nature of the capitalistic organisation of society. At a more strictly theoretical level, the concept of labour value and exploitation are completely disregarded, just as the origin of profits seems to be placed in the sphere of exchange rather than in the production of surplus value. Kalecki's Marxism is therefore atypical, in the sense that, while rooted in his own way of thinking, it does not materialise in the field of research and in the most characteristic concepts of this approach. Similarly, Keynes's liberal (not liberist) creed leads him to match the rejection of *laissez-faire* with a basic optimism in the capacity of capitalism to reform itself from within, which rests on belief in the progressive prevailing of ideas over vested interests, and which is poles apart from Kaleckian materialism.[21]

With respect to this background of different outlooks, the income adjustment principle is *neutral*, in that its acceptance is compatible with different basic explanations of the level and dynamics of income. Indeed, the true difference in the two authors' cultural and ideological background becomes clear once the stage of seeking immediate explanations of the phenomena is replaced by the investigation of the basic aspects inherent in the nature of the system. The ideas of the two economists may thus appear both very similar and very distant at the same time; for the same reason the relations between them may lead to opposing conclusions and be instrumentalised.

In dealing with this aspect, it is therefore appropriate to distinguish two levels of analysis, whose discriminant is a different ideological bias; while meaningful elements of affinity are evident as to the identification of the phenomena to be dealt with and their immediate explanation, the different outlooks emerge in all their force when one goes on to consider the nature of the system, the influence of class relationships, the inner mechanisms regulating the working of the system, and the long-run prospects.

With this in mind, Keynes and Kalecki are brought together, first of all, by the common indication that market economies are subject to two serious, not contingent shortcomings: the inability to ensure a satisfying level of employment of resources and their instability. They also agree in attributing immediate responsibility for both these defects to the nature of investment decisions, insofar as they are *autonomous*, i.e., not coordinated with consumption, and *unstable*; the first characteristic is the core of the theory of effective demand, the second is the premise for the theory of the business cycle.

The diagnosis they share of the chronic defects of capitalist economies is accompanied by differing attention to each of them. In the *General Theory* Keynes focuses directly only on the more innovative of the two, leaving instability in the background. Kalecki follows a rather more conventional path, coming to underemployment equilibrium through the theory of economic fluctuations; although the two problems would later be treated separately as well, his interest in the dynamic aspects, together with his scepticism about the relevance of analysis centred on the notion of steady growth, led him to develop this dual line of investigation jointly and to reconsider the theory of economic fluctuations until the end (without, however, reaching fully satisfactory solutions). The overlapping of these two aspects is probably the reason why even today the more original part of Kalecki's work is little appreciated.

As mentioned earlier, the above analogies are made more and more evident by the 'low profile' of the analysis. When, instead, one looks into the basic causes of these phenomena, the different viewpoints inspiring the two economists become immediately apparent.

In Kalecki the idea is deeply rooted, typical of Marxist tradition, that over and above the insufficiency of investments – which frequently appears as the most evident cause – the very origin of unemployment rests on chronic underconsumption due to the poverty of the masses. This diagnosis derives from the asymmetry that, according to Kalecki, would characterise the effects of investments, inasmuch as they would affect productive capacity more markedly than demand; this circumstance (as we shall see later) makes it useless, and even contradictory in the long run, to step up investments in order to create full-employment demand.

It is this asymmetry, in that it leads the economy to oscillate between overaccumulation and underaccumulation, that is the basic cause of cyclical fluctuations. Kalecki does not overlook the role of the congenital instability of confidence, but he considers it an element grafted (thereby amplifying its importance) on to a background of causes which have an objective justification and which are permanently at work in the *laissez-faire* economy. In line with Marxist thinking, according to Kalecki instability is the way of being of capitalism, and the sign of its inner contradictions.

Not even Keynes denies that underinvestment or overinvestment lie at the root of the phases of expansion and depression, but he does not consider them incurable causes of instability. He observes that over-investment is mostly a *relative* state; it is rarely, he argues, a situation in which the return from capital goods is insufficient to cover the 'cost of substitution', but rather one in which investments 'are destined to disappoint the expectations which prompted them' (Keynes, 1936a, p. 320) – i.e., destined to give a positive yield but less than expected, and therefore less than the interest rate at which they were decided. In this case the compromise between expectations and results – and, therefore, the maintenance of investments at a level such as to protract expansion – can be attained through a compensatory drop in the interest rate.[22]

The competitive framework of the *General Theory* becomes evident here: excess capacity might not occur (at least not in the dimensions it would otherwise assume) if prices were flexible relative to wages, since the redistribution of income would raise consumption; in this case, there would be only a reduction of profit per unit of product and therefore, by extrapolation, of marginal efficiency of capital, which might be offset by an adequate drop in the interest rate. It follows that the 'objective' causes of instability (the asymmetry of the effects of the investment) can be neutralised by flexible prices and by a proper monetary policy; instead, what is an ungovernable and irremediable cause of instability is the psychological fragility of the investors.

It is more difficult to ascertain the basic causes of underemployment according to Keynes. In reviewing the debate on this point, Keynes distinguishes between authors stressing underinvestment from others focusing on underconsumption, and argues that the contrast is difficult to resolve,[23] first of all because the indication of the causes cannot be abstractly separated from that of the remedies; furthermore, Keynes (as we have seen) appears less concerned than Kalecki about the asymmetry of the effects of investments, so that he lacks an objective criterion for discriminating between the concepts of underconsumption and underinvestment; finally we can see in Keynes different levels of reflection, depending on the time perspective involved.

There is no doubt that Keynes looks at the weakness of the mechanism of accumulation as a permanent obstacle to achieving high employment; this point of view has implications which go far beyond the short term, almost to theorising a sort of law of movement of the *laissez-faire* economy: the emphasis on the monetary nature of the economy should be considered in the light of the obstacles the existence of money raises to the accumulation of capital in the long run. From these limits Keynes derives the need to proceed to 'a somewhat comprehensive socialisation of investment' (1936a, p. 378); on the other hand, it was precisely with this idea in mind that Keynes, as early as the 1920s, began to challenge the high rates of interest, seeing them as the mainspring of the relative stagnation of those years.

Obviously, the lack of incentive to invest could be counterbalanced – for employment purposes – by stimulating consumption: Keynes is not prejudiced against this course, nor does he judge it ineffective, but he questions it on the basis of convenience. In his opinion, the social benefits deriving from the growth of capital 'until it ceases to be scarce' (1936a, p. 376) are so many and great that this way to full employment is far preferable to that relying on a rise in a propensity to consume.[24] The choice between the two alternatives is, nevertheless, a question of expediency since, he adds 'this is a practical judgement, not a theoretical imperative' (1936a, p. 325).

Keynes does not indicate *a priori* the causes of the insufficiency of effective demand in either underconsumption or underinvestment; with strict regard to employment, it makes no difference technically whether one policy or the other is pursued. Considerations of a different nature (the social advantages inherent in a high rate of accumulation) bring him to advocate the speeding up of investments; indeed he sees no danger of overaccumulation ('for a generation or two'), obviously, provided the system exhibits the flexibilities mentioned above:

> I should readily concede that the wisest course is to advance on both fronts at once. Whilst aiming at a socially controlled rate of investment with a view to a progressive decline in the marginal efficiency of capital, I should support at the same time all sorts of policies for

increasing the propensity to consume. For it is unlikely that full employment can be maintained, whatever we may do about investment, with the existing propensity to consume (1936a, p. 325).

Keynes's pragmatism derives from his natural aversion to rigidly adhering to preconstituted schemes, whether ideological or theoretical, an aversion he shares with Kalecki. However, where his liberal roots and the enlightenment of his mentality lead Keynes to differ from Kalecki is in holding that the relationship between consumption and investments can be defined in a 'neutral' way and resolved to the benefit of all the 'productive' classes; in other words, the belief that it does not represent an uneliminable conflict within the capitalist system. On the contrary, for Kalecki, behind that problem lies an irremediable class antagonism, which excludes a satisfactory solution, i.e., a solution matched by stable full employment.

1.2.3 Unemployment in the Long Run

These different approaches are confirmed, together with other similar aspects, when the two authors address their attention to the long run. The main common point is that both of them seem to conceive stagnation or a state of semi-stagnation as the ultimate stage of the capitalist economy, the cause of which they both regard as substantially outside the economic mechanism. This conclusion flows directly from conceiving long-run growth as determined by exogenous factors, so that both the process of growth and the ending of it are assumed to be determined by a set of external causes. Beyond these similarities one finds significant differences of view, especially with regard to the judgements on the stationary situation that emerge.

According to Keynes, the main factors that would drastically change the long-term perspectives are the slowing down of the increase in population (a situation he had already noticed) and the saturation of needs. These factors would result in stationary conditions of the economy, a situation Keynes regards as compatible with the survival of a 'reformed capitalism'.

Analysing the English economy for the period 1860–1913, Keynes concluded that the accumulation of capital in that span of time had been determined: (1) about 50% by the growth in population; (2) about 50% by the increase in the standard of living; (3) by an insignificant percentage by the increase in capital intensity.[25] Since the growth of population will soon come to an end, Keynes argues, the accumulation of capital will then rely on (2) and (3):

> With a stationary population we shall, I argue, be absolutely dependent for the maintenance of prosperity and civil peace on policies of increasing consumption by a more equal distribution of income and of forcing down the rate of interest so as to make more profitable a substantial change in the length of the period of production. [Consequently] If capitalistic society rejects a more equal distribution of incomes and the forces of banking and finance succeed in maintaining the rate of interest somewhere near the figure which ruled on the average during the nineteenth century ... then a chronic tendency towards the unemployment of resources must in the end sap and destroy that form of society (Keynes, 1937d, p. 132).[26]

With these remedies in mind, Keynes outlines the 'natural evolution' of society:

> The natural evolution should be towards a decent level of consumption for everyone; and, when that is high enough, towards the occupation of our energies in the non-economic interests of our lives. Thus we need to be slowly reconstructing our social system with this end in view (Keynes, 1937c, p. 393).

Keynes strikes against the copresence of unused resources and unsatisfied needs, and refuses to accept that effective demand, as generated by market forces, sets up a barrier to the growth of production. At the same time he rejects the idea that the frontier of needs must be 'artificially' and continually shifted forward to feed a steadily increasing production. Like John Stuart Mill, Keynes was in no way a supporter of endless growth; on the contrary, for him the stationary economy would be the highest stage of evolution of society (of course, a stationary state caused not by the fact that needs fail to be converted into effective demand, but by the fact that they are stationary in themselves).

Keynes is aware that managing a society appeased with needs 'worthy to be satisfied' will require far-reaching measures going beyond the economic sphere and aiming at the transition towards a 'reformed capitalism': 'Drastic social changes directed towards increasing consumption', he argues (1934, p. 491), will be necessary, together with new attitudes towards labour and free time – since 'three hours a day is quite enough to satisfy the old Adam in most of us' (1930b, p. 329).[27]

Obviously there are several doubtful points in Keynes's reasoning where Kalecki would radically disagree. One can argue against the realism of this outlook or question the sense of continuing to label as 'capitalist' a society in which accumulation has lost its place in the scale of social values and its quantitative importance, a society in which the suppression of the rate of interest virtually implies the disappearance of financial capital. Another debatable aspect concerns the possibility of reconciling the high propensity to save – prompted by passing from a society founded on needs to a society founded on wants (where the latter are not induced) – with low rates of accumulation. Finally, the possibility of introducing reforms necessary for permitting capitalism to coexist with the new situation, and their nature, can be questioned. Keynes's opinion in this regard is strongly biased by ideology; characterised as it is by the enlightenment of his mentality (as well as by a strong optimism of the will) it is equivalent to the statement that ideas are destined to prevail over vested habits and interests.[28]

Kalecki sees the tendency towards stationary situations emerging at two levels. First, there is an *inherent tendency* which accounts for the contradictory nature of investment and which results in the 'pure economic cycle'; the system can be released from this situation by counter-tendencies generated by 'semi-exogenous' factors – i.e., factors that cannot be functionally reconnected to its inner mechanisms:

> Our analysis shows that long-run development is not inherent in the capitalist economy. Thus specific 'development factors' are required to sustain a long-run upward movement (Kalecki, 1954, p. 161).

Even if, thanks to the combined support of public action and sufficient vitality of the 'development factors', the capitalist economy were capable of overcoming the impulses towards a slow and erratic growth, it would be extremely unlikely that a secular decline could be avoided, especially because of the slowing down of the intensity of innovations.[29] In Kalecki's view, innovations play a leading role for the long-run perspectives of capitalism; however, in the same way that they constitute the predominant factor of growth, they are also decisive in bringing about its halt. At the same time, their alleged exogenous nature leaves the causes of both growth and its arrest largely unexplored.

To conclude, for Kalecki the threat of stagnation is here and now, always imminent and always opposed by 'antagonistic' forces; in the very long run, however, this course is destined to prevail under *laissez-faire* conditions. The long-term growth being not 'inherent' to the capitalist economy, systematic intervention by the state becomes necessary: (1) on the one hand, in order to integrate and stabilise private investment at the pace set by the growth in population and in the productivity of labour; (2)

on the other hand, in order to raise overall demand to a full-employment level.

Unlike Keynes (who considers the semi-stationary state as virtually inevitable and as something to be hoped for), for Kalecki the trend towards that state is not the outcome of a law of necessity, nor is it to be wished for, at least as the saturation of the needs of the masses is not within the range of capitalism; on the contrary, Kalecki argues, it would be the masses who would pay the price with growing unemployment and poverty. The reforms that Kalecki, at a certain point in his life, judged feasible and suitable, would – unlike Keynes's viewpoint – permit capitalism to survive in the only way it can, as a system in perpetual expansion.

1.3. FULL EMPLOYMENT

1.3.1 Ways to Full Employment

According to Kalecki, as well as Keynes, full employment and economic stability are objectives *technically* attainable through policies of demand control, by combining measures on investments and consumptions; with different emphasis, both concede that the spur to private investments would not be sufficient to guarantee full employment (and even less its stability) and that, therefore, it would be necessary, on the one hand, to apply a certain degree of socialisation of investment and, on the other, to broaden mass consumption; finally, both of them subordinate the support of consumption to investments. These affinities, however, also conceal deep divergences between the two authors.

Kalecki favours social policies aimed at supporting demand, through subsidies and measures bound to change the distribution of income, but he is sceptical about the opportunity of stimulating private investments to raise employment directly. He observes that the task of private investment is first to broaden the productive capacity of the economy and only subordinately to sustain employment by increasing demand; naturally investments bring about both effects, but nothing ensures that they will be symmetrical.

Indeed Kalecki argues that a policy of full employment carried on by stimulating private investment is bound to give rise to a gap between the dynamics of capacity and that of demand – the first exceeding the second[30] – so that instability would be increased rather than repressed. Indeed:

(a) If investment were established so as to give rise to a level of effective demand consistent with the full employment of labour (as suggested by Keynes), this would entail an excess of installed capacity. A decrease in investments would then ensue and the employment target would be missed. To avoid this, a steadily declining rate of interest would be necessary, a course Kalecki considered impracticable.[31]

(b) If, instead, efforts were directed to increasing investments in step with population and labour productivity (in order to guarantee full-employment conditions from the supply side), the insufficiency of effective demand which would follow would leave both workers and plants idle.

(c) Nor could an escape from this *impasse* be found in the hypothesis that the conflict between the two effects is reabsorbed by increasing capital intensity; first, because the thrust in this direction comes mainly from new inventions, while the stimulus exerted by the rate of interest is weak;[32] furthermore, even if the latter had some influence in this direction, it would have to decline steadily to defeat a tendency that is continuous.

(d) Similar results would also be met even if technical progress were accompanied by a growing capital/output ratio (given the degree of utilisation of capacity), since once again a decline in the rate of return on capital would occur which would have to be compensated by a continuous decline in the rate of interest.[33]

To conclude, according to Kalecki, even if private investments were completely under control, it would still be impossible to ensure a state of prolonged full employment by means of investments alone because, no matter how they are manoeuvred, excess productive capacity would in any case emerge. Given these circumstances, the basic cause of unemployment can only be found in underconsumption. Therefore:

> Private investment must be pushed up to the level sufficient to expand the productive capacity of capital equipment *pari passu* with the increase in population and productivity of labour ... Government expenditure on public investment and subsidies to mass consumption (financed by income tax or borrowing) must be such as to create full employment in combination with this level of private investment. The division of public spending between public investment and subsidizing consumption should be based on the principle of social priorities (Kalecki, 1944, pp. 57–8).

Kalecki thus suggests a clear-cut division of tasks: on the one hand, investments addressed to guaranteeing the conditions for accumulation and growth in the long run at a pace set by external parameters (the dynamics of population and productivity); on the other, public spending and income redistribution to the extent that effective demand associated with those investments proves to be below the full-employment level. The priority assigned to investments has a well-definite basis that also enables its limits to be defined: not an indiscriminate favour (as sometimes appears in Keynes), but the recognition of a constraint which is to be respected for pursuing the objectives of social policy.

Keynes's opinion differs in many ways.[34] First of all, the bias for the short run leads him, as a rule, to overlook the relative consequences of investments on demand and capacity; on the other hand, as we have seen, justifying this view is the conviction that the mechanism of competition, integrated with a flexible monetary policy, would be able, the former, to reabsorb possible asymmetries in these effects, and, the latter, to offset their repercussions on investment activity. With these premises, it was natural for Keynes to set the 'right' rate of investment, consistent with 'sustained enjoyment of prosperity', taking into account primarily the demand side,[35] and to believe that the subordination of consumption to investments (until capital is no longer scarce) is subject only, on the one hand, to the capacity and the will of present generations to undergo sacrifices and, on the other, to the congenital weakness of the incentive to invest.

Once quantified, Keynes suggests, private investment should be promoted by keeping the long-term interest rate steadily at a proper level and refraining from using monetary policy as an anti-cyclic device.[36] It follows that the maintainance of a state as close as possible to full employment, in spite of fluctuations in private investment around the long-term level, rests primarily on fiscal policy.[37] It is worth stressing Keynes's scepticism about the possibility of relying on private investments entirely, which led him to believe in the necessity of 'a somewhat comprehensive socialization of investment' as 'the only means of securing an approximation to full employment' (Keynes, 1936a, p. 378).[38]

In summary, the choice of the means for ensuring full employment is conceived by Kalecki and by Keynes in terms reflecting their different emphasis on implications over the long run and their different evaluation of price flexibility. For Kalecki, investments must be addressed to securing the requisites for full employment (the conditions on the supply side), so that the proper rate of investment is related to the growth of population and productivity, while the regulation of the effective level of employment (the conditions on the demand side) is entrusted to fiscal and redistributive measures. Keynes conceives investments also as an instrument for directly controlling demand and leaves instead the task of completing or stabilising the effects to fiscal measures.

1.3.2 The Problem of Controls

Obviously, Kalecki's strong criticism of capitalist society leads him to interpret adversly not only the economic mechanisms as such but also the behaviour of public authorities who, even in countries with democratic regimes, would express the values and interests of the ruling class. It is for this reason that certain problems, while capable of solution at a purely technical level, become difficult to solve when they conflict with vested interests.

This conflict occurs at three levels:

(a) over the *actual content* of employment policies;

(b) over the *economic consequences* of full employment;

(c) over the *political consequences* of maintaining it, from which Kalecki derives a contradiction between full employment and democratic capitalism.

Kalecki questions the possibility of governing private investments effectively through the long-term interest rate, not only because investments are not very sensitive to the interest rate, but also because this is relatively sticky (and as such, scarcely suitable for carrying out anti-cyclical policies) and cannot drop below certain values, even accounting for the spread it has to maintain over the short-term rate. For this reason Kalecki is convinced that monetary measures must be matched by fiscal devices, i.e., by tax relief on reinvested profits. Indirect measures, Kalecki continues, are in any case to be excluded as a means for bringing private investments towards the above target, so that large public investments are necessary.

At the same time, public spending on investments is constrained by limitations. It must avoid invading the field reserved to private 'productive' investments, as otherwise it would be considered the 'Trojan horse of socialism ("creeping socialism")'.[39] But investments in the services sector have a limited scope, probably not enough to ensure full employment; furthermore they are unpopular with entrepreneurs since they might even generate temptations to nationalise certain services to make more room for public investments. Because of this complex of limitations, public spending for investments is fatally channelled in the direction where it meets the least resistance or, better, in the direction it is pushed towards by a powerful block of interests, which might include not only capitalists but also trade unions, the political class and, above all, the national conscience.[40]

As for measures devised to support demand, Kalecki is sceptical about the possibility of manoeuvring foreign trade for this purpose, not because he disregards its influence on the economy but because he does not believe that approaching economic policy in this way would be either decisive or desirable. The basic reason for this view (which leads him to consider foreign exchanges as a *datum* in policies supporting demand) is, on the one hand, that measures acting on foreign trade cannot lead to recovering the world economy from depression; on the other hand, as he never identified himself with the interests of single countries, he was not favourable to partial solutions.

The most promising 'external market' for capitalist economies, Kalecki believes, is to be found in public expenditure, in particular in social spending; it is through this channel – along with measures modifying income distribution – that mass consumption must be raised to the point of generating full-employment demand.

The social content of measures favouring employment is limited, however, first by the 'capitalist ethic' which is averse to supporting mass consumption (by means of subsidies or administered prices), since:

> here a moral principle of the highest importance is at stake. The fundamentals of capitalist ethics require that 'You shall earn your bread in sweat' – unless you happen to have private means (Kalecki, 1943a, p. 351).

Themes peculiar to neo-Marxist literature, therefore, come into Kalecki's criticism of how aggregate demand is actually governed in capitalist countries: internally, waste of resources, increases in the standard of living of the masses to a level far below the potential of the economy (and, in any case, their relative impoverishment), degradation of values, moral misery; internationally, imperialism and war (hot or cold) as indispensable to supporting consensus.[41]

Keynes is less worried by considerations of this type; not that he is unaware of the existence of contradictions, conflicts and pressures on public authorities, but he trusts that in the long run the force of reason[42] will prevail over everything else. As for relations between the public and private spheres, Keynes adheres to the principle that the authorities must never supplant private initiative wherever it is present.[43]

The second point to consider is the possibility of maintaining full employment without imposing more selective controls than those required to govern aggregate demand. On this matter there are two overlapping levels of reflection, where a comparison with Keynes's point of view is interesting; one concerns the capitalist economy's capacity in general to allocate resources efficiently and to distribute them fairly, the other the specific problems raised by full employment.

It is widely recognised that allocative aspects are hastily dealt with in the *General Theory*, confined within problems that, as a rule, the free forces of the market can handle satisfactorily alone.[44] It would not be correct, however, to infer that Keynes ignores the need for public intervention to go beyond a generalised support of demand. In many writings (especially in the 1920s[45]) Keynes proves rather sceptical about the market's capacity for self-regulation and harshly attacks the philosophical conception and premises on which *laissez-faire* is grounded,[46] by positing a clearly different view:

> For my part I think that capitalism, wisely managed, can probably be made more efficient for attaining economic ends than any alternative system yet in sight, but that in itself it is in many ways extremely objectionable. Our problem is to work out a social organization which shall be as efficient as possible without offending our notions of a satisfactory way of life (Keynes, 1926, p. 294).

In 1939, he confirms:

> The question is whether we are prepared to move out of the nineteenth-century *laissez-faire* state into an era of liberal socialism, by which I mean a system where we can act as an organized community for common purposes and to promote social and economic justice, whilst respecting and protecting the individual – his freedom of choice, his faith, his mind and its expression, his enterprise and his property (Keynes, *CW*, XXI, p. 500).

Also accounting for the difficulty in getting rid of old ideas, Keynes's apparent neglect for allocative questions throughout the *General Theory* seems to be due not so much to a change in opinion as to the need not to shift the interlocutor away from the central message or, if we prefer, to the need to limit the upset in the 'profession' to the extent that the core of the work would inevitably cause.

This is confirmed by the legitimation of policies of redistribution to create employment, i.e., by the lack of in-principle preclusions against putting this field under public control. Keynes argues that the need to act in this direction becomes more urgent as full employment approaches (and even more as this state is maintained for a long time), mainly because of the bottlenecks in the supply of certain products and the tendency of wages to rise. Keynes is perfectly aware that this situation will require abandoning exclusively macroeconomic policies[47] and necessitate imposing controls on the dynamics of wages.[48]

The fact remains, however, that Keynes's different levels of reflection find in the *General Theory* an unsatisfactory synthesis which reduces the strength of his argument. Kalecki's scepticism on the market's capacity to regulate itself is supported, instead, by a theoretical model consistent with his vision. In the economic system he takes as a benchmark, the conditions of an economy that regulates itself to attain the position of a social optimum are absent: the competitive framework is banned, market power is not atomised but real and palpable; maximising behaviours are replaced by more complex motivations; prices do not reflect conditions of relative scarcity; the myth of consumer sovereignty falls away; the equality of opportunities, basic to social mobility and justice, is lacking.

When full employment comes about, specific objections are further added to the general ones, such as the difficulty of reconciling this situation with the external equilibrium, the tendency of wages to rise and the sharpening of conflict in the factories. Overcoming these problems is not impossible in itself but, Kalecki argues, it requires an entire set of controls which come up against the opposition of the ruling class. Full employment is therefore doubtly incompatible with capitalism: first, because of the problems it raises and, second, because of the measures which would be required to surmount them. The incompatibility, therefore, is by nature fundamentally political; with this we come to the third aspect to be examined.

1.3.3 Political Aspects of Full Employment

The political aspects of full employment are among the best known Kaleckian themes. The thesis according to which after the Keynesian revolution full employment is essentially only a political problem is scattered throughout Kalecki's writings, but receives organic treatment in an article published in 1943 (see Kalecki, 1943a) which summarises conclusions matured over the years on the employment policies of the thirties. Kalecki's basic argument is that the solution of the problem of unemployment cannot be isolated from that of other problems; the central point is not whether full employment can be achieved abstractly, but whether it can be attained while maintaining the existing order – the existing mechanisms of income distribution and resources allocation – and whether this order can withstand a state of prolonged full employment. It is from the awareness of these implications, he asserts, that the greatest resistance to realising that objective comes.

In (1943a) Kalecki argues that the main obstacle to full employment is entrepreneurs' deep aversion to State intervention in this field, in spite of the advantages they would gain on the economic ground. This opposition finds justification, first of all, in the fact that:

> Under a *laissez-faire* system the level of employment depends to a greater extent on the so-called state of confidence ... This gives to the capitalists a powerful indirect control over Government policy: everything which may shake the state of confidence must be carefully avoided because it would cause an economic crisis (Kalecki, 1943a, p. 350).

The systematic use of policies supporting demand, therefore, deprives entrepreneurs of the basis of their power of pressure on public authorities, since they would be demoted to merely one of the many subjects on whose decision the satisfactory course of the economy depends.

This deep hostility is further enhanced by the maintenance of full employment over time, a situation which would be considered a forerunner of social and political changes. The weakening of the employers' position in such a case would undermine their leadership while reinforcing the conscience of the working classes and making them aware of their strength. Nor is the business world's aversion mitigated by the considerable economic benefits this situation brings, for:

> 'discipline in factories' and 'political stability' are more appreciated by the business leaders than profits. Their class instinct tells them that lasting full employment is unsound from their point of view and that unemployment is an integral part of the 'normal' capitalist system (1943a, p. 351).

For Kalecki, therefore, unemployment is a phenomenon inseparable from capitalism since it performs a role of social control and consequently safeguards the values and relations on which capitalism rests. However, the feeble optimism still marking his social philosophy on capitalism at that time led him to believe that incompatibility with full employment might be reabsorbed, or at least governed in an acceptable way; and that this goal might be pursued without abolishing political freedom, which had been the path followed historically up until then.

The latter solution (accomplished by fascist regimes) emasculates the conflict by political pressure on the masses that replaces the social control exercised by unemployment.[49] This case being generally excluded, capitalist economies would probably opt for a solution consisting in intervening only to smooth the extreme phases of the cycle, leaving the market to handle the rest. In the resulting cycle, full employment is attained only during the boom, while recessions, too, are rather brief and of moderate intensity; the working of the system is thus the outcome of a deliberate political choice addressed to preventing the worsening of social tensions generated by the excessive hardship of recessions or by the prolonged state of full employment, and through this choice to preserve the social and political structure of the system.[50] In this scheme – which reproduces the 'artificial restoration of the position as it existed in nineteenth-century capitalism' (1943a, p. 355) – the behaviour of public authorities, far from attaining the claimed purpose of stabilising the economy, becomes on the contrary a factor of instability.[51]

As a 'progressive', Kalecki claimed dissatisfaction with the political business cycle solution and this led him to consider a third possibility, consisting in an extensive social policy, which in turn would require a radical reform of the system with the development of 'new social and political institutions which will reflect the increased power of the working class'(1943a, p. 356). At the same time, 'full employment capitalism', precisely by virtue of the reforms it requires and involves, would generate in the long run the political consensus necessary for its maintenance as a social priority. At this stage of reflection, Kalecki's conclusions were still open:

> If capitalism can adjust itself to full employment, a fundamental reform will have been incorporated in it. If not, it will show itself an outmoded system which must be scrapped (1943a, p. 356).[52]

The fact that this acknowledgement of the possibility of a reformed capitalism was not incorporated into a theoretical model is probably due to Kalecki's lack of conviction in the feasibility of a compromise between 'monopoly capitalism' and social needs, and to the disillusion that suddenly replaced his albeit cautious hopes. Indeed, starting from the end of the 1940s Kalecki's attitude in this regard became more and more pessimistic as he saw western societies embodying the worst features of capitalist organisation. His disappointment grew as the gap widened between the means then available to economic policy and the will to use them systematically; further motives for dissatisfaction were the increasing importance of public expenditure for armaments – cause and effect of international tension[53] – instead of for social consumption or aid to backward countries, economic and political imperialism, and the degradation of the social and political conscience of the masses (which appeared to him to conform with the teaching of historical materialism).[54] Kalecki became convinced that the post-war experience of the leading capitalist countries, where in his view these phenomena were on the rise, reflected an inevitable and irreversible trend for all capitalist economies, which led him to abandon his earlier cautious optimism.[55]

1.4 METHODOLOGICAL ASPECTS

1.4.1 The Notion of Equilibrium

A feature Keynes and Kalecki share in methodology is the separation of the problem of underemployment from that of instability, an approach justified primarily by the perception that unemployment is a phenomenon logically distinct from the business cycle. This leads to several remarkable consequences, first of all that of bringing the analysis of unemployment within the framework of equilibrium, which marks a first important departure from the traditional approach.

On the notion of equilibrium, too, Kalecki and Keynes share some meaningful aspects. Equilibrium, whether short- or long-period, is conceived by Keynes as a situation occurring at a given time, logically springing from factors predominant in that moment; it is not an actual position nor one the system tends to, but just a position bound to persist once it has been reached (of course, provided that parameters and exogenous variables remain unchanged).[56]

Kalecki's position is based on the same notion. When speaking of 'quasi-equilibrium' (1934b, p. 215) or of 'conditional equilibrium' (1939a, p. 139) he distinguishes between decisions and realisations of investments, assuming that decisions cannot be changed during the current period since they were made at an earlier time. The separation of the two acts allows Kalecki to pursue two objectives: (1) underlining the causal relationship between investments and savings; (2) denying that changes in income, brought about by investments, affect the latter within the same interval, which would otherwise prejudice the restoration of equilibrium. It is precisely this time lag that allows Kalecki to conclude that current phenomena do not affect existing equilibria but only, by stimulating new decisions, those to come.[57]

For both authors the relevance of equilibrium does not rely on it being a situation which actually comes about, i.e., a situation where *ex ante* values are verified *ex post*. Nor is it necessary in this framework to take into account the existence of tendencies towards equilibrium; one can speak of equilibrium only as a situation of rest, meaning that there are no endogenous forces acting to move the system from that state, however it may have materialised. Indeed the adoption of this concept by Kalecki and Keynes appears to have been prompted exclusively by the opportunity of singling out the *final* effects of the outstanding factors operating in a given situation rather than a criterion induced by the belief that the very relevance of equilibrium relies on the existence of forces able to bring the system towards it.[58]

1.4.2 The Way to Dynamics

In Kalecki's dynamic analysis the economic process is conceived as a 'chain of short-period equilibria each of them prevailing during time *t*' (Kalecki, 1937b, p. 83), where all changes come to maturity when passing from one interval to another. The transition occurs by virtue of differently dated variables, so that those which are supposed independent within each period (first of all investments) are in turn assumed to be a function of variables of preceding periods; the variables investments mainly interact with are income and capital stock, in relation to which the expected marginal rate of profit is set.[59] It thus becomes possible to distinguish a primary causal chain (from investments to income), which acts within each interval, from a second one, acting between the periods, which takes the form of a feedback.

Though not interested in dynamics, Keynes probably has in mind a similar structure, as evidenced especially in Chapter XVIII of the *General Theory* where he summarises his theory by dividing the 'determinants of the economic system' into independent and dependent variables, the distinction being made 'so as to correspond ... to those factors in which the changes are found in practice to exercise a dominant influence on our *quaesitum*' (1936a, p. 247).

Keynes's purpose is to isolate the dominant causal factors from other less important ones, and this is done through a sequence scheme, in which a main causal chain is taken as distinct from feedbacks: given the 'psychological variables', the wage unit and the money supply determine the rate of interest, and then the *equilibrium* level of investment and income; only at this stage may the latter affect the *subsequent* level of the rate of interest,[60] and so on, but it is legitimate to speak of feedbacks ('repercussions') and not of interdependence between equally important variables.

Of course, Keynes's arguing is formally weak because of the dependence of the demand for money on income: once this step is made, the road is open to the possibility of reworking the *General Theory* in terms of Hicks's *IS–LM* framework. Though *formally* correct, this general equilibrium interpretation appears to miss the method and the spirit of Keynes's theory as outlined above.

The similarities outlined between Kalecki's and Keynes's sequence analysis, however, do not go much beyond a first impression. First of all, the analysis of the feedbacks is for Kalecki the starting point for studying economic fluctuations, whereas Keynes contents himself with a hint; second, feedbacks involve different variables: Kalecki focuses on the repercussions of changing income and capital stock (via the expected rate of profit) on the subsequent level of investment, while Keynes mainly considers the effects of changes in income (via the demand for money) on the subsequent level of the rate of interest.

Kalecki generally tends to keep the problem of economic fluctuations distinct from that of the 'regular' long-run tendency, the former being regarded as fluctuations around a stationary position characterised by zero net investments, whereas the ascending trend is dealt with subsequently by introducing 'factors of development'.[61] While economic fluctuations are meant to be the effects of primarily endogenous forces (the basis of the cyclical mechanism is the alternation of phases of overaccumulation and underaccumulation), the key to Kalecki's conception of development is that it requires constant support of 'external' factors (such as innovations) which 'transform a static system into one subject to an upward trend' (1954, p. 158).

According to Kalecki the external origin of these influences is important not only because it demonstrates the lack of self-propulsive impulses in the economy, but also because it shows that:

> the rate of growth at a given time is a phenomenon rooted in past economic, social and technological developments rather than determined fully by the coefficients of our equations as in the case with the business cycle.[62]

In the dynamic process the 'factors of development' thus assume that historic-institutional traits which – in the framework of determination of income at a given time – are assigned to the 'factors of distribution'[63] and to investment decisions.

The differences separating Kalecki from so-called 'Keynesian' dynamics are self-evident, but differences can also be found in the conception of the long period.

The short period, Joan Robinson remarks, 'is not a length of time but the position at a moment of time' (1978, p. 211); it is 'here and now, with concrete stocks of means of production in existence' (1962a, p. 101)'.[64] Consistently, the short-period equilibrium represents a situation at a given moment, i.e., a state resulting from the independent variables and data, where forces considered prevalent in that specific contest take form. As we have seen, there is substantial accord between Keynes and Kalecki on this notion of equilibrium.

The two authors differ instead with regard to the long period. Contrary to the viewpoint prevalent in economic thought, this concept does not constitute for Kalecki an 'independent entity' on the methodological ground but the mere succession of short-period situations;[65] it follows that long-period analysis provides the direction of movement and nothing else. From this comes Kalecki's marked preference for business cycle phenomena and for dealing with long-period dynamics within this frame.

Keynes's approach is different,[66] and Joan Robinson once again seems to grasp it correctly:

> Long-period equilibrium is not at some date in the future; it is an imaginary state of affairs in which there are no incompatibilities in the existing situation, here and now (1962a, p. 101).

The discriminant between the short and the long period is therefore for Keynes not the time horizon but the different nature of situations taken into consideration, and the task of long-period analysis is to bring out tendencies and stylised facts that are not made apparent by the short-run analysis. Long-period equilibrium in any case no way represents a centre of gravity, but only a hypothetical situation which permits a grasp of relevant features emerging under the particular conditions prevailing in that context. According to this reasoning, the steady-state growth models (commonly considered as the legitimate dynamic extension of the Keynesian theory) bring to dynamics the concept of long-period equilibrium mentioned above, i.e., as a situation of full adjustment of the economy to *dominant* forces.

Kalecki denies the significance of the notion of long-period equilibrium, that is, its capacity to take into account phenomena which are of outstanding importance in reality, and therefore rules it out as an analytical device; for the same reason he is strongly critical about the utility of steady-state growth models. Taking explicitly into account both cyclical and trend phenomena, without treating the latter as independent of the former, Kalecki counters the method of dynamic equilibrium with that of the *dynamics of short-*

period equilibria. This approach can be profitably followed in extending Keynes's theory to dynamics; with respect to Harrod's approach there is perhaps less affinity as concerns method (better: as concerns the method followed in the *General Theory*), but there is undoubtedly greater affinity as concerns the vision of the working of the capitalist process.

1.5 THE FRAMEWORK OF KALECKI'S THEORY

Kalecki's research was carried on within a framework already outlined in its essential features in the early 1930s while other aspects were further developed and still others more thoroughly examined later. Thus in the forty years that followed he concentrated on a core of original ideas, part of which remained substantially unchanged while others were incessantly revised over time. Save from details, however, strong continuity in his paradigma can be traced.

To begin with, it is therefore worth outlining this framework in order to grasp its essential features, at the same time being free not to respect too strictly one or the other of the many formulations of its components that Kalecki put forward from time to time. This second aspect is developed in subsequent chapters, in which an analysis is attempted of the principal stages in the evolution of Kalecki's thought about single pieces of his paradigma. Indeed, certain positions are better understood by examining them as they matured, particularly in view of the debate they inspired, which in turn certainly influenced their development.[67]

Synthetically, Kalecki's theory is framed in two logically independent parts – a theory of the *level of profits* and a theory of *distributive shares* – from the synthesis of which the theory of effective demand derives.[68] In drastically simplified hypotheses[69] let us consider:

$$Y = P + W, \qquad s_p > 0; s_w = 0 \tag{1.1}$$

$$P = C_p + I \tag{1.2}$$

$$C_p = (1 - s_p)P \tag{1.3}$$

where Y, C_p and I are overall income, consumption out of profits, and investments (in monetary terms); P and W, profits and the wage bill; s_p and s_w, the propensities of the two classes to save. By substituting we have:

$$P = I\frac{1}{s_P} \tag{1.4}$$

which (besides expressing the condition of equilibrium of income) states the *theory of profits*, according to which the overall level of profits is determined by the spending decisions of capitalists as a class. Indeed, Kalecki argues, the causal connection operates from the right since:

> capitalists may decide to consume and to invest more in a given period than in the preceding one, but they cannot decide to earn more. It is, therefore, their investment and consumption decisions which determine profits, and not vice versa (Kalecki, 1954, p. 46).

Moreover, if we assume:

$$Y = pX$$

$$W = wL$$

$$L = X/a$$

with p indicating the price level (we can also think of it as the price of a standard commodity representing the overall production); X, quantity produced; w and L, the wage unit and the number of employed; a, the product per worker, made constant up to full employment of productive capacity. By substituting in (1.1) we have:

$$\frac{P}{pX} = 1 - \frac{w}{ap}$$

or:

$$\frac{P}{Y} = \frac{p - w/a}{p} \tag{1.5}$$

By itself (1.5) is but an identity; it turns to a theory of distributive shares once coupled with an explanation of prices and wages, i.e., what Kalecki calls the 'factors of distribution' and which he considers exogenous with respect to the process of income generation – given the hypotheses of underemployment of capacity and constant returns (which become essential here, but not for (1.4)).

From the synthesis of (1.4) and (1.5) we have:

$$Y = pX = \frac{pI_x}{s_p \dfrac{p - w/a}{p}} \tag{1.6}$$

(with I_x, investments in real terms), which defines the mechanism determining the equilibrium level of income: given the distributive shares, this will be pushed to a level creating an amount of profits equal to capitalists' expenditure decisions.

In Kalecki's view of prices and distribution as data within the process of determination of income – according to a logical causal order where they occupy a stage upstream – we find reflected the priority he assigns to the political and institutional aspects compared to the more specifically economic ones. This priority is confirmed by the fact that when his ideas were at last organically presented (mainly in 1954) the factors of distribution and the determinants of profits were analysed before coming to the theory of income and the study of monetary aspects. In the treatment that follows we have used the sequence suggested by Kalecki.

2 The Theory of Pricing and Distribution

From his earliest writings in the 1930s until 1954 Kalecki's analysis of prices reflected the trouble which marked the discussion of this subject at the time. Sraffa's criticism (1925, 1926) of the marginalist theory of prices started a period of transition rich in ferment but lacking in really innovative proposals.[1] For at least twenty years no alternative schemes embodying sufficiently-defined theoretical settings were presented: Hall and Hitch's contributions in Great Britain and Sweezy's in the United States date from 1939,[2] but modern versions of the theory of prices in oligopoly were not to come until many years later.[3]

Among the most important reasons for the traumatic nature of this transition was the reluctance to accept the idea that, once the marginalist scheme was rejected, one would have to be satisfied with theories devoid of the same degree of completeness and 'objectivity'; the reverse side of the discretional element in the price policy under oligopoly is the difficulty in winding up the theory of prices. Much has been written in an effort to eliminate the area of indeterminacy (or 'plurideterminacy'), but an uneliminable *quid*, embodying the political–institutional element, still remains. This conclusion which many today consider a proof of maturity of economic science, was at the time difficult to accept given the habits that marginalism had instilled in scholars.

The evolution of Kalecki's view on prices lends itself to different interpretations, none entirely free of doubt and so all somewhat questionable; the choice of one or the other must therefore aim at minimising the elements of contradiction (which, however, persist), i.e., being the most reliable and coherent *on the whole*. The review that follows takes into consideration Kalecki's outstanding contributions on this theme; we will argue against the prevailing interpretation according to which there was, within the development of Kalecki's thought, an early marginalist phase followed (starting with 1954) by a non-marginalist one. The thesis put forward here, instead, is that Kalecki was sceptical from the beginning about the traditional approach, and that from his earliest works he was inclined to shape his analysis by making use of different theoretical frameworks according to the market forms assumed; the marginalist toolkit, adopted for competition, thus appears to be abandoned for other approaches when different market situations come into consideration.

This approach might be explained by the need to verify the generality of the macroeconomic reasoning in relation to different microeconomic hypotheses; this seems confirmed by the fact that Kalecki continued to follow this dual approach even after his alleged marginalist phase was undoubtedly over. While the consideration of competition and the parallel use of marginalist analysis were meant to cover his ideas on a ground which was an obligatory point of reference at that time (but which he judged not very promising), his true interest was in implementing a scheme more sympathetic to his view of reality. Kalecki's endless task was to argue with increasing rigour and realism on behalf of explanations of prices different from the traditional one; at the same time, the lack of clarity often affecting his treatment should not be understood as unconfessed acceptance of marginalist principles, but as a result of his difficulty in giving a definite theoretical content to alternative criteria.

Kalecki's reluctance to clearly specify the theoretical background and the premises from which he moves is, however, a constant in his analysis of prices, and though this might be justified in the beginning (i.e., in his writings in the 1930s and 1940s) by the state of economic theory, it was no longer so for his subsequent works. In effect, a kind of indifference to the views of other scholars and an apparent lack of interest in taking advantage of the progress in economic theory seem to mark Kalecki's attitude in this regard, and has made the theory of prices one of the most discussed and (albeit with certain excesses of criticism) least happy parts in his work; this is even more disappointing when one considers, as we shall see, its considerable potential.[4]

Kalecki generally deals with the question of prices with a view to the explanation of distributive shares and their dynamics in the business-cycle or in the longer period. As stated earlier, dynamic analysis is not within the scope of this study; in the pages that follow we shall consequently leave out an albeit important part of Kalecki's thinking in order to concentrate on its basic characteristics, as they emerge from the identification of the causes of the price level and of the distributive setting at a given moment in time.

2.1 THE ESSAY OF 1933

Our review starts with the 1933 essay (1933a, 1933b) in which the outstanding aspects of Kalecki's theory are more or less explicitly drawn: on the one hand, the theory of effective demand and profits, along lines close to those illustrated above, on the other, a non-competitive price theory outlined in terms which already seem outside the marginalist framework.[5] The main purpose of the essay is to provide a theory of the business cycle; subordinate to this purpose is the explanation of the equilibrium level of income at a given moment; the two aspects, however, are separable so that (in line with our intention) we will reverse the order of importance Kalecki attributed to them.

In the 1933 essay the microeconomic aspects are examined for two reasons: (1) to clarify the relationship between investments and the level of production (i.e., to pass from the theory of profits to the theory of aggregate income); (2) to examine the dynamics of distributive shares in the business cycle.

The essence of Kalecki's reasoning can be illustrated as follows.[6] Starting with a situation at a given point of the cycle, capital stock and capitalists' expenditure (in real terms) can be assumed as given, both being established by decisions taken earlier; the profit equation, therefore, is:

$$\frac{P}{p} = I + C_p \qquad (2.1)$$

where, for the sake of simplicity, a single price for consumer and investment goods is considered. Since[7]

$$P \equiv \frac{P}{Y} Y$$

and:

$$Y = pX$$

we have:

$$\frac{P}{p} = \frac{P}{pX} X \qquad (2.2)$$

in which P/pX is both the gross profit margin in the value of each unit of product and the share of profits in national income.[8] By the preceding equations Kalecki aims at the objectives mentioned above, i.e., explaining the level of activity (X) and the distributive shares. To fulfil this purpose a further relation is introduced in addition to (2.1) and (2.2), which (depending on the underlying price theory) takes, alternatively, the form:

$$\frac{P}{pX} = f(X), \qquad f' > 0 \qquad (2.3)$$

or:

$$\frac{P}{pX} = \text{cost} \qquad (2.4)$$

Equation (2.3) applies to the case of free competition (with or without 'imperfections'), (2.4) to 'cartelised' markets (1933b, p. 107). In both cases the underlying microeconomic basis is so obscure that it is necessary to guess the author's reasoning.[9]

Though it can be interpreted in different ways, Kalecki's belief that in competitive markets profit margins and the share of profits vary in direct relation to the level of activity relies, in our opinion, on the traditional marginalist framework (or, in any case, is consistent with it). In a short-period context, with rising costs and maximising behaviour, profit margins rise with output because of the progressive divergence of marginal from average costs; therefore, demand-determined variations in the general level of business, by shifting the functions of demand for each firm (in both perfect and imperfect competition) cause changes in the same direction of profit margins and the share of profits in the aggregate income.[10]

Kalecki shows concern for clarifying the microeconomic premises of his reasoning only when he distinguishes, within the firms, those he calls 'marginal' (1933b, p. 99), meaning those earning lower profit margins. During recessions, he argues that: 'competition sharpens through reductions in gross profit margins, shifting the fall in utilization to marginal plants' (1933b, p. 99).

Kalecki's reasoning here is not in contrast with the marginalist approach and the interpretation proposed above; reference to 'marginal' firms seems to rely on the idea that they are those which undergo greater losses in profit margins during recessions, as their gap between marginal and average costs is smaller.[11]

The conceptual frame Kalecki resorts to when considering a 'cartelised' system (1933b, pp. 106–8), a situation, he seems to mean, in which firms more or less openly agree on the price policy, is far from the marginalist approach. Kalecki could have adopted the marginalist scheme of monopoly (the purpose of cartels being to make the firms act like a monopoly) here, but he argues along quite different lines. He asserts that in this kind of market profit margins, through cartels, are kept constant when business activity changes[12] and the productive capacity is generally underemployed. The explanation of this point, however, is left to conjecture, since Kalecki is unconcerned about making it clear.

Constant margins are not in themselves incompatible with the hypothesis of profit maximisation, but such particular conditions are necessary in this case as to make it negligible.[13] The constancy of the margin must therefore have a different explanation, i.e., not the effect of the free play of the market but the result of firms' *price decisions*. These decisions would be centred on two points: the determination of a certain margin (on which Kalecki will always be evasive), and the maintenance of it when short-term variations in the production level occur. From this price policy the constancy of the distributive shares in a completely cartelised system, as the level of activity changes, is derived as a corollary.[14]

If the preceding considerations are correct, Kalecki would have applied different theoretical models to different market situations without it being strictly necessary on the theoretical level, since the *oligopolistic* case (conceived as a cartelised system) could have been treated as a variant of monopoly and as such enter into the general scheme put forward by marginalism; this is then a first instance of a method which, as we shall see, will be systematically applied in subsequent writings.

2.2 THE DEGREE OF MONOPOLY IN THE ESSAY OF 1938

An obligatory step in reviewing Kalecki's theory of income distribution is the article which first appeared in *Econometrica* in 1938 (1938a) and was later republished with changes in (1939a). This essay drew strong criticisms which probably negatively influenced the appraisal of subsequent contributions. In what follows we will argue that these criticisms were founded on overly reductive interpretations, albeit they were amply justified by the confused and incomplete manner – the 'rather imperfect form', as the author himself would later admit (Kalecki, 1971b, p. vii) – in which the subject was treated.

The purpose of the 1938 article is to investigate the factors determining the share of manual labour in aggregate income[15] and the causes of its stability in time, as brought out by several studies in Great Britain and the United States.[16]

After recalling Lerner's index of the degree of monopoly:[17]

$$m = \frac{p - MC}{p} \tag{2.7}$$

Kalecki (1938a, p. 102) demonstrates that m is 'with great approximation' equal to the share of gross profits and salaries in the 'aggregate turnover' T (i.e., the gross tradeable production),[18] from which:

$$\frac{P+S}{Y} = 1 - \frac{W}{Y} = m\frac{T}{Y} \tag{2.8}$$

with S, the amount of salaries; $T = Y + M$, and M the value of raw materials; m, average (weighted) degree of monopoly of the firms operating in the economy. Equation (2.8) shows that the share of profits and salaries in the gross national income is in a direct relationship with the degree of monopoly and with the 'rate of turnover' (T/Y), which measures the incidence of raw materials on final production.

Kalecki arrives at this equation after assuming that the short-period cost functions are such that:

(a) depreciation and salaries are substantially fixed costs;

(b) marginal and average costs for wages and raw materials are constant up to full employment of 'practical capacity', as capital and labour are (at least in the short period) *limitational* instead of *substitutional* factors; from this it follows that the prime and marginal costs functions take the shape of an inverted 'L' and coincide each other along the 'horizontal stroke';[19]

(c) firms normally work below 'full practical capacity' (1939a, p. 23), i.e., along the 'horizontal stroke' of their cost functions.

Equation (2.8) is a variant of (1.5), the diversity arising (apart from considering S) from the different method of derivation;[20] both of them are but identities deprived of explicative capacity. These definitory aspects are premises for giving a solution to the following problems: (1) explaining the factors the degree of monopoly depends on, and how this determines the distributive structure; (2) demonstrating that the theory, though derived from short-period hypotheses, holds even for the long period.[21]

Point (1) raised major criticisms; two types of objections have been moved,[22] each corresponding with a different interpretation of the concept of degree of monopoly: according to one interpretation, the degree of monopoly is *determined* by the elasticity of demand and *coincides* with its inverse, which precludes it from providing a macroeconomic explanation of distribution; according to the other, if the tie with elasticity is discarded, the Kaleckian approach loses explanatory power or even becomes tautological.

As Kalecki himself warns (1938a, p. 100) *if* marginal cost equals marginal returns – i.e., *if* maximising behaviour is assumed – then the degree of monopoly coincides with the inverse of price elasticity of demand by definition. As recalled before, the possibility of using the concept of degree of monopoly to explain the distributive phenomena in this case has undergone important objections.

One of these, advanced by Kaldor (1956), is based on the idea that:

> the very notion of a demand curve for products of a single firm is illegitimate if the prices charged by different firms cannot be assumed to be independent of each other (p. 225).

Such an hypothesis would nevertheless be untenable because of the interdependence of firms' decisions in non-competitive markets and, more generally, because of Kalecki's intention to lend his theory of distribution a macroeconomic scope. In other words, the use of the concept of price elasticity of demand entails considering all the other prices and incomes as given – i.e., it requires a partial equilibrium framework – and cannot be correctly generalised to the macroeconomic level; the Kaleckian approach, therefore:

> encounters the same problems as neoclassical theory, namely the use of microeconomic concepts to explain a macroeconomic problem (Nuti, 1970, p. 268).[23]

Another point was raised by Lange (1941):

> The average degree of monopoly for the whole economy being a weighted mean is changed by a shift in output between industries. Thus it has little meaning to say that the distribution of the national income is 'determined' by the average degree of monopoly. Rather the average degree of monopoly is, together with the other variables of the system, determined by more fundamental data such as demand schedules and the shape of cost curves which determine the degree of monopoly of the firms as well as the distribution of the value of the total output between industries and firms (p. 281).

In synthesis, Lange seems to argue, by depending on the structure of production the *average* degree of monopoly is also affected – given the different spending habits of social classes – by the distribution of income.

Lange's interpretation is more subtle and problematic than Kaldor's; in the review of the *Essays* Lange (1941) emphasises the open nature of 'Kalecki's formula' (i.e., equation (2.7)), and hence its being subject to different interpretations. Lange continues (1941, pp. 281–2) by saying that Kalecki's claim that the degree of monopoly *determines* the distribution of income thus requires further assumptions on which the nature of the resulting theory of distribution depends: *if* Kalecki is deemed to have had in mind that firms maximise profits along marginalist lines, then his conclusions meet the objections mentioned above. Alternatively, Lange continues, Kalecki's theory *becomes* 'a social-power theory of distribution' once it is completed – according to the then emerging approaches – with the the *mark-up* principle. He then concludes:

> But this conclusion is based upon additional assumptions and is not contained in Mr. Kalecki's formula. His formula is causally neutral, i.e., it is compatible with various causal interpretations (1941, p. 282).

Among the two possibilities mentioned by Lange, Kalecki inclined, in our opinion, towards the second; this can be inferred, at least, from the fact that the framework of hypotheses put forward seems to exclude the first possibility.

Clearing the field from pure competition (where $m = 0$), Kalecki points out that the proper ground for his theory is non-competitive markets,[24] for which he assumes the existence of a *given* degree of monopoly; therefore, the idea, already put forward in (1933a, 1933b), as to the stability of the margin and share of profits, is confirmed. The hypothesis that the degree of monopoly is given (and therefore invariable with respect to short-period changes in output), joined to that of L-shaped cost functions, leads to the conclusion that the supply functions, too, are horizontal up to full practical capacity.[25] However, the causes of the extent and constancy of the degree of monopoly remain unclear, e.g., whether they derive from maximising or other behaviour, and on this point the shortcomings of Kalecki's argument make it difficult to arrive at definite conclusions.

The marginalist approach does not seem feasible since the constancy of the degree of monopoly would have to rely on the behaviour of the market. In this case, the horizontal shape of the supply function for each firm would be the result of shifts of the functions of demand and marginal returns as the overall level of activity changes; these shifts would have to take place in such a way as to allow the firms to maximise profits at an unchanged price. Given the constraints set by the constancy of the magnitudes in (2.7) and the constancy of the elasticity of demand,[26] in order for the supply function to have the claimed characteristics, the various demand functions associated with it must demonstrate, at the same price, unchanged elasticity whatever output is produced; for this to occur, the demand functions must shift, changing their features in a particular way.[27]

Kalecki does not mention this condition, nor does he refer to the hypothesis of profit maximisation. The second possibility is therefore more likely: namely, that the constancy of the degree of monopoly is not the mere result of the particular way in which the demand curves move, but more simply the effect of the *price policy* implemented by the firms, who apply fixed margins on prime costs; prices, together with the degree of monopoly, are thus determined by production conditions and by margins *set discretionally* in order to cover overheads and to allow a certain profit.[28]

This second way of conceiving of the degree of monopoly overcomes the objections arising from the marginalist interpretation, but it is subjected to a different order of criticism,[29] according to which, once the connection to elasticity has been abandoned (and lacking a price theory), the degree of monopoly would be explained by its own definition after all; in this case, it would represent only an *ex post* variable which does not provide any explanation of the distribution of income, being at the most an indicator of it.

There are certainly defects in Kalecki's arguing, especially because, while dropping the assumption of maximising behaviour, no alternative hypotheses are stated in a sufficiently explicit manner. However, hints about the mainsprings of the degree of monopoly and the way it affects firms' behaviour as regards pricing are not lacking; on the whole these indications confirm the unreliability of the marginalist interpretation and free the Kaleckian approach from the flaw of tautology.

To interpret Kalecki's outlook correctly, the dual nature of the concept of the degree of monopoly should be kept in mind: *stricto sensu*, this coincides with Lerner's definition and as such is an *effect* of price decisions (however taken) and an indicator of the distributive structure; in a more general sense, however, the degree of monopoly marks the market condition that allows firms to *make* a price policy, i.e., not to be merely price takers.

In limiting firms' market power, on the one hand, the extent of losses due to competitors' reactions to changes in prices and, on the other, the public's responsiveness to price differentiations (degree of market imperfection) concur. Influencing the first type of factors are industrial concentration, the existence of tacit agreements or cartels , the strength of the dimensional and sectoral barriers and those due to product differentiation; influencing the second type are the spreading of information, the diversity of products and the habits of consumers, and the phase of the business cycle. All these factors together – the degree of monopoly *lato sensu* – determine the pattern of the demand functions estimated by the firms, so that, by influencing pricing decisions, they come to set the degree of monopoly in the *stricto sensu* of the term.

Kalecki's departure from marginalist logic is confirmed by the causes he adduces for the changes in the degree of monopoly during the business cycle. Drawing from Joan Robinson (1936) and Harrod (1936) (according to the latter the degree of monopoly rises during a boom and decreases during a depression due to the different degree of market imperfection characterising those phases of the cycle[30]), Kalecki (1939a, p. 35) objects that the tendency is just the opposite, as is evident by the fact that during a depression the prices of certain manufactured goods do not decline *in spite of* the fall in the prices of raw materials and nominal wages. This course is explained by various considerations:

(a) by the setting up of cartels designed to protect profits;

(b) because firms are reluctant to reduce prices for fear that competitors will be pushed to emulation;

(c) because there is little room for concern, during this phase, about the entry of new competitors.[31]

Then, if maximising behaviour ruled, firms would be inclined to accept lower prices following the decline in production costs during the negative phases of the cycle; if this does not occur, it means that they behave according to a different logic. Nor can it be objected that increasing uncertainty makes it impossible for firms (1) to know the precise nature of their demand functions, or even (2) to conjecture about them.

In the second case, maximising behaviour fails for lack of presuppositions (even though rebuttal of its logic as such is not implied). As to the first, firms could attempt to *evaluate* the patterns of their demand functions,[32] which becomes more feasible when the setting up of cartels reduces uncertainty about competitors' reactions: therefore, if the marginalist rule applied, prices would be lowered following the decline in costs because, by doing so, profit *expectations* would be maximised;[33] if this does not occur it means that operators have dropped the target of maximum profit in favour of a *satisfactory* profit.

A second aspect Kalecki is concerned with is demonstrating that his theory of distribution, though derived from short-period hypotheses, holds also for the long period, whilst this would not be the case for the marginalist theory, which is based on substitutability between capital and labour. Kalecki argues that changes in the 'basic data' (technical progress, inventions, interest rate), while influencing the relationship between capital and labour – and consequently the long-period position and the price level – nevertheless do not affect the distribution of income which

> remains unaffected by changes of basic data so long as the degree of monopoly is unaltered and the use of equipment in the long-run

> equilibrium does not reach [full practical capacity (1938a, p. 105). It follows that] both the elasticity of substitution between capital and labour, and inventions are, contrary to the prevailing opinion, of no influence on the distribution of income (1938a, p. 103).[34]

This point of view is not sufficiently argued since if the degree of monopoly is the result of entrepreneurial behaviour, then it must be concluded that – similarly to the latter – it is affected by changes in the 'basic data';[35] arguing that the distribution of income is not influenced by these factors *since* the degree of monopoly is (without justification) independent of them, means falling into the tautological trap.

What Kalecki probably really wants to demonstrate through this hypothesis is a more general thesis: namely, that the degree of monopoly is a permanent feature of the capitalist market, as such not imputable to the slowness in the processes of adjustment and therefore not bound to be reabsorbed in the long run; it would consequently be illusory to seek *definite* analytical relationships, even with variables which come into play in the long period.[36] In this way Kalecki emphasises his basic conviction, being the distribution of income beyond market automatisms and relying instead on *social power*.

2.3 THE WRITINGS OF THE EARLY 1940s

In an essay that followed in (1940a), Kalecki's detachment from the maximising approach with regard to non-competitive markets appears more marked. Kalecki distinguishes here (p. 91) between 'pure imperfect competition', which allows a large number of small enterprises, and oligopoly. In the first case each firm is supposed to know the precise pattern of the demand function for its product since, by virtue of the nature of the market, its behaviour does not arouse appreciable response by competitors; the marginalist categories would consequently apply here.[37]

Kalecki's reasoning is different when imperfect competition assumes the guise of oligopoly. He warns that

> an equilibrium theory of oligopoly ... is entirely beyond the scope of this article and I rather doubt whether it is practicable for the short period at all [; consequently, everything he aims at is] to assume as data what we call the degree of oligopoly or certain elements in the selling policy, and examine only how these data change under the influence of

> short period factors, in particular in the course of the trade cycle (1940a, p. 97).

In oligopoly, Kalecki argues, the small number of enterprises prevents them from knowing the precise pattern of the demand functions for their products; firms do not consequently equate the marginal return with the marginal cost. Instead, the entrepreneur:

> fixes its price at a certain point where the former is *greater* than the latter [(1940a, p. 97);[38] this price is kept constant since the entrepreneur] does not reduce its price below this level because he assumes that this will induce his competitors to reduce their prices and so the average price sufficiently to render his operation unprofitable. But neither does he raise the price above this level because he assumes that his competitors will not raise their prices sufficiently to make *this* operation profitable (1940a, p. 97).

A contradiction needs to be pointed out in the above reasoning, since the very fact that firms set prices in such a way as to earn marginal returns greater than marginal costs entails that the 'imagined' demand function is derivable also in correspondence to the price fixed; on the contrary, Kalecki's argument about the stability of price requires that the demand curve be kinked at the price set,[39] i.e., exactly where marginal returns cannot be appraised.[40] However this constrast is worked out, the maximising approach is ruled out in any case; in fact, if the considerations on stability are discarded (if usual demand curves are assumed), the conclusion remains that firms give up maximising profits even though they are in a position to do so; if, instead, the demand curve is supposed to be kinked, then the explanation of prices must lie outside the marginalist categories. In the one case the maximising behaviour would be excluded as a consequence of a *choice* by entrepreneurs, in the other as a consequence of the lack of conditions necessary to make it practicable.

The elements brought forward to give substance to the price theory (those determining the value of a_i) are, as always, quite meagre; the essence of Kalecki's reasoning is that firms take competition into account *empirically* by applying a discretionally set margin above prime costs.[41] As in (1938a), more elements, derived mainly from changes in the degree of monopoly, are adduced by Kalecki when dealing with the causes of price variations during the course of the business cycle.[42]

During the negative phases of the business cycle, firms react in two ways to the decline in profits resulting from the fall in the price of prime factors and the level of activity:[43]

(a) By lowering their degree of oligopoly in order to expel the weaker enterprises from the market and to gain their share:

> the 'stronger' firms (low-cost producers) try to improve their situation by lowering their degrees of oligopoly in order to drive out the field the 'weaker' ones (high-cost producers) who already are on the verge of ruin as a result of the 'natural' fall in gross profits. A necessary (though not sufficient) condition of this state of affairs is a considerable dispersion of the level of prime costs between the different firms (1940a, p. 101).

(b) By stipulating tacit agreements to prevent ruinous price wars, allowing them to maintain their degree of oligopoly or even to raise it to offset the increased incidence of overheads:

> In the case of a 'tacit agreement' the single entrepreneur in the slump arrives at the conclusion that if his degree of oligopoly *a* falls, or even remains constant, he will inevitably reach a position of not being able to cover his overhead expenditure ... Thus he raises *a*, his only hope being that his competitors will do likewise. If they do not he is lost, but so he would be if he did not raise *a*. If such is the prevailing attitude a tacit agreement is established and the supply curve shifts upwards (1940a, p. 101).

It is easy to see that the above lies outside the standard of maximising behaviour, and that instead the degree of oligopoly is a variable subject to the control of firms rather than being fully determined by the parameters of the demand function; in this sense, the introduction of this concept is a step forward towards the translation of market situations into behavioural hypotheses.

An element conflicting with this interpretation (but also marking a regression from Kalecki's previous positions) is represented by some remarks in (1943b, pp. 9–31),[44] which more than others lend themselves to a reading in the traditional vein. Here Kalecki's purpose is to demonstrate that *gross margins* $((p - APC)/p)$,[45] together with the share of wages in the output of each industry, are constant during the course of the business cycle *unless* the degree of oligopoly or the degree of market imperfection change.

The field of analysis is the short-period equilibria of the industry's price system, understood as situations in which each firm – which sets the price according to customers' mobility and the expected reactions of rivals – 'is satisfied that the price p_i fixed is more advantageous than a higher or a lower level' (1943b, p. 10). This point sets the basis for exercises in comparative statistics, designed to demonstrate that after perturbations (such as changes in variable costs or overall output) the price system returns to equilibrium, the previous margins remaining unchanged.

The equilibrium prices mentioned above can be interpreted in either the traditional manner, as Marshallian normal short-period prices, or (as later in 1954) as prices that are maintained, being considered all in all satisfactory. The arguments underlying the restoration of equilibrium can likewise be interpreted in either traditional or non-traditional ways; there are, however, statements here (even if relegated to the notes) which suggest that Kalecki was thinking of the traditional way.

In case of a change in the overall level of activity (let us suppose upward), the gross margin, Kalecki argues (1943b, p. 15), remains unaltered till productive capacity is in excess, unless increased demand affects the degree of oligopoly or the degree of market imperfection. Now, if the margin is exogenously established, *nulla questio* for it to keep unchanged; if instead it is set according to the rule of maximisation, then its constancy implies constancy of the elasticity of demand: indeed, this is the case Kalecki refers to when asserting that 'in terms of individual demand curves this means an iso-elastic shift of these curves to the right' (1943b, p. 15n.). The constancy of the elasticity is derived from (2.10), the shape of which in (1940a) took into account only the degree of market imperfection, while it now also allows for the degree of oligopoly: if these two factors do not change along with changes in demand and if all the firms behave in the same manner (so that $(p_i/\overline{p})$ remains unaltered), the elasticity, too, will remain constant.

Another possibility concerns the effects of proportional cost variations for all the firms in the industry; Kalecki's conclusion in this regard (1943b, p. 10) is that proportional changes in prices will occur so that the new equilibrium price system will be characterised by unaltered gross margins. In this case, too, the keystone is the constancy of elasticity.[46]

Besides indicating a return to earlier theses, which appeared overcome by the hints traceable in other writings (Kalecki, 1938a, 1940a), this way of arguing is highly unsatisfactory since its conclusions are contained in its premises. The core of the reasoning is that firms continue to maximise profits in correspondence with unaltered margins *since* elasticity does not change; however, for this not to change requires (1) that the ratio $(p_i/\overline{p})$

does not change, that is to say that the margins remain unaltered,[47] and (2) that it be influenced by no other elements except for $(p_i/\overline{p})$. The first condition is clearly tautological, since it represents both the hypothesis and the conclusion, besides being unrealistic in that it implies that the firms all behave as though they were one. The second condition, too, is unacceptable since elasticity also depends: (a) on the level of activity, so that it is incorrect – except in a very special case – to hypothesise iso-elastic shifts of the functions of demand upon its variation; (b) on the ratio of the prices of the particular industry to the prices of the *other* industries, so that it changes even if $(p_i/\overline{p})$ remains constant.[48]

2.4 THE MOST RECENT FORMULATIONS

In (1954, pp. 11–41) Kalecki's theory of prices and distribution takes almost definitive physionomy in spite of some persisting, unsatisfying aspects. In opening this work, Kalecki makes an important distinction about pricing:

> Short-term price changes may be classified into two broad groups: those determined mainly by changes in cost of production and those determined mainly by changes in demand (1954, p. 11).

The first case applies to the industrial sector where excess capacity allows firms to meet changes in demand by adjusting output at unaltered prices; this condition being absent in the second (the primary sector), the short-period adjustment runs mainly from the price side.[49] It worth noting that the influence of demand on the price of primary products does not necessarily entail competitive conditions but only short-period inelasticity of supply; consistently, it would not be correct – as often happens[50] – to identify the dual criterion of determination of prices with the distinction between *price leader* and *price taker* firms.[51]

Once this line of demarcation has been drawn, Kalecki turns to focus on the industrial sector because of its greater impact on national income, the space monopolistic elements find in it, and the possibility it offers to free the analysis of prices and distribution from the influence of occasional factors.[52] Thus circumscribed, Kalecki's investigation is developed along three levels of increasing generality: (a) that of the single firm; (b) that of the single industry; (c) that of the complex of manufacturing industries, and so on up to spanning the entire private sector, in order to explain the causes of the share of wages in private output.

The guidelines are those made familiar in earlier writings: the scope of the analysis is the short period and productive capacity is in excess; unit prime costs are constant within the relevant range; firms' behaviour is bound to profits but without assuming maximising targets.[53] Given these conditions, prices must be such as to allow earning a satisfactory gross margin, the determination of which is also influenced by the state of competition.[54] The price equation is:

$$p = mu + n\bar{p} \tag{2.13}$$

with u unit prime cost and $\bar{p}$ a weighted average of the prices charged by the firms belonging to the same industry; m and n represent the decisional parameters 'characterizing the price-fixing policy of the firm [and] reflect what may be called the degree of monopoly of the firm's position' (1954, p. 13).[55]

It is clearer here than in earlier writings that by 'degree of monopoly' Kalecki means the market situation which allows firms to carry on their own pricing policy; the magnitude of the parameters of the price equation – and hence the ratio of price to prime cost – is no longer identified or *defined* as the degree of monopoly but is instead regarded as an *effect* of it. Kaldor's misinterpretation of Kalecki's point (as it is argued here) is therefore surprising when he accuses the author of being:

> content with a purely tautological approach according to which the ratio of price to prime costs was *defined* simply as the 'degree of monopoly' (Kaldor, 1956, p. 225).[56]

Kaldor's criticism is even more unfounded if one considers that Kalecki did not leave out references to the main causes of the degree of monopoly. First of all he indicates the structure of the industry (its greater or lesser concentration), since the greater the firm's share in the market the more its price incidence on the average price of the industry, and therefore the less it can be influenced by competitors. Furthermore, this state of things favours the making of cartels and price agreements which can also take the form of tacit recognition of the larger firms as *price leaders*. Another factor affecting the size of the degree of monopoly is the 'development of sales promotion' so that 'price competition is replaced by competition in advertising campaigns, etc.' (Kalecki, 1954, p. 17); this refers, as a factor of monopolistic positions, to the policy of innovation and product differentiation and finally to technical progress and the accumulation of capital.

Control of the price–cost ratio is carried out by the trade unions,[57] since 'a high ratio of profits to wages strengthens the bargaining position of the trade unions in their demand for wages increases' (1954, p. 18); firms are consequently induced to content themselves with the objective of 'reasonable profits' by the fear of the wage struggle.[58]

Less definite conclusions are attained concerning the effects of changes in overheads on p/u, since the shifting in margins of an increase in these costs could not be taken for granted but largely depends on the phase of the business cycle; in reproposing earlier theses,[59] Kalecki holds that the spur to protect profits by means of agreements emerges chiefly during a depression, while competition is more vigorous during expansion.[60] A factor neglected among the causes of monopoly are intersectoral barriers – an omission that appears based on the conviction that the competition which really rules is that among the firms actually present in the market, rather than that with new firms willing to enter it.[61] The degree of monopoly seems consequently to be a phenomenon entirely within single industries, while it is evident that this view becomes less plausible as the analysis is extended to the long period or towards a less partial framework.[62]

While Kaldor's criticism appears to be unfounded, in view of the above considerations, it is nevertheless true that Kalecki's approach is weak on the explanatory ground, due mainly to his failure to state criteria of entrepreneurial conduct. In this regard, Kalecki suggests some guidelines – on the one hand, the search for 'reasonable' profits and, on the other, the degree of monopoly and market imperfection setting the boundaries of freedom for the entrepreneur – but nothing more than approximate criteria; in fact, he does not go much beyond suggesting that the parameters m and n *reflect* the firm's degree of monopoly[63] and singling out some values within which these parameters must range.[64]

From single firms Kalecki (1954, pp. 15–16) goes on to consider the industry, whose price system consists of $(k+1)$ equations:

$$
\begin{aligned}
p_1 &= m_1 u_1 + n_1 \bar{p} \\
&\;\cdot \\
&\;\cdot \\
&\;\cdot \\
\bar{p}_k &= m_k u_k + n_k \bar{p} \\
p &= \bar{m}\bar{u} + \bar{n}\bar{p}
\end{aligned}
\tag{2.16}
$$

where $\bar{m}$, $\bar{n}$ and $\bar{u}$ are weighted averages of the respective variables appearing in the price equations of each of the k firms;[65] the equation of the average price can be rewritten as:

$$\overline{p} = \frac{\overline{m}}{1-\overline{n}}\overline{u} \qquad (2.17)$$

From the characteristics of the price system it ensues that its solution interacts with the structure of the industry: by settling the relative importance of the firms, the structure of the industry affects the average price and consequently the single prices, which in turn determine the distribution of production among the firms. Given the demand function for each firm, the set of costs and parameters of the price equations, and the equations expressing the average values $\overline{m}$, $\overline{n}$ and $\overline{u}$ – Kalecki seems to argue – system (2.16) provides the equilibrium prices of the industry, i.e., those that lead to a structure of demand (as reflected in the average values of the parameters and in $\overline{u}$) such as to give the various firms exactly those weights which determine an average price compatible with the prices fixed individually by each of them.[66]

Having proved the existence of an equilibrium price vector for the industry, Kalecki then turns to demonstrate the *convergence* towards it. This point is pursued by assuming that the parameters *m* and *n* are uniform among the various firms, while unit costs differ; only the latter therefore appear as weighted averages in (2.17), while *m* and *n* are present as single values, coincident with those actually fixed by the firms. Kalecki's arguments to prove the tendency of the price system towards equilibrium[67] are scanty, as they rest on the condition that changes in unit costs (which represent the disequilibrating impulse that gives rise to the process towards a new equilibrium) leave the relative importance of the firms unchanged, and therefore bring about only an *una tantum* modification of the average cost $\overline{u}$; it is on this basis that Kalecki is able to derive (2.18) and conclude in favour of convergence towards new equilibrium prices.

It must be opposed to Kalecki's reasoning that changes in unitary costs affect firms' prices to a different extent, modifying the relative importance of each of them within the industry and, in this way, the relative weight of their unitary cost on the average cost. It follows that the new average price is the result both of the changes in the single costs and of the changes in the incidence of each one on the average ($\overline{u}$); furthermore, the new average price becomes in turn the cause of further different changes in the single prices so that the relative importance of the firms, and with it the influence of their costs on the average, are altered again, and so on.[68] And again, the above considerations imply that variations occurring in the weight of the firms, as prices shift, are determinable; this in turn requires that the individual demand functions be stable, a condition which cannot be fulfilled since they necessarily shift as the price structure changes.

The interaction of the price system with the structure of the industry also complicates another aspect Kalecki cares about, namely the *singling-out* of the degree of monopoly as the determinant of the distribution of income within the industry, which would make it necessary to make it free from being influenced by variations in the level of activity. To this end it is not enough for firms' costs and prices to be independent of their level of production, since if firms have different margins the distribution of income can also change by virtue of the simple shifting of their importance in the industry. It follows that in order to neutralise the influence on distribution of variations in the level of activity it must be further assumed that these variations have to be shared equiproportionately among the firms.[69]

In practice, this amounts to assuming that industry behaves as a single firm, and that is actually the step Kalecki takes by introducing a *representative firm*, 'for which the coefficients m and n are equal to $\bar{m}$ and $\bar{n}$ for the industry' (1954, p. 16) and whose degree of monopoly is that of the industry.

Kalecki implicitly makes reference to a representative firm when analysing the distributive implications of his price theory. The relationship between average price and average prime cost of an industry is presented as follows:

$$\frac{\bar{p}}{\bar{u}} = \frac{R}{M+W} = k \qquad (2.20)$$

with:

$$R = M + W + (P + C_c) \qquad (2.21)$$

where R, total proceeds or overall value of industry output; M, W, P, C_c, respectively overall cost of consumer materials, wages, profits and overheads (including salaries). Since the value added of the ith industry ($Y_i = R–M$) can be expressed:[70]

$$Y_i = W + (k–1)(M + W) \qquad (2.22)$$

it is easily deduced that:

$$\frac{W}{Y_i} = \frac{1}{1+(k-1)(j+1)} \qquad (2.23)$$

with $j = M/W$. According to (2.23) the share of wages in the value added of industry is determined by the degree of monopoly (as reflected in k) and by the ratio of the expenditure for raw materials to wages.[71]

The next step is extending (2.23) to the manufacturing sector as a whole and finally to the entire private sector. In this case, the share of wages depends not only on k and j of each industry but also on the industrial structure. By assuming k and j as weighted averages of the coefficients of different industries, Kalecki concludes that:

> the relative share of wages in the value added of manufacturing is determined, apart from the industrial composition of the value added, by the degree of monopoly and by the ratio of raw material prices to unit wage costs (1954, p. 29).[72]

Finally, the conclusions concerning the manufacturing sector are generalised to the entire private sector; this is done so roughly and hastily as not to be justifiable, even allowing for the approximate meaning they are given by Kalecki:

> It may now be shown that this theorem can be generalized to cover the relative share of wages in the gross national income of the private sector (i.e. national income gross of depreciation exclusive of income of public employees). In addition to the sectors of the economy accounted for above, we have still to consider (besides construction, transport and private services assimilated to the manufacturing industry) agriculture and mining, communications and public utilities, trade, real estate and finance. In agriculture and mining the products are raw materials and the relative share of wages in the value added depends mainly on the ratio of prices of the raw materials *produced* to their unit wage costs. In the remaining sectors the relative share of wages in the value added is negligible. It will thus be seen that, broadly speaking, the degree of monopoly, the ratio of prices of raw materials to unit wage costs and industrial composition are the determinants of the relative share of wages in the gross income of the private sector (1954, p. 30).[73]

2.5 CONCLUDING REMARKS

The approach to prices and distribution outlined so far raises several aspects worthy of further reflection. A first point is Kalecki's extending to the general and macroeconomic level conclusions drawn from partial analysis. In generalising (2.23) to the entire manufacturing sector, Kalecki assumes k as an average reflecting the degrees of monopoly of different industries, each one being given independently of the others. As already noticed, this hypothesis probably rests on the idea that the competition ruling the market occurs among firms already operating in the industry, which makes the degree of monopoly a phenomenon which springs entirely from relationships within each industry. This point of view, however, can be accepted only within the frame of partial analysis, or (with the *caveat* below) in a short-period context, in which barriers may be supposed to be effective and each *industry* can be assumed legitimately to pursue an autonomous price policy.

Instead, Kalecki can hardly extend his method to the economic system as a whole or to the long period, since interdependencies which cannot be ignored come into play.

When the analysis is brought to the multisectoral level, the degree of monopoly of each industry, besides reflecting the extent of the agreement among firms within it or the power relationships among them, becomes fundamentally an effect of the protection of its market from the others, i.e., of the existence of intersectoral barriers.[74] Accordingly, the degree of monopoly of the ith industry – thus the term $(\overline{p}/\overline{u})_i$ can no longer be considered independent of the conditions ruling in the kth industry. Nor does it helps to support Kalecki's claim that his reasoning *prevalently* concerns the short period, for even if barriers are effective in this context, firms will still take into account the potential competition stimulated by high-profit policies if capital mobility is allowed. Kalecki's view is even more implausible when the long period is concerned: barriers no longer hold and there must here be some mechanism of intersectoral compensation with regards to pricing, that is to say, a mechanism which tendentially leads the *key variables* the firms pursue to uniformity. This takes us to a second aspect.

According to Kalecki, firms *expend* their degree of monopoly on profit per unit of output, the index being roughly identified as p/u. Instead, the search for profits (at least in the long run) should be related to capital invested rather than to production. Accordingly, it is the rate of profit and not the margin the objective firms pursue, which brings the former to uniformity when capital mobility is allowed; on the contrary, persisting differences in rates of profits are due to barriers and thus to particular power positions of industries or firms. Concluding, it is reasonable to believe that the target the degree of monopoly and the market power strive for in the long run is the rate of profit.

It can be argued, of course, that profit per unit of output is a plausible target for the short period, especially when considering that – capital stock being given (and disregarding effects on the degree of utilisation of equipment) – it is positively related to the rate of profit and may be viewd as a rough approximation of it; moreover, aiming at the margin instead of the rate of profit simplifies things, by freeing firms of the burden of continually reappraising the capital invested. However, if the rate of profit represents the *strategic objective* over the long period, it must also lead to consistent behaviours during the short period.

While referring to section 4.1.2 for a variant of the price equation along these lines, we can now appraise the consequences of this different approach for Kalecki's scheme. These are inferred, starting with:

$$\frac{P}{Y} \equiv \frac{P}{K}\frac{K}{Y} \qquad (2.26)$$

from which the conclusion can be drawn that, given the rate of profit (as the objective pursued), the distribution of income also depends directly on technological choices (as reflected in long-period changes of K/Y) and, therefore, the degree of monopoly ceases to be the sole factor of distribution.[75]

Probably just to avoid this conclusion, the Kaleckian reading of (2.26) is based on the short-cut that distribution – i.e., P/Y – is *directly* determined by the degree of monopoly; this relegates the rate of profit to a secondary position, being subject to the consequences of the manner in which technological choices and the degree of utilisation of equipment affect the capital–output ratio.[76] Kalecki is thus able to conclude:

> the *relations* between prices and unit prime costs can be affected by changes in equipment and technique [i.e., by the factors Kalecki considers outstanding in the long period] only to the extent to which they influence the degree of monopoly (Kalecki, 1954, p. 19).[77]

It is apparent that these conclusions mark no advances compared to Kalecki's preceding contributions (especially 1938a), which now as then can be summarised as follows:

(a) the distributive setting depends on the relationship between prices and costs;

(b) this relationship relies on firms' market power;

(c) this conclusion holds for the long period, too, since factors acting in this span of time can influence distribution only insofar as they affect that power.

The keystone of the above is obviously point (b), that is to say, how the degree of monopoly and the factors operating in the long term are embodied into hypotheses of entrepreneurial behaviour; lack of clearness weakens the entire construction in this regard, though not to such an extent as justify the criticism of tautology. This is particularly disappointing considering that Kalecki (as we will see[78]) had developed elements which would have allowed him to overcome these shortcomings.

A last point we should consider is the relationship between the Kaleckian theory of prices and distribution and the marginalist one. This interest is inspired in particular by the criticism (see Messori, 1977) according to which Kalecki's approach did not involve a 'categorical' break with marginalist tradition, being founded solely on the substitution of perfect competition (deemed unrealistic) with imperfect competition.[79] According to this interpretation, therefore, there would be no rejection of the theoretical foundations of marginalism but only the recognition that in reality imperfect competition is the rule; it follows that:

> the Kaleckian theory of prices and the traditional one are not antagonistic at the categorical level; on the contrary, the first only represents a better approximation to reality, which – as such – is unable to question the methodology of the second, but indeed assumes this as point of departure (1977, p. 78).[80]

In our opinion the substitution of the competitive framework for 'imperfect' competition and of the traditional U-shaped cost curves for L curves, is justified, first of all, by considerations inherent to realism (which seems, indeed, a serious way of approaching things), but also joined to the rejection of marginalism on the 'categorical' front.

It is well known that the peculiar and unifying element of the marginalist theory is methodology, based on the principle of maximisation under constraints; the application of this principle in the theory of prices requires that firms be in a position to know (or to estimate) their functions of demand and marginal return and that the cost functions show an appropriate shape.[81]

Even with theoretical arguments Kalecki rejects both the points on which the marginalist construction is founded. As for the first, firms' uncertainty about the reactions of rivals eliminates the condition for pursuing the maximisation of profit (or urges them to mediate this objective with others). As for the second, Kalecki rejects substitutability among factors in the short period, by arguing that capital and labour are limitational factors and that the capital–labour ratio per time unit is substantially constant.[82] The particular shape of costs, drawn from observation, is therefore explained by the indivisibility of capital – an argument which is opposed to those of marginalism.

The rejection of the theory of marginal productivity, underlying this conception of capital, is confirmed by the theory of distribution in which

Kalecki reaches the conclusion (whose general significance is clear, albeit not sufficiently argued) that:

> both the elasticity of substitution between capital and labour, and inventions are, contrary to the prevailing opinion, of no influence on the distribution of income (1938a, p. 103).

3 The Theory of Effective Demand

In Kalecki's works, the theory of effective demand was the least troubled part; it was free of the troubled course of the theory of distribution or the many revisions the theory of investments and economic fluctuations underwent. Its structure has remained basically unchanged since its original formulation in (1933a, 1993b),[1] while the author's efforts were directed to clarifying connections with earlier theories (namely, with Marxian schemes of reproduction) and with other contemporary theories (i.e., Keynes), to specify its microeconomic premises and some methodological aspects, and to investigate further the implications of the new scheme for economic policy.

It has often been noted that an essential aspect of this analysis is the separation of the problem of underemployment from that of instability, in that they are logically distinct phenomena. This conviction was initially accompanied by greater interest in the second of the two aspects, which was the more conventional one but, at the same time, better mirrored Kalecki's view (then coming from recent Marxist readings) on the ineluctability of the crises as the 'supreme expression' of the contradictions of capitalistic system.[2]

Consistently, in Kalecki's writings in the early thirties the adjustment between profits and capitalists' expenditure – behind which lies the equilibrating role of income – is mainly conceived as a response to conjunctural impulses, that is to say, as a part of the mechanism of cyclical fluctuations rather than as a part of a process of convergence towards hypothetical positions of underemployment equilibrium. In other words, Kalecki does not yet appear interested in focusing on the equilibrium of income as such, though that concept is clearly stated. Even the articles (1934a) and (1935d), which deal with how foreign trade and the government's budget affect the country's level of activity, are oriented to providing a framework for a policy of stabilisation rather than a policy for curing a chronic deficiency of the economy.

Only later – probably after the *General Theory* was published – did Kalecki seem to realise that the outstanding problem was the systematic waste of resources, and that dealing with it required separating the analysis of equilibrium from that of the dynamic process. From this moment on, the two stages of analysis were to become a constant of his methodology, the second stage being increasingly characterised as an extension of an *autonomous* conceptual system. Kalecki's mind in this sense is reflected in the structure of his more significant writings,[3] where the theory of national income is subjected to autonomous analysis and always precedes – with the interposition of the theory of investments – the theory of economic fluctuations.

The structure of the present chapter reflects this interpretation, dealing first with the theory of national income (investments being given), followed by the analysis of the determinants of investments and monetary phenomena, and ending with questions concerning economic policy.

3.1 THE THEORY OF NATIONAL INCOME

In Chapter 1 we outlined Kalecki's theory of national income and indicated its core in two equations: (1.4) in which profits depend on capitalists' overall spending decisions, and (1.5) which shows that the relationship between profits and aggregate income is determined by the 'factors of distributions'; a third equation (1.6) relative to the equilibrium level of income was derived from the first two.

The meaning of (1.5) was considered in Chapter 2. As for the profits equation, Kalecki argues that the causal link acts from the right, since capitalists can directly decide expenditure but not the amount of their income.[4] Therefore:

> Capitalists as a class gain exactly as much as they invest or consume, and if – in a closed system – they cease to construct and consume they could not make any money at all ... In a way they are 'masters of their fate' (Kalecki, 1933a, pp. 12–13).

The dependence of profits on spending does not rest merely on time lags – as might be deduced from the fact that capitalists' investments and consumptions are the result of decisions taken in a preceding period (spending decisions still being dependent on income); more fundamentally this dependence relies on the existence of a banking system which makes credit available for financing expenditure, thereby rendering investments independent of the *prior* formation of profits and savings. From the beginning, Kalecki was careful to clarify that it is not the flow of savings as such but the supply of credit which is the pre-requisite for expanding investments, and that investments, by widening business activity, bring about the amount of savings necessary for being offset:

> It is possible for the capitalists to step up their investment even though their profits are not increased ... nor have they curtailed their consumption *ad hoc* ... The financing of additional investment is effected by the so called creation of purchasing power. The demand for bank credits increases and these are granted by banks ... The entrepreneurs who engage in additional investment are 'propelling' into the pockets of other capitalists profits which are equal to their investment, and they are becoming indebted to these capitalists to the same extent *via* banks (Kalecki, 1935d, p. 29).

As for the equilibrium level of income:

> Given that profits are determined by capitalists' consumption and investment, it is the workers' income (equal here to workers' consumption) which is determined by the 'distribution factors'. In this way capitalists' consumption and investment conjointly with the 'distribution factors' determine the workers' consumptions and consequently the national output and employment. The national output will be pushed up to the point where profits carved out of it in accordance with the 'distribution factors' are equal to the sum of capitalists' consumption and investment (Kalecki, 1954, p. 47).

It should be added that both the process of the multiplier and its role in restoring the equilibrium had already been described in (1933)[5] and in (1934b).[6]

There is not much to add analytically to the basic model referred to above; that model, to a certain extent, was a free reconstruction of Kalecki's theory, made necessary for integrating a scheme Kalecki was reluctant to formalise in a complete manner.[7]

Taken alone, (1.6) is an identity; as such it is not peculiar to the Kaleckian theory (the use it makes of it is peculiar), but embraces a plurality of cases according to the specifications introduced. Once the propensity to save, monetary wage, techniques and investments in real terms are given, real income and the price level remain as unknowns, so that the equation resolves either one or the other variable according to which of the two was set exogenously.

Therefore (1.6) leads to the *Keynesian case* when assuming uniform propensities to save and adding a marginalist price equation, or to the *Kaleckian case* if price is fixed independently of quantities; if instead full capacity is supposed, it is then the structure of distribution which comes out as the equilibrium solution (*post-Keynesian case à la Kaldor*[8]).

Finally, the equation can be used in order to 'close' the Marxian schemes of reproduction (we will return on this point later).

Equation (1.6) is also useful in illustrating the mechanism of adjustment between savings and investments in a planned economy. In this regard, Kalecki writes:

> In order to bring into focus the nature of this process in the capitalist economy it is useful to consider what the effect of a reduction in investment in a socialist system would be. The workers released from the production of investment goods would be employed in consumption goods industries. The increased supply of these goods would be absorbed by means of a reduction in their prices. Since profits of the socialist industries would be equal to investment, prices would have to be reduced to the point where the decline in profits would be equal to the fall in the value of investment. In other words, full employment would be maintained through the reduction of prices in relation to costs (1954, p. 62).[9]

Keeping the conceptual framework of a capitalist economy, the case considered here is analogous to the Kaldorian one: changes in prices relative to monetary wages ensure that income – whose level is now set as an objective – is not affected by variations in investments.

Kalecki's attention to the institutional aspects also reverberates in attributing to social classes different spending habits, a consequence of their different motivations and opportunities.[10] This viewpoint, which is in line with classic and Marxian tradition, is substantiated in the hypothesis of different propensities to save and, in the disaggregated schemes, in the identification of specific goods the various classes demand.[11]

The idea that workers' income is for the most part bound to consumption is historically linked with the notion of subsistence wage, even if meant as a relative concept; in classical economics and in Marx this concept was important in supporting the view of capitalism as a system grounded in class barriers: the workers' low propensity to save excluded them from the accumulation of capital, thereby perpetuating their condition; hence the identification of dependent workers with wage earners and of profit earners with capitalists–entrepreneurs.

In more recent approaches – from the post-Keynesians to the neo-Marxists, to Kalecki – the lack of social mobility (i.e., of interchangeability of roles), which with different emphases would keep representing the basic feature of capitalism, has been aptly distinguished from what to the classical economists appeared to be its inseparable cause, but which is today outdated. The central point is no longer the disavowal of workers' capacity to save, and thus to share the ownership of capital (of *financial capital*), but their exclusion *de factu* from *direct* participation in investment activity – from the possibility of becoming entrepreneurs – because of the obstacles to taking control of the means of production; this situation, moreover, is in itself a powerful disincentive to save.[12] The traditional causal relationship between spending behaviour and the permanence of class barriers is thus upset; it is no longer, fundamentally, the workers' low propensity to save that prevents their access to the 'club' of capitalists, but the lack of social osmosis that keeps them from saving.[13]

The statement that capitalists (a class which should now be redefined) hold the exclusive power over investment activity is based on considerations symmetrical with those that exclude workers – that is to say, on the key position they enjoy in the productive process, which gives them motivations and possibilities lacking to the others. As we shall see below, this aspect is strongly rooted in Kalecki, who claims tirelessly that 'business democracy' is illusory and that 'the most important prerequisite for becoming an entrepreneur is the *ownership* of capital' (1954, pp. 94–5).

3.2 THE THEORY OF INVESTMENT

According to Kalecki (1968c, p.165) the theory of investment is the central 'pièce de résistance' of economic theory. Kalecki's personal case makes no exception, since he struggled over this subject over a period of thirty years. His effort was developed along two parallel lines: one addressed to grasping the basic determinants of the incentive to invest, the other to improving the formal scheme in order to make it more apt for explaining cyclical fluctuations. While valid suggestions and results have come from the first line, the same does not apply, all in all, to the second, which often suffers from a redundant, mechanistic analytical apparatus, overambitious in claiming to offer empirically verifiable explanations.[14]

With these coordinates in mind, we shall first examine the informing principles and then the analytical framework into which they have been embodied; as our purpose is to focus on the determination of income at a given time, rather than on dynamics, we shall not go deeply into the theory of economic fluctuations.

3.2.1 General Features

We have already seen that according to Kalecki the weakness and instability of the incentive to invest are aspects grafted onto the process of accumulation; it would be incorrect, however, to blame these shortcomings only on the fragility of the state of confidence or on the mere lack of coordination among centres of spending, which are instead factors reinforcing the working of other structural causes, such as:

(a) the distribution of income which, given its ruling mechanisms, is generally insufficient for ensuring adequate outlets to production;

(b) the *productive* nature of investment and, more precisely, the fact that its impact on productive capacity tends to overcome its influence on aggregate demand;

(c) the lack of systematically self-propelling impulses.

These weaknesses emerge in different ways: (1) in a *spontaneous* level of investments which is insufficient to bring about, at a given moment and with the given distribution of income, full employment; (2) in the instability of investments, which is the mainspring of economic fluctuations; (3) in the tendency of the economy, free of external shocks, to gravitate around stationary positions.

A careful policy designed to control accumulation could overcome these difficulties,[15] but as this solution is opposed by the business world, it becomes inevitable for investments to fluctuate, while their long-run growth has to rely on occasional stimuli coming from outside the economic mechanism. Though these impulses are an integral part of the working of the capitalistic economy, they cannot be referred organically to its inner mechanisms; this is an important point for Kalecki, as it underscores the absence of endogenous forces acting systematically and continually for progress.[16]

The definition of these propulsive elements as *development factors* (to which Chapter 15 of (1954) lends its title), for the sporadic nature inherent to the concept, rightly grasps the lack of steady self-propelling stimuli and, instead, the precariousness and the irregularity of a process entrusted to contingent elements. This view inspires Kalecki's splitting of dynamic analysis into two parts: the study of *intrinsic* tendencies, which are reflected in the gravitation around a stationary trend, and the subsequent inclusion of the development factors which break the static situation by setting off an ascending trend.

Among these factors, primary importance is given to innovations[17] whose effect, similar to that of an increase in profits, is to make investment projects more attractive. As *process-innovating* factors, their impact on investment is greater the larger the existing stock of capital goods, since a greater amount of such goods will become obsolete; positive effects on the incentive to invest stimulate other forms of technical progress – from the introduction of new products to the discovery of new sources of raw materials (Kalecki, 1954, pp. 158–9).

The flow of innovations is exogenous in the sense that it cannot be brought back to the working of the economy through general and systematic relationships;[18] in general, this flow is the product of competition among firms for gaining new markets or expanding their share in the existing ones.[19] The operating of competition through investments and its consequences for the working of the economy are argued by Kalecki, for example, by opposing Luxemburg's thesis of the ineluctability of simple reproduction (due to the lack of incentive to invest – external markets being absent) that 'capitalists do many things as a class but they certainly don't invest as a class' (1967b, p. 152); investment is the means whereby capitalists endlessly struggle, so that it can also generate, as a whole, self-justifying conditions.[20]

According to Kalecki, one important factor counters the above stimuli: 'entrepreneurial capital'. The theory of entrepreneurial capital has undergone various formulations – from (1937a) to (1954) – but its core has remained substantially unchanged. In extreme synthesis, Kalecki argues (1937a, pp. 442–3; 1954, pp. 91–2) that firms' investment programmes are constrained by their own capital. This constraint works in two ways:

(a) since internal saving is an essential source of financing, the risk of the investment is greater the higher the amount invested in relation to the entrepreneur's capital;[21]

(b) since access to the financial market is limited by the investor's own capital,[22] firms below a certain size are completely excluded.

The general implications of this viewpoint and its detachment from Keynes's views are evident. Keynes's (not to speak of the traditional theory's) lack of attention to the different ways of financing investments implies indifference on the part of investors, which in turn means that accumulation of capital is within the range even of those who do not personally owe capital;[23] evidently, this is the aspect where social mobility comes into play. Keynes's full liberal optimism leads him to conclude that entrepreneurial capability (or, more generally, 'enterprise') is sufficient for attaining the ownership and control of the means of production. For Kalecki, instead, ownership of capital is the only condition that counts:

> Many economists assume, at least in their abstract theories, a state of business democracy where anybody endowed with entrepreneurial ability can obtain capital for starting a business venture. This picture of the activities of the 'pure' entrepreneur is, to put it mildly, unrealistic. The most important prerequisite for becoming an entrepreneur is the *ownership* of capital (Kalecki, 1954, pp. 94–5).

The importance of self-financing does not exclude an important role for the financial market; however, compared to Keynesian economics, the separation between decisions to save and to invest becomes less acute, and the financial flows and the relationships between real and monetary sectors are less emphasised.

The relationships between the real and the monetary part of the economy is a rather controversial aspect of Kalecki's theory, in which more attention is clearly paid to the first, whereas the second is given an almost passive role.[24] However, the current explanation of this reversal (compared to the Keynesian approach), according to which the reason lies in the weak response of investments to the rate of interest and to credit availability, cannot be shared.

This interpretation is not convincing, first of all, because it mistakes for small influence of the (long-term) rate of interest as such what is instead only a consequence of its stability; in Kalecki's analysis, the interest rate is considered as a factor concurring to determine the *level* of investments in a given moment, though being deemed – owing to its stability – of little importance in explaining investments' *variability*.[25] Moreover, Kalecki gives central relevance to the credit system, too, for its role both in making investments independent of saving and in stabilizing the interest rate.

The *primacy* of the real sector, therefore, derives not from investments not being responsive to monetary impulses, but rather from the stability of the long-term rate of interest (due to technical reasons) and, basically, from the flexibility of the banking system in adapting monetary circulation to changes in income and in liquidity preference.[26]

3.2.2 The Investment Functions

Coming to the main analytical formulations of the theory of investment Kalecki put forward over time,[27] the first we need to consider was presented in (1933a, 1933b). The analysis of investments is shaped, according to a constant frame, in two stages: one concerns the determinants of investment *orders* and thus the production of capital goods (called 'gross accumulation'); the other concerns how changes in capital stock, as a result of the *delivery* of new equipment, affect the incentive to invest.[28]

Kalecki argues initially (1933a, p. 6) that orders are an increasing function of the 'anticipated gross profitability' of investments and a decreasing function of the rate of interest;[29] the distinction is not yet drawn between short- and long-term rates. Through subsequent simplifications expected profitability is approximated to the current profitability of the equipment in use; the rate of interest is discarded, being directly related to the profitability of investments by virtue of the causal nexus featuring the economic preocess – from investments to the level of income and to the demand for money.[30] Accordingly, the investment functions is defined as follows:[31]

$$\frac{I}{K} = F\left(\frac{P}{K}\right), \qquad F' > 0 \tag{3.10}$$

The reasoning underlying (3.10) does not permit determining a *specific* level of investments; as expected profitability – being a datum – does not (*ex ante*) interact with the amount of *programmed* investments, there is theoretically no limit to investment decisions. In other words, under assumed conditions of expected positive net profitability (independent of the scale of investments programmes), rational agents should be eager to invest to an unlimited extent.[32] If this does not occur, it must be because of some limitational factor: starting with (1937a), this would be identified as the *increasing risk*, but at the stage we are dealing with now nothing was explicitly proposed in this regard,[33] so that the investment function turned out to be void of theoretical justification.

Assuming (3.10) as linear, and overall profits proportional to ($B°$+A),[34] Kalecki (1933a, pp. 7–8) obtains:

$$\frac{I}{K} = m\frac{B^{\circ} + A}{K} - n \tag{3.13}$$

or:

$$I = m(B^{\circ} + A) - nK, \qquad m, n > 0^{35} \tag{3.14}$$

from which he concludes that:

> the volume of investment orders I is an increasing function of the gross accumulation A and a diminishing function of the volume of capital equipment K (1933a, p. 8).

The completion of orders, therefore, results in contrasting effects on the incentive to invest: positive, since gross accumulation affects overall profits favourably; negative, further on in time, since it leads to increased capital stock. Investment fluctuations are thus the result of the dialectics between these opposing forces and of their acting out of phase.[36]

The search for a limitational factor is pursued later (1937a, 1937b), stimulated by the Keynesian theory of investment and by Kalecki's remarks in this regard (1936). The author sifts several possible factors limiting investment, from that suggested by Keynes, which would act primarily from the supply conditions of capital goods,[37] to the decrease in physical productivity, to that focusing on the conditions of demand.

Kalecki notes that Keynes's solution 'does not say anything about the sphere of investment *decisions*' (1936, p. 230) since the rise in the supply price of capital goods acts only *ex post*, once the investments have been made. For the single investor the price of investment goods is a datum whereby he assesses the profitability of his programmes; the eventual rise in their price is instead the effect of the realisation of programmes – an unpredictable result, since it depends on decisions taken by investors as a whole, which as such cannot be claimed as an *ex ante* limitational factor. Then 'the starting point' for a valid approach to the theory of investment, Kalecki concludes, must be 'the solution of the problem of investment decisions, of the *ex ante* investment' (1936, p. 231).

For this purpose the other limitational factors mentioned above might be considered, but they are discarded one by one for lack of realism.

It is not plausible, according to Kalecki, assuming 'large scale diseconomies', i.e., that an increase in the size of firms brings about decreasing returns, since investments lead to an increase in both equipment and the employment of labour (workers being unemployed, which is the basic hypothesis throughout Kalecki's reasoning); the capital–labour ratio being constant, a further limitational factor might be seen in the 'difficulties of management arising out of the large scale of enterprises', but this may concern only 'industrial giants' and so cannot provide a general explanation of the phenomenon.[38]

Not even the case of 'imperfect competition' – or, the 'limitations of market' in relation to the size of the firm, as Kalecki puts it (1954, p. 91) – is an exhaustive justification of the limits firms meet in their investment programmes (though, he concedes, it is more realistic than the factors mentioned above). First of all, the degree of imperfection becomes relevant only for very large-scale firms (1937a, p. 442); moreover, this is not a deterrent to the firm's investments *as such,* but only to their concentration in a single sector: the limits set by the size of single markets can be overcome by spreading investments over various fields (1939a, p. 98); finally, this factor 'leaves unexplained the existence of large and small firms in the same industry' (1954, p. 91).

After dropping the current explanations, the constraint to investment decisions is approached 'by taking risk over from the demand side to the supply side' – as Joan Robinson notes (1964, p. 96) – i.e., from the market to the internal conditions of the investor. The principle of increasing risk (already outlined in (1937b)) is fully worked out in (1937a), and then many times restated without relevant changes in the essential lines. It is a generalisation of an idea suggested by Breit (1935)[39] in analysing the consequences of the lender's risk on the structure and dynamics of interest rates;[40] while not neglecting this factor, Kalecki's variant consists essentially in shifting the risk to the borrower.

As already seen, Kalecki's idea is founded on the following considerations:

(a) the danger an investor undergoes in case of failure will be greater the greater investments are in relation to his wealth;

(b) access to credit and the financial market is more difficult – or more costly[41] – the greater is indebtedness compared to the investor's own capital;

(c) as a result of point (b), the risk of suffering illiquidity rises with the expansion of initiatives not backed by an adequate volume of capital belonging to the firm.

Given these conditions, the appraisal of risk is sharper the higher the ratio of programmed investments to the value of entrepreneurial capital, so that, to be offset, it requires a growing difference between expected marginal profitability and the interest rate. Conversely, with a given spread between these two variables (and with given entrepreneurial capital), investment decisions will be taken up to the point where the marginal risk balances this gap.[42]

The above considerations provide the elements for identifying the equilibrium level of investment decisions in a given moment, that is to say, the amount of these decisions that *exhausts* the convenience of investing in the given conditions. Further decisions may take place only as a result of changes in net marginal profitability or in the risk factor: from this point onward Kalecki's entire research on investments focuses on the causes of change of these factors, and on their consequences for the business cycle.

In (1937a), major attention is given to factors affecting the risk constraint, identified in the firms' accumulation of gross savings (depreciation and undistributed profits) whereby entrepreneurial capital increases;[43] investments will be stimulated since 'the entrepreneur can invest the new accumulated amount without reducing his safety or increasing illiquidity' (1937a, p. 446). Furthermore, given a *desired* ratio of indebtedness to capital – determined by the firms' propensity to risk, which is in turn influenced by profit expectations, and subject to a maximum fixed by creditors – the flow of internal savings potentially gives rise to even greater investments by increasing the possibility of raising external financing.

With d the desired debt ratio (i.e., net debt divided by own capital – and being $d=d(Emi - i)$), s the flow of internal savings in the time unit, v a coefficient depending on 'the velocity of change of marginal net profitability', the rate of the investment decisions (in monetary terms) will be:[44]

$$I_t = s(1 + d) + v \tag{3.16}$$

whence the conclusion:

> the rate of the investment decisions of a single entrepreneur depends on his capital accumulation [here meant as accumulation of entrepreneurial capital] and on the velocity of change of marginal net profitability (1937a, p. 447).[45]

The general framework of the principle of increasing risk remains substantially unchanged in subsequent works which focus mainly on improving the analytical formulation of the investment function – especially by investigating the causes of change in profitability – in order to make it more suitable for explaining investment fluctuations.

In (1939a), Kalecki generalises the risk factor by extending it from investment programmes to 'commitments'[46] and argues that risk is a function of the ratio of such commitments to private capital; within the short period, however (considering that private capital is not subject to marked changes over that span of time) risk is more simply supposed to be a function of the total *amount* of commitments. It follows that:

> The investment plans undertaken today must be such as to 'push' commitments to the point at which marginal risk is equal to the difference between the marginal rate of profit and the rate of interest (1939a, p. 106).

Kalecki is here applying to the stock of commitments the same conceptual frame earlier applied to their flow; however, this is only the starting point for working out a theory of economic fluctuations. For this purpose, Kalecki elaborates a more simple aggregate relationship between investment decisions and net marginal profitability, namely a relationship which can prescind from the stock of commitments; complications are thus soon ruled out by *ad hoc* hypotheses, such as the usual splitting of investment activity into two phases – the order and the production of capital goods – and, above all, the attribution of the formation of savings to entrepreneurs only.[47]

With these assumptions it is easy for Kalecki to conclude that commitments *as a whole* vary only in the phase of *order* (i.e., by virtue of I in (3.17)) since investment orders, being executed (I°), are balanced by an identical flow of savings which increases private capital by the same amount.[48] It follows that neither realised investments nor changes in capital stock alter the burden of risk, while only the not-yet-fulfilled investment decisions do so: therefore they can still be related to the marginal profitability, independently of commitments:[49]

$$I = f(Emi - r) \tag{3.18}$$

Once the simple relationship between investment decisions and profitability has been restored[50] – similar to that stated in (1937a) – then the reasoning is to be framed in dynamic terms; leaving the more formal aspects aside, Kalecki's argument can be summarised as follows (1939a, pp. 133–6):

(a) because of the stability of the *long-term* interest rate (r), assumed to be approximately constant, investment decisions are an increasing function of the expected (gross) marginal profit rate alone;[51]

(b) the latter is *roughly* determined by the level of national income[52] and by the stock of capital equipment, so that these two variables become the factors explaining the investment decisions in the time unit;

(c) national income, in turn, is a function of the investment decisions, with a time-lag (e) depending both on the length of the period of construction of capital goods and on the lag between income and consumption.

Between national income and the investment decisions, therefore, reciprocal relationships run on a line which is a constant for Kalecki:

$$I_t = f(Y_t, \bar{K}), \qquad f' > 0 \tag{3.19}$$

$$Y_{t+e} = g(I_t), \qquad g' > 0 \tag{3.20}$$

Figure 3.2 depicts the interplay of the above relations[53] and shows the system tending toward point *B*, which represents a hypothetical situation of equilibrium, that is:

> ... a conditional equilibrium, in the sense that at this point the system has no tendency to change provided that there is no change in capital equipment (which has so far been assumed constant). However, as investment is generally not at the level of wear and tear, equipment *does* change, and ... the state of 'conditional equilibrium' cannot be permanent (1939a, p. 139).

Figure 3.2

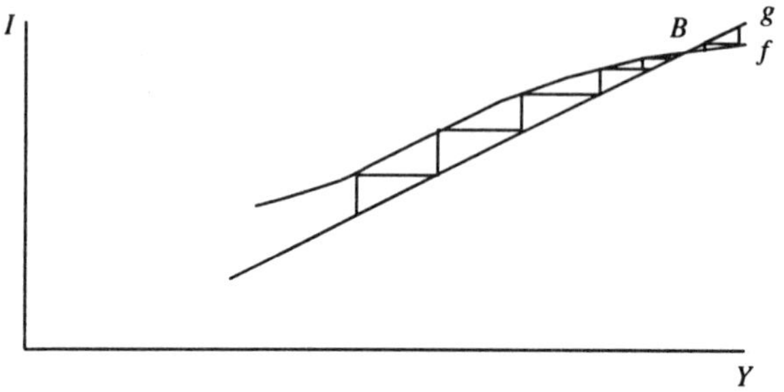

The growth of capital stock shifts function *f* to the right, so that – though ruled out as a factor of risk – *K* comes back into play as a limitational factor on the rate-of-profit side. The self-stimulating process of growth toward equilibrium and the consequent change in equipment, interact with each other, giving rise to 'automatic' fluctuations in income and investments. This course can be disturbed by the influence of exogenous factors such as changes in the state of confidence (1939a, p. 140); or (which Kalecki seems to forget) variations in the capitalists' propensity to save can take place which exert opposite effects on the level of income, moving the two curves in the *same* direction: curve *g*, since they affect the income multiplier, and curve *f*, since they modify commitments.

Subsequent writings – particularly (1943b) and (1954) – continue to examine closely the causes of change in investments, the distinction being made between those responsible for the cycle and those driving the system along the trend. From this point of view these causes are classified as endogenous and semi-exogenous, the first being a by-product of investment activity and the second being those which cannot be related systematically to the current working of the economy or which, in any case, act over the long period. To the first set of causes belong the flow of overall gross savings and variations in profits and capital stock; within the second fall the long-run changes of capitalist–entrepreneurs' consumption and rentiers' savings, the growth of population and, above all, the stream of innovations.

This set of elements is grafted onto the theoretical framework of the principle of increasing risk to which two important specifications are added: the explicit restoration of the centrality of the relationship between the size of the firm and the entrepreneurial capital, and the extension of saving to other components of society, with the distinction – within profit earners – between entrepreneurs and rentiers.

The first endogenous factor of change – as already in (1937a) and in (1939a) – is the 'gross accumulation of capital', drawn from the gross savings of firms (depreciation and undistributed profits) and from the 'personal' savings which the controlling groups invest in their own companies through subscriptions to new share issues (1954, p. 97). Since this concept of firms' saving is 'somewhat vague', Kalecki overcomes the difficulty by 'assuming that the gross savings of firms as conceived above are related to total gross private savings' (1954, p. 97); consequently, as investment decisions depend on firms' savings, they are also – *ceteris paribus* – 'an increasing function of total gross savings' (1954, p. 97).[54]

As to the other endogenous factors, the agents' propensity to turn current data into expectations leads them to look at the variations in profits as a tendency bound to last, at least in the near future; consistently, given the stock of equipment, changes in profits convert into changes in expected profitability. Finally, considerations similar to those in (1939a) are made as regards variations in the stock of equipment, which act inversely on the incentive to invest.

On this basis Kalecki (1954, p. 98) obtains the equation:[55]

$$I = aS + b\frac{dP}{dt} - c\frac{dK}{dt} + q \qquad (3.21)$$

with $0 < a < 1$;[56] only as a first approximation does (3.21) coincide with the analysis based on the principle of increasing risk,[57] but nevertheless it follows the logic of that formulation.

3.2.3 The Trend

Coefficient q in (3.21) includes the trend factors or 'development factors' mentioned earlier; we have also seen that, within these factors, particular importance is given to innovations, since they:

> tend to increase the long-run level of the investment and thus make for a long-run upward trend [Kalecki, 1954, p. 158; on the other hand] the accumulation of capital ... increases in turn the scope of the influence of the 'development factors' and thus contributes to the maintenance of the long-run trend (1954, p. 151).

The continuity of this *virtuous circle*, however, is not granted since the spreading of innovations brings later a decline in the benefits gained by innovators, so that the initial stimulus to invest is soon followed by a fall in the incentive.[58] Both the positive and the negative effect of innovations are proportional to the existing volume of equipment, but since the second is delayed, the *net* effect will be positive if the system is growing (i.e., if capital stock rises) and, all the more so, if the rate of technical progress is increasing.[59] There is no reason, however, to conclude that regular growth is normal for the capitalistic economy; a uniform trend, Kalecki objects to the theorists of steady-growth models, is a particular case resting on the condition that the influence of the development factors increases proportionately with the stock of capital (1954, p. 156).

The *effect* of development factors being dependent on variables inherent to the system does not make the long-period trend endogenous, since the causes of these factors cannot be referred, through functional relationships, to the working of the economy[60] (indeed, they remain largely unexplained throughout Kalecki's theory). Nevertheless, the author argues for a progressive slackening of the propulsive drive of these forces, both because of a rising degree of monopoly (which weakens the propensity to consume), and because of the slowing down of the rate of innovations for the sharpened monopolistic nature of the economy and for the increasing importance of mature sectors;[61] consequently, in the long run the ascending drives would be replaced by a stationary tendency.

Concluding, the tendency toward stationary situations emerges at two levels: there is an intrinsic tendency, springing from the contradictory character of investments, which comes to light in the *pure economic cycle*; the system is freed from this situation by counter-tendencies brought about by 'extra-economic' factors bound, however, to weaken in the long period: consistently, the upward shifting of the centre of gravity of economic fluctuations slackens increasingly, until it comes to an end in a secular perspective.[62]

Kalecki returns to the relationships between technical progress and the trend in (1968c), where he reverses the approach followed till then and aims at integrating the study of the business cycle with that of the trend, this being 'the only key to the realistic analysis of the dynamics of a capitalist economy' (1968c, p. 165). Reasons for this new conviction are that:

> [on the one hand] the long-run trend is but a slowly changing component of a chain of short-period situations; it has not independent entity [; on the other hand,] by this separation of short-period and long-run influences I missed certain repercussions of technical progress which affect the dynamic process as a whole (1968c, pp. 165–6).[63]

These commendable purposes, however, are pursued in a rather obscure way,[64] so that the main interest for this contribution seems to lie in intentions themselves, i.e., in Kalecki's attained awareness of the need for a change in approaching the dynamic process, as well as in the basic conviction – which is in part both premise and conclusion of the analysis – that:

> the rate of growth at a given time is a phenomenon rooted in past economic, social and technological developments, rather than determined fully by the coefficients of our equations (1968c, p. 183).[65]

It is interesting to compare Kalecki's outlook on long-period tendencies with other approaches of economic thought, chiefly with those of Keynes and the neo-Marxists.[66]

Keynes is primarily concerned with short-run aspects, and when he comes to the longer period he proves to trust the potentiality of capital accumulation; this faith is accompanied, however, by equal scepticism about the possibility of realizing those potentials under *laissez-faire* conditions: without the systematic support of public policy, Keynes argues,[67] the economy is bound to gravitate around a path characterised by underemployment of resources, though this path is not necessarily (nor historically) represented by a stationary trend

Only in a still-too-far-off time horizon do elements emerge which render the possibility of stagnation concrete. This aspect is dealt with in one of the few works in which Keynes considers long-period tendencies (1937d),[68] in which he outlines the economic consequences of a declining (or of a stationary) population, a phenomenon he then considered imminent. Since, until that time, about half the accumulation of capital was to satisfy the needs of a growing population (1937d, p. 139), a halt in this process would – *ceteris paribus* – give rise to overaccumulation and a chronic tendency toward stagnation. Acting on the other factors of investment[69] – primarily on income distribution in order to raise the propensity to consume – would then be necessary in order to offset this situation.[70]

For both Keynes and Kalecki, therefore, stagnation is a situation the *laissez-faire* economy may undergo in the long period; moreover, both of them ascribe the long-run ascending tendencies to semi-exogenous (or policy-governed) factors, such as 'external markets' (first, public expenditure), population dynamics and technological change, a more equal distribution of income – though different emphasis is given to one factor or the other. There are certainly differences in their views, but they are more apparent in their visions – in their trust or scepticism about the possibility of carrying out reforms able to curb the causes of stagnation – than in the analysis of these causes as such.

Neo-Marxist thought has drawn from Kalecki many suggestions for reflection[71] – ranging from the consideration of monopoly in the process of accumulation and the antagonistic character of the latter, to the relationships between distribution and the level of income; at the same time neo-Marxists differ from Kalecki in referring the dynamics of the capitalistic economy and its decline to internal mechanisms, organic to the economic process,[72] refusing therefore to resort to the *deus ex machina* of semi-exogenous factors such as innovations.[73] Indeed, while the external pattern of development factors emphasises the lack of self-propulsive spurs in the economy, it becomes instead an obstacle to definite conclusions when attention is turned to the very long-period tendencies.

The exclusion of semi-exogenous elements by neo-Marxists is mainly explained by arguing that innovations 'affect only the *form* which net investment takes' but 'they do not act on it as a propelling force'.[74] This conviction – which appears difficult to reconcile with that according to which in monopoly capitalism competition runs through innovations – was subsequently abandoned by Steindl,[75] by assigning to innovations the role of 'random shocks' (1981, p. 46), whose positive effect mingles with the opposing ones[76] caused by the oligopolistic structure of the economy.[77]

3.2.4 Kalecki and the Marginalist Analysis of Investments

A further aspect calling for brief investigation is the relationship between the Kaleckian and marginalist analysis of investments. In marginalist theory substitutability among productive factors is conceived in two ways: there is a short-period 'substitutability' – with given techniques and equipment – which takes place under the pressure of demand for goods and which makes it possible to combine fixed with variable factors in different proportions; and there is a long-period substitutability (among methods of production) which is a function of the relative prices of factors.

As we have seen, Kalecki denies the first type of substitutability, at least as the general rule; not so clear-cut is his departure from the concept of long-period substitutability. On the contrary, he at first seeks to maintain continuity with the conclusions of the traditional approach; later the links are in fact broken by arguing that this substitutability does not work in practice and that it plays a marginal role in investment decisions; this reasoning, however, has not been coupled with a direct challenge on the theoretical ground.

Kalecki separates the investments for increasing the *scale* of production – independently of changes in methods – from those destined to modify *methods* independently of the consequences for the scale of production; both types of investments are sensitive to variations in the interest rate and undertaking one or the other depends on the circumstances: as a general rule, Kalecki argues, changes in the interest rate can affect methods of production in so far as the expansion of capacity is precluded by the narrowness (or 'imperfection') of the market; the choice between *extensive* and *rationalizing* investments depends therefore on whether or not there is room to make increases in productive capacity advantageous.

Thus, in (1937a) Kalecki writes:

> *So long as we can consider the influence of imperfect competition as negligible and thus have constant returns to the scale the change in the rate of interest does not affect the method of production admitted by the entrepreneur in his plans but only the size of investment planned* (p. 444, emphasis in original).[78]

This view, Kalecki points out (1937a, pp. 444–5), is not in contrast with the 'classical theory of marginal productivity'; rather, it covers a ground the latter left bare. The traditional theory applies, indeed, to situations of 'long-period equilibrium' (characterised by the equality of the marginal productivity of factors to their prices), but it is unable to explain investment decisions when 'disequilibrium' rules, since:

> [this] theory says nothing about the immediate influence of the fall of the rate of interest on the *plans* of the entrepreneur [(1937a, p. 444). On the other hand:] Our statement that the fall of the rate of interest does not affect the method of production but only the scale of investment plans referred only to the *plans* but not to the situation arising out of their realization (1937a, p. 445).[79]

With increased clear-cut insight Kalecki returns to this theme in (1944), dealing with the consequences of employment policies based on stimulating private investments: the potential for these policies to cause overaccumulation of capital, he argues, would be avoided if the lowering of the interest rate acted to increase capital intensity instead of productive capacity. In this regard, Kalecki writes:

> The idea that the reduction of the rate of interest stimulates the application of more capital per worker is based on the assumption that the planned *output* of the investing entrepreneur is given. On this condition a lower rate of interest makes it profitable to use more capital and less labour. If we assume, however, that *capital* available to a firm for financing investment is given, the reduction of the rate of interest has no influence on the choice of the method of production when planning investment, because it affects the expected net profits equally whatever the method of production adopted (1944, p. 51).

Kalecki definitely opts for the second possibility and concludes that the most important influence of the interest rate is as an incentive to vary the scale of production; of course, this does not imply excluding investments to bring about changes in methods, but this is not important once it has been ascertained that the existence of a *systematic* relationship between the rate of interest and the level of investments principally rests on the other aspect.[80] Rather:

> the main stimulus to use more capital per worker is provided by new inventions. The advantage offered by them is usually so high that it will be taken whatever (within a wide range) the level of the rate of interest (1944, p. 51).

3.3 MONETARY ASPECTS

3.3.1 General Features

The monetary part of Kalecki's work has generally received little attention, being considered a minor aspect, marginal with respect to the central themes of his writings. This view – which inspires the 'post-Keynesian synthesis'[81] – appears only partially justified. To give an evaluation in this regard, it is worth distinguishing in Kalecki's monetary thought the general conception from the theory of interest; while the first is remarkably broad and innovative, the second draws substantially from Keynes (even though it differs from Keynes in a number of aspects) and does not appear in full accord with the general premises.

It has already been remarked that, according to Kalecki (1933a, p. 13), the autonomy of investments from prior accumulation of profits and from prior flow of savings is due to the existence of a flexible credit system, which plays an even more important role when investments proceed at an increasing pace; the condition necessary for this to occur is the *creation* of additional financial means, i.e., means exceeding the amount offset by the real resources available at the given level of income and at the given propensity to save. It is therefore not saving in itself, but rather the supply of finance, that constitutes the essential prerequisite for investment; later, it will be the latter that, by broadening business activity, gives rise to the volume of savings necessary to equilibrate it. This two-phase framework for 'covering' investment – the prior availability of finance and the subsequent offsetting by an equal amount of saving – is manifest from Kalecki's earliest writings, and is one of his most original perceptions.[82]

Kalecki's path to a monetary theory of interest coincides with that of Keynes; for both, once it is acknowledged that the adjustment between savings and investments does not occur along the traditional lines, it follows that the explanation of the interest rate must be sought elsewhere:

> It has been stated above that the rate of interest cannot be determined by the demand for and the supply of capital because investment automatically brings into existence an equal amount of savings. Thus investment 'finances itself' whatever the level of the rate of interest. The rate of interest is, therefore, the result of the interplay of other factors (Kalecki, 1954, p. 73).[83]

Like Keynes, therefore, Kalecki arrives at a monetary explanation of interest after modifications had been brought into the real part of the theoretical scheme.

It is plausible that the conciseness with which Kalecki deals with the theory of interest, as well as the relatively short time within which he conceived it (primarily between 1939 and 1943), are to be explained – as Joan Robinson suggests[84] – by his being free of orthodox biases. Nevertheless, neither this circumstance nor the overlapping with Keynesian research can justify the small importance the author seems to give to the subject and to his own work in this regard;[85] in this attitude we find evidence of a certain detachment from monetary phenomena as such, in spite of their recognised general importance.[86]

Although a monetary explanation of the interest rate is already implicit in (1933a, 1933b), only later is a theory of the demand for money as an *asset* clearly worked out (probably not by chance, not until after Keynes's *General Theory*). Only starting with (1937b) – and then more in detail in (1940b), (1943b) and (1954) – did the way open for an approach to monetary problems within the framework of the theory of capital, whereas in earlier writings the demand for currency, while allowing for its elasticity to the rate of interest, continued to be viewed in strict relationship with needs deriving from the financing of investments and from transactions in general.

The monetary theory Kalecki puts forward in his maturity draws inspiration from Keynes, but shows remarkable differences. First of all the distinction is made between short- and long-term rates, and great attention is given to the relationships between the two. Moreover, choices as regards portfolio are mainly inspired by the search for income, so that speculation is given minor importance compared to Keynes; finally the assessment of risk depends not only on the probability as such that an unfavourable event will occur but also on the degree of concentration of investments in similar assets: thus the principle of increasing risk also finds application to the financial field.[87]

Among the consequences of the public's attitude is that portfolio choices are made within homogeneous assets and in successive stages. Given their different characteristics and the limited importance of speculative motives, *direct* substitutability between money and long-term bonds is ruled out; substitutability ranges instead over similar assets, and therefore occurs by stages – i.e., between money and short-term securities ('bills'), whose value is stable, and between the latter and long-term securities. It ensues that long-term rates are affected loosely and slowly by changes in money supply and in the liquidity preference, since the impact of monetary impulses is weakened by the intermediation of short-term activities. Changes in monetary magnitudes thus bring about a chain of substitutions whose intensity gradually lessens as it moves away from the origin of the impulse: it is also for this reason that monetary policies for employment are not very effective.

3.3.2 Specific Aspects

Two phases stand out in Kalecki's research on monetary theory. Initially (1933a, 1933b and 1935d), money as an asset does not yet explicitly appear, and attention is mainly focused on the effects of the pace of economic activity on monetary variables, particularly on money demand for transactions and finance. Then, starting with (1937b), another phase follows in which the theory of the demand for money and the theory of interest are worked out in terms of portfolio selection.

In the first group of works Kalecki is concerned with two themes: first, 'where the capitalists find the "means" to increase the production of investment goods'; second, the interplay between the interest rate and the demand for money – an aspect he will clarify only later.

Dealing with the first aspect, Kalecki aims at proving wrong 'the common conviction that the more is consumed the less is saved' (1933a, p. 12) by demonstrating that investment, once realised, brings about savings and profits necessary to restore the equilibrium:[88]

> The question may still arise, where the capitalists find the 'means' to increase the production of investment goods or their personal consumption. If we abstract from the 'technical' elements of the money market, we may say that the capitalists as a whole do not need money in order to achieve this since, as shown above, the expenditure of some capitalists is converted into profits for others ... If during a particular period more money is spent, e.g. out of bank deposits, then *pro tanto* more money flows back into the banks in the form of realized profits, so that the sum of deposits remains unchanged (1933a, p. 13).

Kalecki points out (1933a) that credit expansion is actually inevitable because of the 'technical elements' of the money market, consisting in the increased demand for money to finance investments – which is a function of the volume of projects and of the length of the period of execution[89] – as well as in the increased transaction demand for money brought about by the rise in the level of activity.

It is worth noting that what Kalecki calls 'technical elements' do not refer to mere details but to fundamental requisites, since the response of the banking system to the demand for finance is an essential condition for the autonomy of capitalists' spending; this inclination to undervalue the limits within which capitalists are 'masters of their fate' is confirmed by the fact that this component of the demand for money (which is the most original aspect of the monetary part of that essay) was omitted in subsequent editions in English.[90]

At this early stage Kalecki's ideas about the determinants of the rate of interest are not yet clear-cut; there is no precise explanation of this variable, which is referred chiefly to banking policy, while its relationship with the demand for money lacks symmetry. The dependence of the rate of interest on the demand for money is clearly stated,[91] even if the mechanism is not yet well specified; however, no reverse relationship is pointed out, except very indirectly, which entails that money was not yet conceived as an asset, i.e., that liquidity preference was not yet considered as such, but only in relation to specific requirements of transactions and financing of investments.

It is in (1937b) that the demand for money is related to the state of confidence,[92] and liquidity preference appears; from here to the demand for money as an asset and a theory of interest within the frame of portfolio choices it is, in principle, but a short step. In so doing, Kalecki (1940b and then 1943b and 1954) distinguishes three kinds of financial assets: money (including current accounts), short-term assets ('bills') – time deposits, commercial bills, Treasury bills – and long-term securities ('bonds'). The distinctive features these assets share in different proportions are *liquidity*, which belongs to money only, *risk*, to which bond holders alone are exposed, and *profitability*, enjoyed by both short-term and long-term assets.

Portfolio adjustments take place among similar assets, that is to say, between money and bills (both being substantially riskless) and between the latter and bonds, which share income and illiquidity. Hence the separate determination of the short-term and of the long-term rate of interest, the first being the remuneration for giving up liquidity 'in its pure form', while the second must include also the reward for risk;[93] the cost of reinvesting short-term sums must also be taken into account when defining the equilibrium condition between the two rates.

The basis of the structure of interest rates is the short-term one:[94]

> The higher the short-term rate the greater is the inducement to invest money for short periods rather than to keep it as cash reserve. Or, to put it more precisely: transactions can be managed with a larger or a smaller stock of money; however, a larger stock of money in relation to turnover means on the average a smoother and more convenient handling of transactions. The higher the short-term rate of interest the more expensive is this convenience as compared with the alternative of investing in short-term assets (Kalecki, 1954, pp. 73–4).[95]

With T the total volume of transactions, M the supply of money (notes and current account deposits), V the (*ex ante*) money velocity of circulation, and i the short-term rate of interest, we have (1954, p. 74):

$$V = V(i), \qquad V' > 0 \tag{3.22}$$

$$V(i) = \frac{T}{M} \tag{3.23}$$

Equation (3.22) also defines the demand for money as an inverse function of the rate of interest, for a given amount of transactions; its characteristics depend on habits and the state of confidence, making it potentially a highly unstable function.[96] The short-term interest rate is therefore determined by the volume of transactions, the money supply policy and the liquidity preference; if we disregard Kalecki's neglect of the speculative motive (justified in effect by the nature of assets), the Keynesian inspiration is quite evident.

Kalecki then goes on to analyse (1954, pp. 81–2) the relationships of the short-term rate with the long-term rate[97] which originates from substitutability among assets.[98] The assumption is made that the public takes as reference the estimated length of a long-term investment, and on this basis evaluates the relative advantage of investing in short-term or in long-term securities. The terms for comparison are, on the one hand, the present rate of interest (r) on long-term bonds and, on the other, the sequence of expected short-term rates (i) spanning the entire period of the investment, i.e., those accruing by reinvesting the sum every time until the end of the reference period; from this sequence an average short-period interest rate (i_m) is derived which represents the term of comparison with the long-term rate. Other elements to consider are the cost (e) of reinvesting in short-term securities every time they come to maturity[99] and the risk of depreciation (u) involved in possessing Consols. In equilibrium, the difference between the two rates has to be:

$$r - i_m = u - e \tag{3.24}$$

The most delicate aspect of the question is the assessment of the risk; in this regard, Kalecki writes:

> If the present price of Consols is p and the holder has a certain, more or less definite, idea based on past experience about the minimum to which this price may fall, p_{min}, it is plausible to assume that u is roughly proportionate to $(p - p_{min})/p$, i.e. to the maximum percentage by which the price of Consols is considered apt to fall (1954, p. 81).

It follows that:[100]

$$u = g\left(1 - \frac{p_{min}}{p}\right) \tag{3.25}$$

or, given the inverse relationship between the price and the rate of interest of Consols:[101]

$$u = g\left(1 - \frac{r}{r_{max}}\right) \qquad (3.26)$$

from which the conclusion is inferred that in equilibrium:

$$r = \frac{i_m + g - e}{1 + g / r_{max}} \qquad (3.27)$$

Given coefficients g and e, and given r_{max}, equation (3.27) expresses the long-term rate as a function of the series of expected short-term rates; there is, therefore, a substantially univocal relationship between the two rates, which rests after all on the short-term one being – as the 'remuneration for forgoing the convenience of holding cash in its pure form' (1954, p. 74) – a fundamentally psychological variable, as in Keynes. The tendency of rates toward equilibrium not only relies on adjustments of the long-term interest rate but also on the fact that the risk for Consol holders increases:

(a) with the gap between the present long-term rate and that viewed as 'maximum' (equation (3.26));

(b) with the rise in the weight, within portfolios, of long-term assets compared to the short-term ones and to money.[102]

Finally, from (3.27) the stability is deduced of the long-term rate compared to the short-term, since:

(a) changes in the short-term rate only partially affect the estimate of i_m;

(b) given the parameters of this equation and r_{max}, the long-term rate varies to a smaller extent than i_m.[103]

There is therefore a long sequence to cover before the impulses generated by changes in liquidity may affect the long-term rate , and their shock is dampened on the way. This is one of the reasons why Kalecki is sceptical about the efficacy of monetary policy on investments; its effectiveness, of course, also depends on the tools employed, and in this regard Kalecki's points out that things go better if action on long-term rates is carried out by resorting to large-scale open market operations.[104] There remains, however, the inconvenience that:

> there are limits to the reduction of the long-term rate because (in longer periods) this rate always exceeds the short-term rate by some margin and the short-term rate cannot fall below zero (Kalecki, 1944, p. 48).

3.4 CONCLUDING REMARKS

A contradiction can be traced between Kalecki's general monetary conception and the theory of interest. As for the first, we have seen that the condition necessary for investments to be autonomous is the availability of financial means created by the banking system and, therefore, the elasticity of money supply in relation to demand; in other words, the supply of money is to be considered – within boundaries set by monetary policy – endogenous. On the contrary, the theory of interest implies that liquidity is exogenously fixed since, in order to derive the interest rate from equilibrium between supply and demand, these two functions must be independent of each other; if instead the demand for money gives rise to an equal supply, the determination of the interest rate is to be sought elsewhere.

In reality, between the two extreme cases – i.e., complete adaptability (within the *ceiling* fixed by monetary authorities) versus a complete exogeneity of money supply – fall intermediate situations: for instance, bank credit (and hence liquidity) can expand beyond certain levels at increasing cost to the banking system, or can involve higher interest rates due to market imperfections or to impulses in that direction by monetary authorities.[105] The fact remains, however, that Kalecki's theory – like that of Keynes's[106] – presupposes a completely inelastic supply and that this is in contrast with the general premises of Kalecki's analysis.

The endogenous nature of the money supply implies after all a monetary policy devised to set the level of interest rates directly, leaving the supply to adjust to the demand corresponding with those rates; while Kalecki's interest theory is oriented differently, nevertheless this seems to be the strategy envisaged for the monetary authorities, and the concomitant cause of the stability of the interest rate and of the apparent primacy of the real over the monetary part of the economy.[107]

Another point worthy of mention is the capacity of Kalecki's theory to withstand attempts to reabsorb it within the traditional theory – a theme that characterised the Keynesian debate. We have already seen that it is incorrect to deduce from Kalecki's scheme that investments are insensitive to changes in the interest rate, which would have sheltered his theses from reabsorption in the old schemes; instead, it is logically possible to conceive a level of the long-term interest rate that is sufficiently low to induce investments equal to full-employment savings.[108] Then, as in the Keynesian debate, the central point is whether forces can be hypothesised within this model able to promote that condition, and if their being inactive is to be ascribed to 'imperfections' or institutional constraints (the rigidity of money wages), or instead to the structure of the theory itself.

The difficulties that would be met in attempting a 'synthesis' of the type the Keynesian theory has undergone are evident. Because of the length and the structure of the financial circuit, the *spontaneous* impulses of the market weakly reverberate on the long-term interest rate; the fact that this shows no tendency toward its full-employment level – even if considerable drops in money wages occur – is therefore not a consequence of imperfections or external constraints but of the nature of the economy. It should also be added that deflation of monetary wages may act on the interest rate *insofar as* the supply of money is given; if, instead, this is made endogenous, liquidity varies *along with wages*, so that the effect on interest is further weakened.

4 A Synthesis

4.1 A SCHEME OF REFERENCE

4.1.1 The Basic Model

A simplified model which brings together the most important points outlined in the preceding chapters is proposed here; further considerations will be added subsequently and several possible extensions explored.

The model aims at representing an equilibrium situation at a given moment, while considerations about dynamics are ruled out; accordingly, we will avoid dating variables, those concerning preceding periods being regarded as data.

The basic model rests on the following hypotheses:

(a) a unique commodity produced;

(b) two social classes – workers and capitalists–entrepreneurs – the propensity to save of the latter being greater than that of the former ($s_p > s_w > 0$); *rentiers* are not considered, so that profits accrue entirely into the hands of entrepreneurs;[1]

(c) labour is a *totally* variable factor and its productivity is constant;

(d) fiscal revenues are given, i.e., they are independent of national income.

With the above assumptions in mind, a Kaleckian model can be conceived along the following lines:

$$pX = \frac{pI_x + F}{(s_P - s_w)\dfrac{p - w/a}{p} + s_w} \tag{4.1}$$

$$p = \frac{w}{a}\frac{m}{1-n} \tag{4.2}$$

$$pI_x = S_p\,(1 + d) \tag{4.3}$$

$$d = d(Emi - r) \tag{4.4}$$

$$r = r(i) \tag{4.5}$$

$$L = Tl(i) \tag{4.6}$$

$$L = M \tag{4.7}$$

Equation (4.1) is tantamount to equation (1.6), once the propensity to save from wages, the public budget and the trade balance ($F = (G - T) + (E - M)$) have been introduced. (4.2) is equivalent to (2.17), i.e., the equation of the average price of the sole industry in the economy;[2] m and n are parameters reflecting the degree of monopoly. Equation (4.3) corresponds to (3.16), which appears, among Kalecki's many formulations of the theory of investment, the one most suitable to grasp investment decisions at a given moment; S_p is the flow of savings out of profits (assumed as given as it precedes investments), and d is the *desired* debt ratio, a function of net marginal profitability of investments (equation (4.4));[3] since risk increases along with the ratio of investments expenditure to entrepreneurial savings, investment decisions are set in money terms.[4] Finally, equations (4.5), (4.6) and (4.7) represent the money market, with T being the volume of transactions.[5]

In the model above F, s_p, s_w, w, a, m, n, S_p, Emi, M are given, while X, p, I_x, d, r, i, L are unknown. The precise role played by T is still to be specified, which is naturally linked with the level of activity; in this regard, it is possible to suppose that the demand for money is related to the business activity experienced in the past or expected for the current period (which is true particularly for the demand for finance), so that $T = \bar{T}$; alternatively, the assumption can be made that $T = f(pX)$, which would raise a problem of interdependence similar to (even if less relevant than) that present in Keynes's theory. In both cases, the model gives a solution and confirms the outstanding causal nexus emphasised by Kalecki, that is to say, the priority of the 'factors of distribution' – as reflected in the mechanism of setting prices and distributive shares – compared to the process of determination of the level of activity.

According to the model, distributive shares are invariant in relation to output because of the constancy of the productivity of labour (a); this hypothesis rests in turn on the one that all the labour is direct, so that its employment varies proportionately to the level of activity. If, instead, a portion of labour were assumed as fixed, then it would follow that $a = f(X)$, $f' > 0$, so that – given prices and money wages – the share of profits would rise with output;[6] in such a case the level and distribution of income would be determined simultaneously.

The division of the macroeconomic scheme into three sectors is important to Kalecki in arguing its similarity to Marxian schemes of reproduction;[7] accordingly, we will return to the general aspects of the subject when dealing with the relationship between Kalecki and Marx (Part II, Chapter 5).

Though the model below is in accord with Kalecki's reasoning, the analytical framework is slightly different in order to make it homogeneous with the basic scheme; the only indispensable changes concern equations (4.1) and (4.2). Following Kalecki's hypotheses, the economy is divided into three sectors – investment goods (I_x), consumption goods for capitalists (C_k) and wage goods (C_w).

$$\begin{aligned} I_x &= a_i N_i \\ C_k &= a_k N_k \\ C_w &= a_w N_w \end{aligned} \tag{4.8}$$

$$\begin{aligned} I_x p_i &= wN_i + P_i \\ C_k p_k &= wN_k + P_k \\ C_w p_w &= wN_w + P_w. \end{aligned} \tag{4.9}$$

With $s_w = 0$, in equilibrium we have:

$$I_x p_i = s_p P \tag{4.10a}$$

$$C_k p_k = (1 - s_p)P \tag{4.10b}$$

$$C_w p_w = wN \tag{4.10c}$$

from which it can be concluded that profits are equal to the value of output of the first two sectors. Moreover, from (4.10a–4.10b) we can derive:

$$C_k = I_x \frac{P_i}{P_k} \frac{(1 - s_p)}{s_p}$$

Then, simplifying for $C_k = f(I_x)$, $f'>0$, and taking into account (4.10c), we obtain:[8]

$$C_w = \frac{(w / p_w)(g(I_x))}{1 - w / p_w a_w}, \quad g' > 0 \tag{4.11a}$$

Finally, by aggregating the output of the three sectors, we have equation (4.12) which substitutes (4.1):[9]

$$Y = \frac{I_x p_i}{s_p} + \frac{w(g(I_x))}{1 - w / p_w a_w}, \quad g' > 0 \tag{4.12}$$

These equations confirm that overall profits depend on capitalists' expenditure decisions and that – given the distributive shares and the propensities to consume – the latter also determine workers' consumption and consequently national income; on the other hand, the structure of production is fixed by distributive variables, spending habits, relative prices and the productivity of labour in the different sectors.

So far, we have considered the case of fixed prices and variable quantities, which implies excess capacity within all sectors. Once this hypothesis is discarded, especially as far as wage goods are concerned,[10] then equation (4.11a) determines the price of wage goods – C_w and I_x being given – which leads us to conclude that capitalists as a class not only affect distribution directly, setting the ratio of prices to wages, but also indirectly, insofar as they state a structure of the economy in the long run which results in constraints on distribution.

A further change is to introduce in the model as many price equations as sectors, which have to differ from (4.2) since it is no longer correct to overlook a certain degree of interdependence among price decisions; this aspect, indeed, cannot be appropriately considered by means of equations such as (4.2), since they do not take into account the rate of profit explicitly: we will return to this theme in the paragraph that follows.

4.1.2 Some Possible Variants

The most significant shortcomings pointed out in the above analysis concern the theory of prices; in this section possible variants are suggested in order to rescue Kalecki's approach from its major defaults while keeping, at the same time, its outstanding features.

As far as the price equation is concerned, the simplest change is that suggested by Joan Robinson (1969, p. 260), whereby the profit margin is set according to the expected rate of profit ('the best attainable in the given conditions'), which in turn takes into account the degree of monopoly and an average degree of plants utilisation. In that case equation (4.2) must be integrated with:[11]

$$\frac{m}{1-n} = 1 + \dot{r}k\frac{a}{w} \tag{4.13}$$

where $\dot{r} = P/K$ and $k = K/\bar{X}$ are, respectively, the planned rate of profit and planned capital–output ratio (techniques being given), which reflect long-term expected demand conditions.[12]

In the multisectoral model there must be as many price equations as productive sectors, and a/w must be replaced by $1/u$ – with u, prime cost, which takes into account transactions among sectors – as it is no longer possible to assume that prime costs consist of labour costs only. Moreover, interdependence among profit rates is now to be allowed; in this regard, profit rates might be envisaged as the algebraic sum of two parts: the first, uniform for all sectors and equal to the long-run interest rate increased by a coefficient covering a 'normal' (or average) entrepreneurial risk; the second, sized according to the specific risk and the degree of monopoly of each sector.

Returning to the one-sector scheme, a further possible variant to the theory of prices might be its integration with the theory of investment and financial choices. All the ingredients for this kind of approach (mainly worked out by the post-Keynesians) are present in Kalecki's theory, traceable in the circumstances that firms centralise decisions regarding investments, prices and the financial structure. An obstacle to coordination among these decisions is that internal saving is considered given when taking investment decisions, which is correct from a chronological standpoint, since 'internal accumulation' precedes investment; however, the flow of internal saving is also a result of factors partially under the firms' control, all the more so in the kind of market conceived by Kalecki. Indeed, the volume of internal saving is:

$$S_p = \frac{w}{a} X(\frac{m}{1-n} - 1)s_p$$

or, putting $(m/(1 - n) - 1) = q$[13] and replacing X with $\bar{X}$, planned production:

$$S_p = q\frac{w}{a}\bar{X}s_p \tag{4.15}$$

with s_p, the retention rate,[14] and S_p now meaning the expected flow of internal saving. Substituting in (4.13), we obtain:

$$pI_x = (q\frac{w}{a}\bar{X})(1+d)s_p \tag{4.3a}$$

which, according to the variables which are given, alternatively explains investments, financial choices or prices. Leaving aside s_p, we can conclude that:

(a) given d and $(q(w/a)\bar{X})$, equation (4.3a) explains investments (solution *à la Kalecki*);

(b) given pI_x and $(q(w/a)\bar{X})$, it is the debt ratio that is determined (in this sense see, for example, Kaldor, 1966, p. 98);

(c) finally, given investment programmes and the planned debt ratio, and given the frame of compatibility set by the 'imagined demand curve', the flow of internal means (through margin q) comes forth as the solution; in this regard, it must be added that firms are able to influence to some extent both the position of their demand functions (the markets being characterised by oligopoly) and the value of s_p (which, however, for simplicity is here assumed as given[15]).

Case (c) (like case (b)) changes to some extent the original logic of the principle of increasing risk, according to which net marginal profitability determines investment (otherwise unlimited) *since* it sets the desired debt ratio. According to case (c), instead, investment pI_x and the ratio d are fixed separately, meaning that net marginal profitability exerts a *distinct* influence on them; this in turn implies that investment decisions are limited (*à la Keynes*), even without financial constraint, which therefore does not act so much on investment as such but on the requirements of internal means.[16] The equation below is therefore to be added to (4.3) and (4.4):

$$pI_x = f(Emi - r) \tag{4.17}$$

The revised model, too, is resoluble, as it includes nine unknowns (X, p, I_x, q, S_p, d, r, i, L) in nine equations (4.1), (4.14), (4.17), (4.3), (4.4), (4.15), (4.5), (4.6), (4.7) – to which s_p (4.16) and T (where $T = f(pX)$) can be eventually added.[17] The solution represents a virtual equilibrium, in which the equilibrium level of production coincides only by chance with that expected when the price decisions were taken;[18] if this condition is not fulfilled, then both savings and the debt ratio diverge from the desired values, which affects the subsequent period – for instance, by modifying the relation $d(Emi - r)$ – and so on. Besides these factors of change, others, deriving from the impact of variations in profits and capital stock on investments, receive more attention from Kalecki.

4.2 IMPLICATIONS FOR ECONOMIC POLICY

Two levels of reflection may be singled out in Kalecki's view of economic policy: the first, firmly grounded in theoretical scheme, from which conclusions can be drawn about *if* and *how* capitalism's shortcomings can be overcome; the second, where political and institutional elements come into play and make capitalism's escape from its contradictions even more difficult. The above model enables close examination of the first kind of aspects;[19] of course, the model is devised to fit problems centred on the level of activity at a given time, the analysis of other aspects, like dynamics and allocative processes, remaining beyond its scope.

4.2.1 Wages and Employment

A first point the above scheme highlights (equation (4.1)) is the positive (*ceteris paribus*) relationship between real wages and the level of output.[20]

When underemployment of capacity exists, the impact of changes in wages on the level of output depends on the *relative* effects – both direct and indirect – they exert over the expenditure of profit and wage earners; leaving aside the reaction of the former (whose behaviour is assumed to be unaltered), the workers' reaction depends on the repercussions on prices and then on the nature of markets.

In his outstanding works on the relationship between distribution and effective demand, Kalecki makes use of a three-sectors model[21] and carries out the analysis on both the hypotheses of pure competition and of oligopoly. In perfect competition, changes in money wages give rise to proportional shifts in prices, so that neither profit per unit of output nor the overall level of production undergo variations;[22] similar conclusions hold for imperfect competition and oligopoly if the degree of monopoly is constant,[23] for in this case, too, money wages and prices vary in the same proportion.

The situation is quite different when changes in wages take place in real terms, an occurrence Kalecki considers in relation to non-competitive markets, where the degree of monopoly tends to vary inversely with money wages.[24] This case is best analysed in (1971a), in which relative changes in money wages and prices are referred to workers' power to affect pricing.[25] The consequence of this power is a change in distribution to the benefit of wage earners and then – with excess capacity[26] and given capitalists' expenditure – a rise in overall production. The trade unions' bargain, therefore, far from being a factor of crisis is an antidote which, wisely appraised and controlled, can offset the involutional thrusts coming from inside the system.[27] [28]

The validity of Kalecki's conclusions in this regard rests on the alleged constancy of capitalists' expenditure in spite of changes in distribution. This appears likely to Kalecki, as capitalists' spending decisions are taken on the basis of profits earned earlier: as their expenditure is *predetermined*, profits will not be *immediately* curtailed by adverse changes in distribution; nor will profits be negatively affected afterwards as – precisely by virtue of their initial constancy – there will be no reason for reducing expenditure.[29]

Several comments are appropriate in this connection. Generally speaking, the basic meaning of Kalecki's statement is that the autonomy of capitalists' spending is such that it is not *necessarily* affected by the relative worsening of their position; the situation capitalists enjoy cannot be undermined by external factors but only by their own will or by their own unjustified behaviour, namely, by a reduction in expenditure: it is in this sense that they are 'masters of their fate'. As a result – and this is the most relevant political implication – the responsibility of unemployment is thrown back on capitalists, and the refusal of the criterion of restraining from doing anything which might trouble business' confidence is reinforced, once its irrationality or the instrumental use of it have been proved. In this context, the lack of realism of the hypothesis of constant capitalists' expenditure – i.e., the fact that, it might be argued, not only the volume but also the share of profits affect capitalists' spending decisions – loses importance compared to the general political implications of Kalecki's thesis.

Specifically, from the hypothesis that the increase in wages does not bring about an *immediate* fall in capitalists' demand it follows that the rate of profit is not curtailed on the average, as both overall profits and the stock of capital in real terms[30] remain unchanged for the moment: as a result, there is no reason for justifying even a decrease in investments; on the contrary, these should be stimulated by the increased utilisation of plants.[31] Here, Kalecki appears to run into the same mistake he attributes to Tugan-Baranowski and Rosa Luxemburg (Kalecki 1967b), i.e., he implicitly reasons as if capitalists acted *as a class*, and not individually, when taking spending decisions: since *overall* profits did not fall – he seems to argue – it follows that not even capitalists' spending habits should be affected on the whole. However, the constancy of profits goes along with their redistribution among capitalists,[32] so that the exclusion of negative shocks on aggregate demand has to rest on hypotheses which cannot be regarded reliable *a priori*, namely:

(a) that capitalists who gain increases in income raise expenditure at least to the extent necessary to offset the contraction in the demand of the other capitalists;

(b) or, that each one keeps his decisions unhaltered,[33] the capitalists who find themselves 'in deficit' resorting to bank credit or to direct loans from capitalists 'in surplus'.

To conclude, Kalecki's argument appears to rest on a figure such as the *collective capitalist*; but even accepting this short-cut, his reasoning appears close to tautology, as it is based on the idea that profits and expenditure support each other without any leak and, after all, it ends in mingling premises and conclusions. Kalecki seeks to ward off this objection by introducing logic and time sequences, which are plausible for the short period but which became less and less convincing as the time span lengthens.[34]

4.2.2 The Control of Demand

From the employment standpoint, investments bring about a twofold result, by creating *jobs*, as they act on the supply side, and by widening the *opportunities* for employment, by expanding demand. As a rule, however, Kalecki remarks (especially in (1944, 1945)), the two effects do not coincide, so that it will be necessary to focus on either one or the other, setting up compensative measures for the rest.

As propensity to save rises with income, the rate of growth of the capital stock necessary to keep aggregate demand at full-employment level ($\dot{K}_d$) is tendentially greater than that ($\dot{K}_k$) required to create jobs in step with the increase in active population and labour productivity.[35] Consistently, the economy is fated to undergo an *impasse* which it cannot escape from; indeed:

(a) if $\dot{K} = \dot{K}_d$ then effective demand is adequate to ensure full-employment of labour, but this occurs at the cost of plants' increasing idleness, which inevitably preludes reductions in the pace of investment;

(b) if, instead, $\dot{K} = \dot{K}_k$, then both capital and labour will keep partially idle.

In both cases a squeeze in the rate of profit occurs, which calls for a *steady* reduction in interest rates or taxation to be offset;[36] Kalecki (1944, 1945) is strongly averse to this line of action, both for its ungovernability in the long run and the waste of resources it involves, as well as because it leaves the existing allocative mechanisms unchanged.[37] The fundamental principle that public authorities should comply with as regards both private and public investments is that they be undertaken insofar as they are 'useful' to the supply side; the gap this criterion would cause between the full-employment level of demand and the demand actually prompted by investments growing according to the pace required from supply conditions – i.e., ($\dot{K}_d - \dot{K}_k$) – should be filled by measures of a different nature.

As is natural considering Rosa Luxemburg's influence, Kalecki comes early to the conclusion that additional support for demand in capitalist regimes is to be found in 'external markets' (1934, 1935d, 1935e). While acknowledging the key role of the international market – both historically and for the future – in the development of capitalist economies (as well as in the underdevelopment of the backward ones),[38] Kalecki is reluctant to accept it as a mean for managing aggregate demand,[39] and even less so as the only tool to rely on; rather, he seems to lean towards including trade balance among the data of employment policy, like the pace of capital accumulation.

Only public expenditure therefore remains as a tool for demand management; the favour with which Kalecki looks upon this way draws justification not only from its governability but also from the possibility of assigning it additional tasks, by choosing an appropriate type of expenditure and way of financing:[40]

> What seems to be a rational way of achieving full employment should be based on the following principles: (i) The Government spends so much on public investment and subsidizing consumption of the poorer sections of the population that this secures full employment in combination with that private investment which is necessary to increase the productive capacity of equipment proportionately to the rise in the 'full employment national income'. (ii) Public investment is carried on at the rate actually required for satisfying the needs of the community, while all Government spending above this level is devoted to subsidizing mass consumption (Kalecki, 1945, p. 89).[41]

The above suggests that employment policy should be founded on income redistribution to some extent, by means of price control of wage goods and taxation;[42] the effects of both methods can be derived from (4.1), as both the control of prices relative to wages and the taxation on profit reduce the share of profits on income (in the latter case, the share of net profits), and in this way affect $(p - w/a)/p$.

Kalecki's conclusions about the effects of profits taxation are not far from those deducible from Keynesian analysis as regards a general tax on incomes, as in both cases a fall in the propensity to save occurs. However, Kalecki's approach has the merit of rendering the mechanism of transmission of fiscal policy impulses more transparent, as well as of grounding it in the specific context of oligopoly.

Net profits being determined by capitalists' expenditure, they do not fall overall after a tax has been levied, provided that the tax is assigned to finance greater public spending; instead, it is net profit per unit of output which is curtailed, so that the overall production will be pushed up to a level where equilibrium between demand and capitalists' net income is restored. When profit taxation finances greater public spending, it does not therefore reduce profits but raises the real income of the economy; consistently, government has a tool for offsetting the recessive tendencies inherent in the price leadership power of firms. Of course, firms may struggle to contrast this course by partially transferring taxes on prices, but their effort would be devoid of consequences on net overall profits which are determined by spending decisions only.

As to the indirect effects of profits taxation on employment, Kalecki shifts from an initial conviction inclined to exclusion (due to the balancing of opposed considerations),[43] to a more flexible position. In (1944) he argues that the joint use of fiscal leverage on profits and public spending can, of course, give rise to full-employment demand, but the depressive effects on investments which are likely to occur might hinder the pace of accumulation from keeping step with long-run growth of population and productivity of labour. In other words, as the *maintenance* of full employment requires satisfying both the conditions of a specific *level* and a specific *composition* of demand, public authorities should have two tools at their disposal, which might even be both fiscal in kind: hence the suggestion of introducing a 'modified' tax on income[44] (which results in tax relief on income from investment) or, alternatively, capital taxation (for 'all types of capital'). Kalecki largely prefers the latter possibility as being, on the one hand, the most equitable form of taxation and, on the other, void of negative repercussions on the incentive to invest;[45] the opposition it would meet, however, make this a difficult way to follow.[46]

4.2.3 Inflation

Kalecki was directly concerned with inflation and its remedies mainly in wartime, with reference to the problems of that moment[47] and, more generally, to those springing from the state of full employment; the scope of his ideas, however, goes beyond the specific situations considered.

His basic conviction is that inflation derives from the struggle between entrepreneurs and workers over income distribution – a struggle which, in market economies, is precariously allayed by adjustments in prices. Inflation, Kalecki argues, is a phenomenon that, though changing in intensity from time to time, is inherent to capitalist economies, just as social conflict and the impossibility for it to be governed through *ex ante* coordination are structural. This conflict comes to evidence in various ways – for instance, by the opposition to the maintenance of full employment – and its settlement would call for radical reform; Kalecki's scepticism in this regard, as we have seen, is rooted in his deep distrust in the possibility of changing the rules of game of capitalism – which would result in preventing a *super partes* coordination – without getting rid of capitalism as such. Fed by an endless race of competitive adjustments, inflation would then represent the most emblematic case of the irrationality of the system.

As we have seen, wage dynamics depend not only on being more or less close to full employment, but also on the magnitude of profit margins, so that upward pressures may also occur when considerable unemployment exists. It is needless to remark that this is an important aspect, which goes beyond the conclusions that can be drawn from 'Keynesian' schemes and the Phillips curve, and makes Kalecki's outlook up-to-date.

In a system organised according to rationality and equity, Kalecki argues, the distributive struggle would be reconciled – when unemployment is present – simply by raising output to the benefit of wage earners (i.e., allowing wages to rise in real terms), without curtailing profits in absolute terms. This course does not occur because of capitalists' opposition to accepting a worsening in their relative position and to appearing as the losing party in the social conflict; as a result, a race breaks out between prices and wages, from which everyone (especially in open economies) turns out to be a loser.

Greater attention is given to the case of full employment, a situation that occurs in a war economy, but is also potentially attainable in peacetime precisely by virtue of 'Keynesian' precepts. The fundamental rule for avoiding wage–price inflation is that wage dynamics should be confined to the growth in productivity of labour, with special emphasis on the supply conditions of wage goods that constrain whatever attempt is made at redistributing real income and feed the vicious wage–price spiral.

For wartime inflation, Kalecki argues in favour of rationing which he considers 'the only radical, fair and efficient way', provided it is 'sufficiently comprehensive';[48] according to Kalecki, this is the only way of reconciling equity with the respect for people's preferences.[49]

In peacetime the problem arises that money wages are spurred on by full employment to overcome the dynamics of productivity, while reverting to remedies designed for states of emergency is out of the question. In order to avoid inflationary pressures or drops in investments, the wage trend should be therefore faced by increased taxation and reductions in the government's deficit;[50] in this way bargaining comes into a wider framework of compatibilities:

> This discussion shows that wage bargaining is likely to change its character in full employment. It will have to be linked with 'bargaining' for higher income tax on larger incomes and thus will relate the policy of trade unions more closely to general economic policy (Kalecki, 1944, p. 55).

4.3 CONCLUDING REMARKS

Conclusions about individual aspects have been drawn as they were dealt with; accordingly, in this section we will be concerned only with wider observations.

A first consideration concerns Kalecki's full title for being regarded as an exponent (perhaps the last one) of the great tradition of political economy – from the classical economists to Marx, to Schumpeter, to Keynes – which joined interest in concrete problems and their implications for economic policy with the belief that these should be dealt with within a general interpretative framework of a capitalist economy; as well as with the conviction that the working of the *machine* is strongly influenced by the political, social and institutional setting, which marks, on the other hand, the limits of validity of the conclusions that may legitimately be drawn from economic analysis *stricto sensu*. Finally, Kalecki's conception of political economy as a *moral science* must be stressed – i.e., a science that cannot discard the value judgements and ethical principles of the economist from its horizons; among these, according to Kalecki, primary importance is to be given to the needs of the human beings in their weakest and least protected components, and to their right to a job and a fair distribution of the wealth.

Kalecki's focus on employment and income distribution, far from being inspired only by reasons of scientific speculation, comes from his deep-rooted conviction that full employment and distributive justice are essential requisites for a society which claims to be really free. In this sense, Kalecki must be considered (with Keynes) one of the inspirers of the modern conception of the welfare state – as embodied in the *Beveridge Report* (Beveridge, 1944) – according to which social institutions, far from being a burden for the economy or a cost to be paid on behalf of justice and consensus, become means for a more efficient and full working of the economy. The 'economics of controls' advocated by Kalecki is not a cost to the economy but a condition for joining justice with efficiency. Kalecki's late rebuttal of reformism and his refusal of capitalism *en bloc* was determined only by increased pessimism that this project was attainable within this system.

The effort spanning Kalecki's whole reflection is to grasp the core of the working of capitalism, clearing the ground of short-cuts and canonical hypotheses typical of the neoclassical and Marxist traditions, and at the same time rejecting the apologetic or totally negative picture that these respectively suggest.

So, while his political evaluation of capitalism is negative, Kalecki's conclusions about its perspective (except when he was feeling particularly polemical) are open to doubt, according to his belief that not everything can be brought to economics; hence his refusal to adhere to rigid, mechanistic schemes, whether *catastrophist* (as often in Marxist literature) or *harmonicist*, as also in some post-Keynesian approaches.

In line with these general premises, the key to Kalecki's theoretical framework is income distribution. The whole working of the economy turns to distribution, both from the angle of effective demand and its laws of motion, and from the angle of inflation; on the other hand, distribution is open *par excellence* to extra-economic factors, so that it is to these that the actual course of things is traced back after all.

The comprehensiveness of the scheme (together with its openness) and the way its working is tied to income distribution are the outstanding aspects of Kalecki's theory. Further aspects can be pointed out, of course, but they are but *tesserae* of a framework in which the overall picture is far more interesting than its single parts.[51]

As to the limitations of Kalecki's approach, a distinction must be made between those deriving from specific shortcomings (as such, amendable) and those which are rooted in the nature of the approach itself. The first have been pointed out whenever they arose in the preceding analysis; however, it is worth emphasising that the explanation of distribution is far from satisfactory: the idea that distribution depends on market conditions, and therefore on changing power relationships among social counterparts, is certainly correct in essence but, without further specification, is too generic a guide to understanding the problem.

Moreover, the macroeconomic pattern of the scheme precludes us from dealing with several questions. Even allowing for Kalecki's occasional use of a multisectoral model – mainly in order to illustrate interdependences between the structure of production and the distributive setting – the fact remains that, all in all, the dynamics of allocative processes are foreign to his analysis. Whether or not this represents a serious defect depends on circumstances and on the answers the theory is claimed to give: both criteria lead to the conclusion that, in the Kaleckian context, this deficiency is not disruptive; it should be added, however, that the same characteristics apply to schemes (including disaggregated schemes) which give priority to reproduction over allocation of scarce resources. Questions pertaining to the supply side are foreign as well;[52] in this regard, Kalecki confines himself to supposing that, in a state of underemployment (which is the normal condition of the *laissez-faire* economy), production is elastic to demand at the given price; indeed, under this hypothesis complications deriving from the structure of supply can be disregarded.[53]

The list of problems could be continued: from the drastic simplifications of the labour market to the schematism of behaviour underlying (first of all) consumption functions, to the rigid contraposition of capitalists and workers, clearly dated today, to the hypothesis of closed economies (even though Kalecki does mention the effects of international trade). However, many of these themes have been developed fairly recently, and it should be taken into account that, starting from the fifties (when he returned to Poland), Kalecki abandoned the theory and problems of capitalism. The fact remains, however, that – as it is – his scheme does not fit the above types of questions.

Does this imply that Kalecki's thought is obsolete, unsuitable for facing the problems of today's economies? We believe that, for at least two reasons, the answer should be 'no'. First of all, however intricate and variegated today's problems may be compared to the high degree of abstraction of Kalecki's theory, it can still trace the *general lines* of the working of the capitalist economy (which was precisely the purpose Kalecki had in mind); moreover, Kalecki's theory is able to deal with what has been considered the most disruptive phenomenon from the 1970s onward and, at the same time, has caused the 'crisis' of the Keynesian model, the coexistence of unemployment and inflation.

Certainly, in view of the simplifications on which it is based and its other shortcomings, Kalecki's theory calls for changes and integration with other analytical tools, especially when it is used for purposes quite different from those for which it was coinceived. A further proof of vitality can be traced here, i.e., the contribution its most valid parts can give to the formulation of new theoretical schemes arrived at from different routes. A comparison between Kalecki's analysis and other streams of thought directly or indirectly related to it is developed in Part II.

Part II

Kalecki and Economic Thought

As stated in the Introduction, Part I was devoted to Kalecki's *positive* contribution to economic theory and policy, with special regard to unemployment. Attention was also given to the affinities and contrasts between Kalecki's thought and other approaches, chiefly with the Keynesian one which represents the most obvious, but also the most interesting reference in the field of unemployment equilibrium.

Part II examines specific aspects of Kalecki's position in the history of economic thought; this is rather a complex subject and needs careful attention, as Kalecki's contribution is at a crossroads where threads of thought arrive and others depart. There is a *vertical line* from Marx through Kalecki to the post-Keynesians, and a *horizontal line* linking contributions, from Keynes to the Swedish school, that matured independently in the early 1930s, whose similarities and divergences with Kalecki require closer investigation.

5 Kalecki and Marx

This chapter investigates the relationships between the stream of thought associated with Marx and the ideas conceived by Kalecki starting from the 1930s. An appraisal is made of Marxist ascendancy over Kalecki, on the one hand, and whether, and to what extent, his work contributed to giving a solution to problems unsolved in Marxist tradition, on the other.

This task is complicated by the *ubiquity* of Marx's thought, both on account of the variety of themes he dealt with and on account of the many ramifications he generated or in which he left (sometimes unnoticed) seeds.

It is difficult to disagree with Schumpeter[1] when he argues that vitality is the sign of the greatness of Marx's *system* – a greatness in no way undermined by possible weaknesses of single building blocks, but which is confirmed by its permeation of modern economic thought. It would thus be a mistake to evaluate the Marxian system purely on the basis of what Marx actually said. It would similarly be inappropriate to assess its influence on modern thought solely on the basis of those who profess to be Marxists; all the more so because, as has been observed,[2] perhaps the richest fruits of Marx's doctrine are to be found in the works of scholars who have no explicit ties with Marxist ideology.

5.1 THE THEORY OF EXPLOITATION

Among the questions left open by Marx, the most controversial concern the relationship between values and prices of production, and the problem of effective demand; that is to say, the two moments which mark the Marxian analysis of profit – the *origin* of profit and the conditions for its *realisation*. The first relates to the sphere of production, to the exchange between capital and labour, to the difference between the use value and the exchange value of the labour force; the second to the propensity of economic agents to spend. Each aspect corresponds with a feature of capitalism that Marx denounces but whose theoretical basis he is unable to demonstrate: the exploitation of workers and the systematic waste of resources.

Several generations of scholars have debated these themes, with different emphasis. The professed Marxist component has focused attention mainly (and unsuccessfully) on the problem of transformation, being convinced that this is crucial to validating the theory of exploitation. The second theme has been developed by economists of different extractions, frequently unrelated to Marxism but sharing the aim – by drawing on hints scattered throughout Marx's works – of setting up ideas and tools able to explain the working of modern capitalist economies.

Kalecki belongs to this second group. Indeed his lack of dogmatism and his intellectual independence from Marxian doctrine are apparent. Kalecki's Marxism is unavowed, and he generally avoids using categories and the lexicon typical of the Marxist approach. The concepts of labour-value and exploitation (in Marx's sense) do not recur in Kalecki's works and no attention is given to notions such as prices of production or the general rate of profits. Kalecki sticks stubbornly to the field of market prices (determined by the cost of production and by that ambiguous creature called degree of monopoly), so that his conception of profit appears entirely within the sphere of realisation.

Kalecki's silence on the existence of a *causa causans* of profit, prior to realisation, could naturally be interpreted either as a tacit acceptance or as a tacit rejection of Marx's premises. In the first case, Kalecki would have merely limited his attention to 'phenomenal reality', to the conditions for the realisation of the surplus value, while accepting Marx's points as its ultimate cause (i.e., the law of value and the theory of exploitation). If this were true, however, it would be necessary to verify the compatibility of Kalecki's categories with those of Marx, which would entail switching from market prices to prices of production and then – through any of several paths, according to a still unsolved debate – to the notion of exploitation.

Kalecki's complete silence on the matter suggests a second interpretation, whereby the origin of profit rests entirely on the power of firms to set prices over costs; that is to say, profits originate in the power relationship between producers and workers , the latter being regarded as consumers rather than suppliers of labour. Realisation of profits thus depends on the propensities to consume and to invest. The entire problem of income distribution consequently finds its answer on the market, which means dropping the Marxian analysis of distribution. Naturally, this does not imply that the notion of exploitation is foreign to Kalecki, but rather that he does not follow Marx in attempting to pass from a purely ideological conception to one based on scientific verification. Considering his pragmatism, it is hardly surprising that Kalecki took no step in this direction, for he would have viewed the attempt to provide a *scientific* demonstration of exploitation (i.e., of the origin of surplus value) as an escape from a *reality* which required no demonstration.[3]

Whatever his opinion might have been, Kalecki's silence lets us focus on effective demand and argue that it is in this field that the main elements of convergence with Marx can be traced. Dobb remarks that Kalecki's works 'could be regarded as a formalization of the "realization problem"' (1973, p. 222). This overstates the case in that, although Kalecki's research undeniably centres around the 'realization problem', it should not be regarded as a contribution entirely internal to Marxian theoretical analysis.

5.2 EFFECTIVE DEMAND

It has been written that Marx's schemes of reproduction probably mark the origin of macroeconomics[4] and that with these schemes Marx set up an analytical tool whose potential was to become evident only after the advent of Keynesian theory.[5]

According to a widely accepted view,[6] Marx was unable to follow up his perception of the problem of effective demand with a theory, because he lacked (1) a theory of investment decisions, and (2) a theory of the effects of investment on the overall level of production.[7]

As far as investment decisions are concerned, Marx tended to identify saving and accumulation in the long run, i.e., he considered profit and investment as inseparable over the long period. Saving and investment are, in point of fact, *separate* acts, and they can also be *widely separated* in *time* (hence the hoarding of money as cause and consequence of crises), but they are basically *non-independent* acts. Once the distrust which accompanies crises vanishes, the struggle for survival induces capitalists to accelerate the pace of investment as much as possible.[8]

On the other hand, a theory of aggregate output would have been all the more necessary to Marx since he appears to deny that the level of production is normally determined by the productive capacity of the economy. Indeed, though overproduction becomes manifest only under particular circumstances (namely, during crises), this does not seem to imply that in normal conditions the economy operates at full capacity. On the contrary, Marx observes:

> The periods in which capitalist production exerts all its forces regularly show themselves to be periods of over-production; because the limit to the application of the productive powers is not simply the production of value, but also its realization (*Capital*, vol. II, p. 391n.).

Marx's description of the 'industrial cycle', where 'high pressure' production is but a phase, further confirms this view.[9]

Without going into the schemes in detail, it is perhaps sufficient to recall that the outputs of the various sectors[10] in excess of their internal requirements, must be equal in value[11] and that their mutual demands must also be equal. To achieve this, Marx specifies the expenditure functions of all the wage earners, whereas the expenditure behaviour of capitalists is set forth only for those operating in sector I. The behaviour of capitalists in sector II is determined as a residual, so as to ensure the existence of equilibrium.[12] Marx further maintains that surplus value must be completely spent, so that the share consumed is immediately determined once the share accumulated is fixed; accordingly, the possibility of insufficient aggregate demand is ruled out *ex hypothesis*.

Thus, from the standpoint of the modern theory of effective demand, Marx's approach suffers a twofold limitation: first, it does not allow for independent consumption and investment functions; second, the expenditure decisions of the capitalists of the one sector are taken as fully dependent on the decisions of the capitalists of the other.

Nevertheless, Marx's reasoning is consistent with his own purpose, which was to specify the *conditions* by which the system can reproduce itself – on an unchanged or on a growing scale – without encountering sectoral disproportions or shortfalls in aggregate expenditure; he wanted, moreover, to demonstrate that the possibility for equilibrium to exist rests on the coordination of the behaviour of agents (a coordination which in turn he considered beyond the reach of capitalism). Indeed, Marx argues that 'on the basis of the spontaneous pattern of this production, this balance is itself an accident' (*Capital*, vol. II, p. 571).

The reproduction schemes at least provide a framework of compatibilities which can be developed into a theory of income, once some definitional and equilibrium conditions are replaced by functional relations, i.e., by behavioural equations.[13] Once we fill the gap and add *independent* consumption and investment functions for the capitalists of *both* sectors, equilibrium must be achieved by the adjustment of other variables. Alternatively: (1) *given distribution*, sectoral outputs must adjust so as to reach levels and proportions which coincide with demands – in this way we obtain a theory of output; or (2) *given the levels of production*, it is the distribution that, through changes in prices and their divergences from values, adapts itself so as to bring the structure of demand into line with production. In this way we have a theory of distribution[14] along *post-Keynesian* lines.[15]

'Kalecki', Joan Robinson remarks,[16] 'began at this point' – i.e., by assuming the distributive setting as a given and output as a variable. Yet, Robinson's statement implies more than cultural affinity; it entails that the relationship between Kalecki and Marx can be seen as one of theoretical derivation. Besides prompting the problems to be taken up and providing a background free of in-principle preclusions, Marxian theory would have given Kalecki the tools he needed (i.e., the reproduction schemes) to tackle these problems; and it would have been precisely by virtue of the reproduction schemes that Kalecki would have succeeded in reaching his goal.

This view rests on an *ex post* interpretation of Kalecki's work, which finds no confirmation in the way his thought developed over the years. Indeed, the starting point of Kalecki's theory of effective demand (1933a, 1933b) is based only on the *classical* hypothesis of zero propensity to save out of wages, while no explicit connection with Marx's theory is put forward.[17] Only at a later stage does Kalecki seem to focus the affinity between his approach and Marx's in the reproduction schemes; he became aware of this after fully realising (also thanks to Keynes) the importance of the concept of underemployment equilibrium versus the business cycle, and after he came to the conclusion that his theory provided a solution to a problem left open by Marx. Furthermore, the incidental manner in which Kalecki (in his major works) aligns his reasoning with Marx's reproduction schemes appears as an implicit denial that he considered these schemes as his source of inspiration.

The first time Kalecki mentions Marx's schemes is in (1939a), when he observes that the relations whereby investment brings about an equal amount of saving 'are contained in the famous Marxian scheme of "extended reproduction"' (p. 45). However, he adds, Marx:

> is interested in finding out, with the help of exchange equations, the pace of investment in investment and consumption goods industries respectively, which is necessary in order to secure a steady expansion of output ... He does not pay attention to the problem of what happens if investment is inadequate to secure the moving equilibrium, and therefore does not approach the idea of the key position of investment in the determination of the level of total output and employment (1939a, p. 45).

In (1954) Kalecki makes a further step in translating his own arguments into Marx's terms. After dividing the economy into three sectors (investment goods, capitalist consumption goods and wage earners' consumer goods), he argues that the sectoral outputs ultimately depend on capitalists' expenditure.[18] This reasoning is later formalised in a model (1968b)[19] in which Kalecki concludes that:

> the national income (or product) Y which can be sold and the profits P which can be realized are determined in all circumstances ... by the level of investments I and capitalist consumption C_k (given the distribution of income between wages and profits) (1968b, pp. 460–1).

The novelty of this result stems from elements which Marx essentially lacked (or which he handled in a rather confused manner). Marx would certainly have conceded that profits, i.e., *realised* surplus value, are affected by capitalists' expenditure and that the latter has a certain degree of autonomy from profits.[20] Nevertheless, (1) this autonomy appears to Marx to be confined to the short period (since in the long run saving governs investment); (2) the amount of produced surplus value (as distinct from the amount realised, i.e., from profits) and the overall level of output continue to rely on factors which are prior to realisation.

The autonomy of capitalists' spending is instead clearly asserted by Kalecki, who argues that it rests ultimately on the working of the banking system, which creates financial resources upon request, so that investment is made independent of any previous accumulation of profits and savings. As we have already seen, Kalecki makes it very clear that it is not the flow of saving in itself, but the supply of finance which is prerequisite for expanding investment; and that it is the latter which, by raising the level of activity, brings about an equal amount of saving. Kalecki's conception of the role of money and finance brings to mind Marx's circuit of money capital and his conviction that capitalists as a whole are able to produce the amount of liquid assets needed to realise the surplus value.[21] Indeed, it is most likely that the immediacy with which Kalecki perceived both the *revolving* character of financial capital and the endogenous nature of money supply derives precisely from his familiarity with Marxian reasoning. Undoubtedly, however, the notion of capitalism as a system grounded on class barriers, that Kalecki shares with Marx, is fed by the nature of the financial system and by that circuit of capital which both of them hold irremediably closed to non-capitalists. In no way can workers 'break their chains' and become entrepreneurs themselves, since the ownership of capital is a precondition for carrying out investment activity, all the more so inasmuch as it is an essential requisite for obtaining credit.

5.3 KALECKI ON TUGAN-BARANOWSKI AND LUXEMBURG

The different conclusions which can be drawn from reproduction schemes led Kalecki (1967b) to differ with *both* Tugan-Baranowski and Rosa Luxemburg on the effects of capitalist accumulation. Tugan-Baranowski argued for the necessity of dynamic equilibrium (provided that exact proportions among sectors are ensured), while Rosa Luxemburg attempted to prove that capitalism exhibits an opposite tendency. These contrasted conclusions are, according to Kalecki, consequences of Tugan-Baranowski's and Luxemburg's distorted views of the accumulation process, and of the lack of a definite theory of investment decisions. Both of their theses, Kalecki remarks, are based on the conception of accumulation as a process *coordinated* within the capitalist class. Consistently, Tugan-Baranowski argues that individual investment decisions (precisely because they are coordinated) mutually support each other; while Luxemburg maintains that the excess capacity potentially brought about by these decisions would (for the very same reason) be anticipated by the entrepreneurs, and hence lead to a check in investment. According to Kalecki the weaknesses of such reasoning is due in both cases to deficiencies in the investment theory. The objection Kalecki raises against Tugan-Baranowski is that:

> The fundamental idea of Tugan rests on an error that what *may* happen is actually happening, because he does not show at all why capitalists in the long-run are to invest to the extent which is necessary to contribute to full utilization of productive equipment (1967b, p. 147).

Nevertheless, Kalecki is sympathetic to the 'deeply anticapitalistic' ideological basis of Tugan's conclusions, that is to say, to his conviction that the 'absurdity of capitalism' is such that it would justify the production of machines as an end in itself, in this way making 'its development immune against the problem of finding markets for its product' (1967b, p. 148).

Symmetrical reasoning is opposed to Luxemburg's conclusions about the inevitability of a halt in the accumulation process, due to the lack of a 'third element' represented by non-capitalist markets. This thesis, too, would appear to reflect deficiencies in the analysis of investment decisions, since underlying Luxemburg's reasoning would be the idea that accumulation is the fruit of decisions made by the capitalist class considered as a whole. Since capitalists are aware that there is no final market for the growing output made available by new equipment, why would they bother to invest at all?[22] Here Kalecki objects that:

> capitalists do many things as a class but they certainly do not invest as a class. And if that *were* the case they might do it just in the way prescribed by Tugan-Baranowski (1967b, p. 152).

Hence the conclusion that while, on the one hand, the lack of coordination of investments brings about crises, on the other it permits capitalism to contain the consequences of its own internal contradictions. In fact, the lack of coordination is not only an expression of the anarchy of the market, but is also an effect of competition among entrepreneurs, which takes place through innovations, diversification of products, the search for new sources of raw materials, the introduction of new productive processes, and so on: in short, by means of an endless investment race. Therefore, it cannot be ruled out *a priori* that the capitalist economy is in fact able to generate tendencies towards extended reproduction; but this conclusion in no way implies denial of the existence of a problem of effective demand, as in Tugan-Baranowski.[23] Hence the recognition of the important but not necessarily vital role played by external markets in supporting the process of accumulation.[24]

Concluding, Kalecki rejects the determinism of the conclusions of the two authors, for he recognises that capitalism is such a versatile *Proteus* that it might be able to overcome (at least temporarily) its own limits; and, paradoxically, to succeed in doing so precisely by virtue of its own contradiction.

5.4 UNEMPLOYMENT AND CRISIS

But what can be said about the *ultimate causes*, the very origin of unemployment – as distinct from the principle of effective demand, i.e., from the *possibility* for income to adjust at equilibrium levels below full-employment capacity? Here Kalecki's view, as we have outlined it, strongly resembles that of Marx.

According to Marx, unemployment is a *permanent* feature of capitalism, a phenomenon deeply rooted in it, even though it emerges more or less strikingly according to the phases of the industrial cycle. The fundamental, primitive and endemic cause of unemployment, Marx argues, is mass underconsumption – a cause just as permanent as is the poverty of the working class:

It is no way a contradiction, on this contradictory basis [the increase in the productive forces *versus* the limited basis for consumption], that excess capital coexists with a growing surplus population; for although the mass of surplus-value produced would rise if these were brought together, yet this would equally heighten the contradiction between the conditions in which this surplus-value was produced and the condition in which it was realized (*Capital*, vol. III, p. 353).[25]

Incidentally, Marx's reasoning here provides further evidence that he does not believe that, as a rule, output is set by the productive capacity of the economy or that unemployment is caused by insufficient accumulation of capital.

As we have seen, for Kalecki, too, beyond the lack of investment which is at times the immediate and most evident cause of unemployment, the basic problem is the chronic underconsumption of the masses. This factor is revealed and emphasised by another (also acknowledged by Marx) – the asymmetry of the effects of investment, which affects productive capacity more markedly than demand. As we have seen, this entails two noteworthy consequences: on the one hand, it would be contradictory over the long term to base unemployment policies on expanding investments;[26] on the other, this asymmetry lies at the root of business cycles inasmuch it leads to alternation of overaccumulation and underaccumulation. The *causa causans* of the instability of capitalism is, therefore, an intrinsic feature of accumulation, which marks its limit and internal contradiction – the *productive character* of the investment:

We face here one of the most remarkable paradoxes of the capitalist system. The expansion of the capital equipment, i.e., the increase in the national wealth, contains the seed of a depression in the course of which the additional wealth proves to be only potential in character (Kalecki, 1935d, p. 32).

Again, with particular strength deriving from its being the closing remark of (1939a):

The tragedy of investment is that it causes crises because it is useful. Doubtless, many people will consider this theory paradoxical. But it is not the theory which is paradoxical, but its subject – the capitalist economy (p. 149).

The similarity of this view with that of Marx is evident; the quotation appears to repeat almost word for word Marx's epigram 'the *true barrier* to capitalist production is *capital itself*' (*Capital*, vol. III, p. 358). The 'contradiction' or the 'barrier' to accumulation lies in the fact that the mechanisms governing accumulation and income distribution enter into conflict with each other as far as the realisation of the surplus value is concerned. In other words, the contradiction is that, in capitalist regimes, distribution is ruled by forces acting in a direction which is diametrically opposed to that guaranteeing a relation between consumption and investment suited to equilibrium growth of productive capacity.

In this sense, Kalecki would certainly adhere to Marx's statement (which Marx himself had difficulty in arguing) according to which: 'The ultimate reason for all real crises always remains the poverty and restricted consumption of the masses' (*Capital*, vol. III, p. 615).

As far as the *immediate* causes are concerned, crises arise for Kalecki because of excess installed capacity, and recovery takes place once the excess has been eliminated by a period of negative net investment. In Marx's view, instead, these phases are determined by fluctuations in the general rate of profits due to the ups and downs of the industrial reserve army.[27]

Marx's linkage of the fluctuations in the general rate of profits to those in the *production* of surplus value (i.e., to changes in wages and in the organic composition of capital), rather than to those in its *realisation*, follows directly from his own definition of the rate of profits. Yet, this reasoning makes it difficult for him to argue that the 'ultimate cause' of crisis is underconsumption. The inadequacy of consumption can no longer be regarded as the factor pushing the rate of profits downward; rather, it must be the latter that negatively affects the former via a breakdown of investment and employment.[28] Thus Marx is deprived of the possibility of joining his belief that overproduction *ultimately* originates in underconsumption to the interpretation of the latter as an *actual cause* of crisis.[29]

Kalecki and Marx also share the idea that, ultimately, unemployment has political roots, as is made particularly evident by the Marxian imprint in Kalecki's theory of the political cycle. Unemployment goes hand in hand with capitalism, first of all, because it performs a function of social control by safeguarding the values and relations on which the systen is grounded. Developments threatening those values can only be temporary; in particular, income distribution may indeed undergo changes during the business cycle,[30] but in the long run it is subordinated to safeguarding the mechanism of accumulation (a safeguard which is, however, misconceived bearing in itself the seeds of the contradiction).

Thus, Marx argues that over the long run the dynamics of wages and employment must be

> confined within limits that not only leave intact the foundations of the capitalist system, but also secure its reproduction on an increasing scale' [whence he concludes that:] 'the rate of accumulation is the independent, not the dependent variable; the rate of wages is the dependent, not the independent variable (*Capital*, vol. I, pp. 770–1).

Marx's reasoning here seems to upset the relationship between wages and accumulation which, as we have seen earlier, is the basis of the industrial cycle. Indeed, the *status* of independent or dependent variables depends on the time horizon considered. Every time wages rise and threaten the process of accumulation, they are pulled down abruptly by the restoration of the unemployed army; in the long run, therefore, it is the rate of profits that capitalists regard as normal (hence the ensuing rate of accumulation) , that determines wages, and not the other way round.[31]

The share of wages rather than the real wage is for Kalecki the most meaningful measure of the state of class relations. Obviously, this does not mean that the level of real wages is unimportant; however, while its gradual increase over time is an historically observed fact, yet inequalities persist in the diffusion of welfare and there is not a widely accepted frame of reference for appraising the level reached by wages.[32] The distributive shares, instead, reveal more immediately the conflictual nature of income distribution – the 'size of inequality'. This is the 'hard core' over which social parties struggle, and it is here that the short-sightedness of the capitalist class becomes apparent: being more interested in its *relative* condition (the share of profits) than in its *absolute* condition (the level of profits), it behaves in such a way as to prevent the whole of society from benefiting from a larger level of output.

5.5 CONCLUDING REMARKS

To conclude, the general relationship between Kalecki and Marx appears best grasped by Kaldor (1989, p. 8) in stating that Kalecki was a 'deviationist' from Marx in the same way Keynes was from Marshall. Specifically, beyond their broad sharing of the vision of capitalist society, convergence occurs in the issue of effective demand.

Marx provided Kalecki with the idea (though devoid of theoretical demonstration) that the deficiency of effective demand is rooted in the normal working of the capitalist economy. For his part, Kalecki believed he had solved a problem left open by Marx, by showing that the equations determining the level of total output are 'contained' in the scheme of extended reproduction.

Whether Marx would have considered Kalecki's solution appropriate to his system is obviously quite a different question. As we have seen, Kalecki shifts emphasis from production to the realisation of surplus value, and from the conditions of exploitation to the conditions of the market. Indeed, this is a change Marx would hardly have accepted, and it was probably his reluctance to follow this route that had driven him away from focusing on the problem of effective demand. Taking also into account Kalecki's interest in market versus production prices and his 'strong distaste' for the theory of value, we can easily conclude that the answer to the above question is that Kalecki was not a diligent exegete of Marx, and than his conclusions were not those Marx was aiming at.

It is, therefore, quite understandable that intransigent advocates of Marx's purity should oppose this kind of exercise.[33] The problem remains, however, whether it is preferable to protect a system from infection by spurious elements, though it be incomplete and unable to interpret relevant aspects of the real world,[34] or, alternatively, rid the field of exegetical cures and open the system to integrations and modifications to permit building a new theoretical *corpus*, distinct from the original contributions. This second approach, according to some writers, is not only *legitimate*,[35] but also *necessary* in order to avoid dissipating Marx's insight.[36]

6 A Digression on Keynes's *Treatise*

According to Harrod (1951, pp. 474–5), Keynes's *Treatise on Money* (1930a) did not have a happy career. Within a few months of its publication, many of its ideas had been made obsolete by further discussion within the 'Cambridge Circus' (which was preparing the *General Theory*), and the subsequent appearance of the latter did much to discourage interest by reinforcing the *Treatise*'s image as a transitional work. This lack of attention was later corrected by arguing that the *Treatise*'s importance went well beyond what had been originally thought, i.e., that it was a re-examination of the channels through which monetary impulses are transmitted, in a perspective that went beyond the mechanism of the quantity theory, though remaining fundamentally dependent on it. Arguments supporting 'rehabilitation' ranged from the importance the *Treatise* attributed to institutional factors to its being a forerunner of many of the ideas later developed in the *General Theory*, such as underemployment and the theory of profits.

It is chiefly in relation to the theory of profits that is worth while taking into consideration the *Treatise* when dealing with Kalecki's thought. In that work, in fact, the origin of the idea according to which the income of entrepreneurs is determined by their spending decisions had been indicated: here, Kaldor states (1956, p. 227n), lies the essential difference between Keynesian and pre-Keynesian thought, and here the source of an alternative to the marginalist theory of distribution is to be found.[1]

It will be argued below that excessive attention has been given to the distributive approach theorised in the *Treatise* – a consequence of an interpretation forced by later theoretical developments and of the tendency to widen the Keynesian roots of post-Keynesian economics. The concept that profits depend on entrepreneurial spending decisions, as proposed in the *Treatise*, must be set instead in a right perspective, both in terms of its innovative scope and in terms of the implications that can be strictly derived from it.

Another much debated question is whether the assumption of full employment is to be found in the *Treatise*, and, if so, in what terms. We shall deal with this problem later, it being sufficient for the moment to note that, as far as the theory of profits is concerned, one needs no more than the hypothesis (indisputably made by Keynes) that supply is *rigid*, whatever the causes may be.

6.1 PRICES AND DISTRIBUTION

The *Treatise* focuses on the instability caused by lack of coordination between savings and investments; accordingly, the general framework in which the argument runs is disequilibrium, this being conceived as the process of transition from one equilibrium position to another.[2] The significance of the work, therefore, must be assessed not only in relation to what happens in disequilibrium but also with regard to the characteristics of equilibrium. Concentrating on the first aspect only would be misleading as it would overemphasise the innovative elements – especially in the field of distribution – as compared with the elements of continuity with the marginalist tradition.

Keynes defines national income as the value of final output at production cost, covering wages and salaries (including doles and pensions), entrepreneurs' *normal* remuneration, interest on capital, 'regular' monopoly gains and rents.[3] Extra profits (or simply profits in Keynes's meaning of the term) and losses arising out of the disparity between proceeds on sales and production costs, therefore, are not considered part of income, but rather as *windfalls* which increase or reduce the wealth accumulated by entrepreneurs and, being tied to random phenomena, cannot be classed as additions to current income.[4]

Profits or losses come into existence as a result of the divergence of monetary demand from production valued at cost (or income), or of money expenditure for investments from savings – the latter being defined as the difference between income and money expenditure for consumption.[5] Consequently, the macroeconomic equilibrium – supplemented by equilibrium in all sectors – implies equality between prices and costs of production, at least as average values of the firms operating in each industry.[6] On the other hand, disparities between investments and savings give rise to gaps between prices and costs, whence the emergence of profits or losses:[7]

$$C + I = E + Q \tag{6.1}$$

or:

$$Q = I - S \tag{6.2}$$

where C and I are money expenditure for consumption and investment, E is national income, Q is total profits (losses).

Investment and saving decisions being autonomous, the causal link in (6.2) runs from the right: profits are determined by spending decisions *compared* to production decisions, whether the former concern greater investments or increased demand for consumption goods.[8] As mentioned earlier, too much importance is often given to this statement; appraising it correctly requires initially:

(a) circumscribing the area of application, i.e., the disequilibrium;

(b) clarifying the precise nature of equilibrium positions.

As prices are market-clearing, they move from the costs of production in a direction depending on the sign of the divergence between investments and savings. The first 'fundamental equation' for the price of consumer goods[9] is:

$$p_c = \frac{C'}{O_c} + \frac{I' - S'}{O_c} \tag{6.3}$$

where C'/O_c is the cost per unit of output (including the entrepreneur's normal remuneration) or 'rate of earnings per unit of output'.[10]

A somewhat different approach is taken to explain the price of investment goods. Here Keynes prefigures a theory of portfolio selection,[11] by assuming that demand price is a function of the public's preferences for different assets and the structure of interest rates. Since this price, too, is market-clearing, it follows that 'the actual price level of investments is the resultant of the sentiment of the public and the behaviour of the banking system' (1930s, p. 128).[12] Concluding, since the supply is given for both goods,[13] price is always determined by demand and only in equilibrium between investments and savings does it coincide with the cost of production.[14]

The fact that in equilibrium price is equal to the cost of production (inclusive of a normal rate of remuneration for entrepreneurs) does not clarify the microeconomic basis Keynes has in mind.[15] The most difficult element to specify is the notion of entrepreneurs' normal remuneration, which is defined

> as that rate of remuneration which, if they [the entrepreneurs] were open to make new bargains with all the factors of production at the currently prevailing rates of earnings, would leave them under no motives either to increase or to decrease their scale of operations.[16]

This meaning of the normal rate of remuneration is clearly functional with respect to a notion of equilibrium conceived as absence of pressures to changes in production;[17] as such, what is important is not so much its level as the condition of uniformity.

As defined by Keynes, the equilibrium price closely resembles Marshall's normal supply price[18] and, more precisely, the long-period normal price.[19] The fact that under the condition of equilibrium there is equality between price, on the one hand, and average and marginal costs, on the other, can be deduced:

(a) as regards average cost, directly from the fundamental equations (C'/O_c and E/O, respectively);

(b) as regards marginal cost, from the fact that where it diverges from price, pressures would occur for changes in production; the absence of such stimuli consequently implies equality between the two.[20]

The framework thus created is suited to the marginalist theory of distribution;[21] adding the fact that Keynes's theory of profits applies solely to disequilibrium positions, while nothing is said about the determinants of distribution under long-run equilibrium, it seems legitimate to conclude that – for the latter situation – he intended resorting to the dominant paradigm of the time, the marginalist theory.

If this interpretation of the microeconomic frame of the *Treatise* proves correct, then Keynes's theory of profits needs to be drastically reappraised in terms of both its originality and of its scope. The mere fact that disparities between savings and investments affect distribution is not at all such as to allow considering a theory as *alternative* to the traditional one. Proving the originality of Keynes's approach requires measuring on the very ground of marginalism (the equilibrium between savings and investments, that Keynes associates with the long-run equilibrium of the price system); only in that case would it be possible to argue that Keynes's allegedly different conclusions – namely the dependence of distribution on spending *instead* of productivity – spring from the diversity of the schemes and not merely from the different *contexts* similar schemes are applied to. On the other hand, marginalists would have no difficulty in admitting that the productivity principle is inapplicable to the ground chosen by Keynes.[22]

Concluding, Keynes's theory, being confined to the context of transition between long-run equilibria, does not appear to represent an alternative to the marginalist theory (the principle of which is alleged to apply to these conditions only), but rather provides a ground for integrating those cases that marginalism did not deem worthy of special attention. As regards the view according to which Keynes anticipated the theory of profits of Kalecki and the post-Keynesians, it should be noted that it is a quite different matter to single out the source of profits in capitalists' spending decisions *as such*, or instead in the *divergence* between investments and savings, that is to say, between demand and a rigid supply. Keynes's originality does not lie so much in the theory of distribution in itself, as in the autonomy of investments and, consequently, in the possibility for entrepreneurs to take *discretional* spending decisions which in turn are bound to affect distribution. In other words, the novelty lies in investigating the consequences on distribution of a (relatively) new aspect – the autonomy of investments from savings as a source of changes in aggregate demand.[23]

6.2 EFFECTIVE DEMAND

The arguments so far have been based on the assumption that supply is given, an assumption that, by virtue of its being generic, is widely accepted throughout the different interpretations of Keynes's work. It is now time to verify this point.

Colleagues close to Keynes held the view that he had no interest in investigating the determinants of the level of production in the *Treatise*.[24] This lack of interest has been widely interpreted as acceptance of the traditional thesis of full employment, at least as a trend emerging beyond short-term fluctuations;[25] in this way the lack of a theory of national income (the acceptance of the existing theory)[26] would be reconciled with the presence of fluctuations in overall production. On the other hand, it is difficult to reconcile the short-term variability of production with the requirement of the fundamental equations that production is given.

An explanation of this contrast might be found in Keynes's intention to deal separately with the causes of changes in prices and in quantities, analysing the adjustments of prices given the quantities and vice versa. The periodic pattern of the *Treatise*'s scheme and the effects of profits on production decisions might support this interpretation.[27]

However, two types of objections can be raised against this view. First, the debate within the 'Cambridge Circus'[28] led to the conclusion (accepted by Keynes) that the fundamental equations implied full employment. Second, the rigidity of supply cannot be argued (as Tonveronachi, 1983, p. 43 seems to do) in the same way the Marshallian market day; Keynes makes this point clear when arguing that:

> the period which must elapse before the supply of specialized factors of production can be increased, and the long-time contracts (partially conditioned by the length of life of these specialized factors) into which

entrepreneurs must enter to induce this increase of supply, are the explanations why, for a time, profits can exist (1930a, p. 113).

Two conclusions can be drawn from the above passage. First, it confirms that profits come into being as a result of demand pressures when *scarce resources* are fully employed; regardless of whether scarce resources be labour or capital, we are just outside the proper context of 'Keynesian' unemployment. Second, it argues that increases in output can occur only as a result of changes in the supply of 'specialized factors';[29] as such, they have to be classed as long-term changes rather than short-term fluctuations. This conclusion, which evidently contradicts Keynes's intention, highlights a basic contrast in the *Treatise* between the requirements underlying its formal part and the way of seeing the world as it is.[30]

Keynes was so mindful of concrete problems (and the 1903s provided a wide variety) that he certainly could not disregard the fact that the cycle also affects the level of activity; at the same time, his analysis was aimed primarily at improving the theory of money, which was still considered basically a theory of prices.[31]

6.3 CONCLUDING REMARKS

In conclusion, the contribution Keynes's *Treatise* makes to the theories of distribution and national income cannot, in our opinion, be regarded as truly innovative, that is, a real break with tradition. It is instead the description of the working of the whole 'machine' that is of special interest; to achieve this Keynes drew on the more open and promising lines of thought of the time,[32] and developed their implications with clarity: the monetary nature of the economy and the importance of institutional factors; the autonomy of production decisions and the fact that savings and investments do not coincide automatically; the effects of this divergence on prices and income distribution; the impact of changes in the latter on sectoral and the overall levels of activity. From this standpoint the most important contribution of the *Treatise* is not so much its developing one or the other particular aspect as its grouping of them all together to highlight their intimate causal relationship.

7 The Stockholm School

The economists of the so-called 'Stockholm School' share some of the conditions already noted for Kalecki, namely an education within a cultural tradition less hostile to the new ideas, both as regards theory and economic policy, which made it easier for them to grasp these ideas but at the same time hampered the full appreciation of their novelty compared to the state of economics of the time.[1] The need to distinguish between aggregate demand and national income, the autonomy of investments from savings, the conviction that full employment does not represent a normal state for the economy nor a condition toward which it tends: all these aspects were currently accepted by the exponents of this 'circus' and claimed to be explainable within a frame of ideas which was considered the natural extension of Wicksell's scheme.

This circumstance may help us to understand why the Stockholm School (like Kalecki) did not attribute to the new ideas the same emphasis which Keynes was led to stress for their break with his own tradition. Specifically, Stockholm economists barely focus at the theoretical level on underemplyment as such, even though this problem was fully appreciated for its practical relevance and was the subject of economic policy proposals; as in Kalecki's writings of the same period, their attention was centred on instability and the measures for curing it.

7.1 UNEMPLOYMENT EQUILIBRIUM

In studying the contributions grouped under the label of the Stockholm School, several problems arise: (a) first, only a few of these contributions have been translated into languages more accessible than Swedish, while there is evidence that several non-translated works may be important in giving some essential interpretative keys; for these, reference is to be made to statements made by disciples whose reliability is sometimes doubtful (considering, for instance, the contradictions that often emerge according to the sources); (b) second, the outstanding exponents of this School were both theorists and advisers of the Government, and their analyses and proposals do not always coincide.

As theoretical economists, their concern was to remain within Wicksell's tradition, by developing the potentialities of the analysis of the cumulative process, i.e., by studying *jointly* the fluctuations in prices and output. According to Ohlin:

> Wicksell and later Lindhal ... were interested in the determination of price movements and monetary stabilisation – not the volume of output. But the same type of reasoning can be used if there are unused resources and if, therefore, an increased demand leads to a growth of output (Ohlin, 1977, pp. 152–3).[2]

It is on this common root that the Stockholm School (as it was named by Ohlin[3]) was founded; its outstanding exponents, as far as the aspects dealt with here are concerned, were Myrdal and Ohlin.[4]

The basic framework of a theory of effective demand can be traced in writings of the early 1930s, visible in the distinction between aggregate demand and national income, whence comes the independence of investments from savings and the concept of output as a variable magnitude.

The autonomy of demand is argued by referring consumption and investment to different and non-coordinated factors, the former being a function of expected income, the latter of profit expectations and the money rate of interest.[5] From this, Swedish economists deduced the independence of investments from savings and the absence of crowding-out conditions, by arguing that only credit availability is the pre-requisite for investing while savings follow:[6] the first statement obviously springs from Wicksell's inheritance; as for the second, i.e., the adjustment of saving to investment, we will come back to this shortly. Finally, the explanation of the money rate of interest is not sought within the savings–investments framework but in banking policy, since:

> any rate of interest indicates equilibrium in the capital market simply because net saving and investment always adjust so as to be equal (Ohlin, 1933, pp. 381–2).[7]

While the crucial elements of the theory of employment are clearly grasped by Ohlin and Myrdal in their writings of the 1930s, their approach to the notion of unemployment equilibrium and the adjustment towards it is more questionable. In this regard, a distinction must be made between the two economists, whose disagreement over these aspects seems to originate from methodology, i.e. from their different conception of the *immediate subject* of economic analysis – whether this should comply with a condition closely resembling reality or, instead, be a stylised representation of the latter, grasping its outstanding, though not immediately perceivable, features.

According to Myrdal, the analysis of the dynamic process should be preceded by the investigation of the nature of 'monetary equilibria', the succession of which marks the path of the economy; Myrdal's *Monetary Equilibrium* (1939) is devoted entirely to this 'preparatory step'. Monetary equilibrium, defined as *ex ante* equality between saving and investment,[8] is a hypothetical situation reflecting 'the driving causal factors, i.e., the tendencies at every point of time' (1939, p. 124). Therefore: 'The hypothesis of a monetary equilibrium does not afford a factual appraisal to reality. It is only an instrument by which observed facts can be analysed in certain respects important from the monetary point of view' (1939, pp 40–2).[9]

As equilibrium is not necessarily coupled with full employment, it is possible to speak of underemployment equilibrium, though Myrdal does not make use of this term. On a general plane, the mainspring of unemployment is supposed to be the independence of investments from savings, but its explaination as an equilibrium phenomenon would require pointing out the mechanism whereby the two variables adjust – the role of income as the equilibrating factor – and, as we shall see, Myrdal is not as clear about this aspect as is necessary.

Not only does monetary equilibrium not imply full employment but, owing to the non-competitive setting of markets, it *requires* unemployment as a condition for persisting:[10]

> If ... prices are to some extent tied by contracts and other elements of inertia or are administered prices ... then it would be impossible to keep unemployment low and to maintain monetary equilibrium at the same time ... Because of the monopoly elements which are present in price formation, the position of monetary equilibrium requires certain disequilibria between demand and supply, consisting generally only in differences between their actual and their potential magnitudes. For labour, however, ... this disequilibrium appears directly in the form of unemployment (1939, pp. 153–6).

Unlike Myrdal, Ohlin deals directly with the dynamic process, while little attention is paid to the notion of *ex ante* equilibrium. Fundamentally, the conviction that emerges is that equilibrium, in order to be a meaningful concept, must apply to a state which is both *actual* and *stable*; since it does not actually occur except by chance[11] and in any case it would never be a stable situation, then analyses along this line may serve a pedagogical purpose only but are unable to interpret real facts.[12] It is from this standpoint that Ohlin confutes the criticism according to which he overlooked the (*ex ante*) equilibrating role of income:[13] simply, he was actually uninterested in tackling that theme in terms he did not consider meaningful.

Coming to investigate the nature of the adjustment process between savings and investments, the fact that Swedish economists (including Lindhal) indicate the level of income as the equilibrating variable may give rise to a too 'forward-looking' interpretation, unless the *ex post* adjustment is clearly distinguished from that *ex ante*. Indeed, while all of them exhaustively argue how *ex ante* disequilibria lead to *ex post* equilibria, they are much more evasive when dealing with the process towards new *ex ante* equilibria.

According to the Keynesian scheme, the *ex post* adjustment runs primarily through changes in inventories, the level of income being given, that is, from the demand side. This process is conceived by Swedish economists in a rather different way, as they assume that:

(1) income *immediately* reacts to savings–investments disequilibria, without bringing about changes in inventories; and (2) consumption decisions are a function of *expected* income.[14] It follows that divergences between savings and investments lead to changes in the level of income which, being unforeseen, do not affect consumption decisions and, as such, result in unplanned changes in savings.[15]

Obviously, the restoration of *ex post* equilibrium gives rise to further shifts in consumption and investment plans as soon as the variations in income impact on expectations; this leads to the problem of *ex ante* adjustment, which is outlined by Swedish economists, though with reticencies and ambiguities. In this regard, Myrdal writes:

> Quite generally the relatively fixed consuming habits and the stability of the total demand for consumption goods are forces tending to a restoration of the relation [of equilibrium between savings and investments, 1939, p. 167. Moreover:] After a credit contraction … the new equilibrium position would be characterized by … some, perhaps quite considerable, unemployment …, saving sufficiently reduced to make free capital disposal correspond to real investment (1939, p. 169).[16]

This aspect often recurs in Ohlin's writings, for instance, when he argues that the decision to 'reduce saving', unless coupled with credit restriction, brings about increasing investment (in the consumption goods sector, first); whence the conclusion that:

> Total saving is not reduced but on the contrary increased, despite the fact that consumption is up. What makes this possible is expanding output (1933, p. 368).

This point is stated even more clearly in an 1932 article:

> The real savings required for increasing output arise as a result of better utilization of the productive machinery, which causes production to grow faster than consumption ... The savings are not needed in advance, for they cannot be accumulated; they arise in parallel with the increase in consumption, and are nourished by the increase in output itself, not by a reduction of consumption from a level that is already low in the relation to the production possibilities (Ohlin, 1932, p. 26).[17]

The above suggests that income is charged with the task of equilibrating savings and investments *ex ante*; not immediately evident from the passages quoted (nor from these scholars' theoretical writings), however, is the working of the multiplier; this is a notably weak point since the *modus operandi* of the adjustment cannot be accurately stated without it.

The lack of an explicit treatment of the multiplier has been a cause for incomprehension and criticism of Swedish economists. It has been argued that:[18]

(a) not only did Stockholm's theories aim at investigating the causes of changes in prices rather than in quantities, but variations in the latter were conceived as an *effect* of the former; this approach, therefore, is much closer to Keynes's *Treatise* than to the *General Theory*;[19]

(b) references to the principle of income adjustment cannot be found in Ohlin (1933).[20] but only in Myrdal (1939), though this author did not fully understand its importance;[21]

(c) finally, however interpreted, these contributions would not be truly original, Myrdal being influenced by Keynes's Harris Lectures (delivered in 1931)[22] and Ohlin by 'The means to prosperity' (Keynes, 1933a).[23]

Objection (c) was contested by both Myrdal and Ohlin, who stated that they never drew any suggestions from these writings which were unknown to them at that time;[24] considering the stature of the two authors and the lapse of time from then, this should be sufficient to settle this kind of dispute.[25] As to (b), an initial answer has already been given in the foregoing, arguing that it is substantially groundless,[26] though income adjustment was not the core of Swedish analysis, as it was instead in Keynes and Kalecki: we will come back to this subject shortly. Finally, with regard to (a), though it is undisputably true that prices are given prominence compared to output, yet it cannot be deduced that changes in the latter are only effects of changes in the former: the selection of the aspects attention is primarily focused on does not imply in itself the particular theoretical structure suggested by Patinkin. Relating the Swedish approach to the *Treatise* goes no further than first appearance,[27] as proved, for instance, by Ohlin's many descriptions of the transmission mechanisms of external impulses, where prices are supposed to be more sticky than output (under unemployment conditions), changes in prices being consequence of changes in output, and not the other way round.[28]

However, the lack of a clear specification of the mechanism of the multiplier remains; this can be tentatively explained by arguing either (1) that it was not fully perceived or (2) that the outcome of the process, the *ex ante* equilibrium, was not considered worth a separate analysis.

The first explanation appears ungrounded in view of evidence offered by Myrdal and Ohlin's disciples, who stated that this process was illustrated in full detail in empirical works, particularly in the Appendixes to the 'Final Report of the Committee on Unemployment', prepared by the authors in 1934. The question then arises why this problem was disregarded in the theoretical works, and the answer is to be found in point (2) which, however, can be split into two cases: (a) that the notion of equilibrium was not considered relevant *in general*; or (b) that it was *unemployment equilibrium* that was considered undeserving of special attention. The first case concerns the *method*, the second the *theory*.

As we have seen, divergences about method are claimed by Ohlin, who replies to the criticism that he overlooked the equilibrating role of income by arguing that he was not interested in tackling the question by means of a tool – equilibrium analysis – he believed unsuitable for capturing real facts.

However, beyond methodology (which may well have played a role), the reason for the lack of interest in the notion of equilibrium is, *in primis*, theoretical in that it concerns the interpretation of the nature of unemployment. This helps explain an otherwise contradictory attitude: the fact that unemployment (independently of being or not being an equilibrium phenomenon) was given central attention in the policy-oriented writings only and kept in the backround in the theoretical ones: as both of them were developed in the early 1930s, when depression had hit bottom, one should exclude that the different emphasis on this theme was due to changes in the economic situation.

The theoretical works were bound to analyse general aspects, i.e., basic problems of the working of the market economy, a context in which unemployment appeared to be ascribed to monopolistic factors. If this impediment (as permanent as it is foreign to the rules of the free market) were lacking, they seem to argue, the economy would be able to generate full-employment effective demand in the long run; the multiplier would consequently be of no use for arguing about both underemployment equilibria (being only temporary and therefore irrelevant for studying basic tendencies) and of full-employment equilibrium (being determined by the availability of resources and not by effective demand).

Accordingly, Myrdal and Ohlin focus on price stability in their theoretical writings. Ohlin's purpose in (1933) is to revise the current monetary theory by arguing that changes in prices and output are related to each other, and that fluctuations in output cannot be interpretated as occasional departures from full employment; nevertheless, his main concern is to find remedies against price instability. Myrdal also deals with price stability first of all, and the primary economic policy target he seems to suggest is the maintenance of a monetary equilibrium 'compatible with the least possible movement' of prices (1939, p. 199).

On the other side, in empirical works addressed to providing indications on how to tackle current problems concretely, circumstances brought 'Keynesian' unemployment to the forefront, a phenomenon quite serious at that time but deemed temporary, as an expression of the cyclical instability of the economy. Here economic policy has to develop through the control of aggregate demand, and its multiplying effects must now be carefully assessed.

On the whole, the idea the most representative exponents of the School seem to agree on is that fluctuations in unemployment occur around a base of *permanent* unemployment; and that while fluctuations are ascribed to the instability of effective demand (as such, suitable for Keynesian remedies), a permanent degree of unemployment is rooted in the monopolistic nature of the labour market. This leads Myrdal (1939, p. 155) to argue that:

> To the extent that the long-run monopolistic control both on the demand and on the supply side [of the labour market] is not ... reduced, permanent unemployment will not decrease, in so far as and so long one does not permit an upward Wicksellian cumulative process.

The concern that permanent unemployment is caused by chronic weakness of demand, therefore, appears foreign to these economists.

Consistently, Keynesian policies must be addressed to stabilising the business cycle, not to systematically supporting demand:

> The idea behind the Swedish proposals is not the Keynesian one of the danger of a *permanent* underemployment and the need of some policy to maintain investment on a sufficiently high level. We are, in this respect, old-fashioned in Sweden. The proposed policy was, in 1944–45, based on the assumption that there are business cycle movements and that, in certain periods, we will probably have a tendency towards too large employment, an assumption justified by the development in 1946–48 (Ohlin, 1950, p. 76).

Compared with the twofold order of problems raised by the theory of effective demand – unemployment equilibrium as a situation at a given moment, and its long-run tendencies – Swedish economists, therefore, appear to have perceived only the former, whereas the persistence of unemployment is referred to different factors; obviously, this belief also deprives the notion of unemployment equilibrium of its essential relevance.

7.2 ECONOMIC POLICY IMPLICATIONS

Following these premises Swedish economists (from Lindhal to Myrdal and Ohlin) recommended that measures for controlling demand be temporary, bound principally to spur the recovery but to be abandoned once the cumulative process had started. Fundamentally, public action was deemed necessary to invert expectations and give the initial impulse to make private investments self-stimulating (as described by the Wicksellian process), once the depressionary impasse was over.[29]

There seems to have been broad agreement in the Stockholm School as to the means to be used for this purpose.[30] First, the view is refuted according to which, even when a certain degree of freedom as regards exchange rates exists, wage cuts may represent a way out from depression; this solution, it is argued, would have the opposite effect by further pushing demand downward. It is worth noting that one of the Swedish government's major concerns, soon after the Great Depression, was stabilisation of demand, i.e., preventing distribution from being negatively affected by current economic difficulties, as this would have made things worse: hence the support of wages and the prices of agricultural goods, as well as the abandonement of the Gold Standard (in 1931) and the contextual announcement that the Central Bank would have been charged with the stabilisation of prices and the cost of living.[31]

An essential condition for starting recovery was gaining advantage from the 'international margin', which was made possible by the abandonement of the Gold Standard. This opportunity was stressed by Swedish economists much more than by Keynes and Kalecki, who instead assigned to policies of foreign relations the sole task of preventing them from hampering inward expansionary policies. Indeed, Sweden exploited the 'international margin' at will (the crown was depreciated by 40% and 25%, respectively, in relation to gold and to the British pound) and gained great advantage as far as expansion was concerned; it is widely acknowledged in fact that the first stage of recovery was prompted mainly by the increase in exports over imports.

The depreciation of the exchange rate moreover, made it possible to carry on an expansionary monetary policy, though doubts were raised about its ability to act (at least in the short run) on private investments. Scepticism in this regard was enhanced by the belief that, first, during depression the cost of money was unable to affect investments markedly and, second, that interest rates could not fall enough.[32] Finally, the efficacy of credit expansion was also questioned by arguing that, besides being a *cause*, expansion is itself also a *consequence* of the rise in investments; in other words, credit creation is prompted by the same variable – investments – it is required to stimulate: such a vicious circle, it was concluded, can be broken only 'if the State takes upon itself the risks and starts an upward process by means of a policy of public investment' (Thomas, 1937, p. 144).

The favour public works enjoyed among Swedish circles was justified by the fact that during depressions their social costs are almost nil. It was argued that in advanced countries the wage bill practically represents a fix cost for the society as a whole in so far as 'unemployment relief is borne as a fixed charge on the budgets of all income recipients' (Myrdal, 1933, p. 138); it follows that the additional cost for society consists only in increased imports of raw materials – a cost which is negligible compared to the social benefits.[33] Moreover, no problems of crowding-out could arise in the conditions of the time:

> The condition that the capital which was absorbed by these projects should be financed by the increase in output in the economy which resulted from them ... was likely to be met when there was much unused capacity in the business sector. Then these works might increase

> output on such a scale that the resulting increase in national income would be likely to give rise to the saving required for financing these public works (Lindhal, 1932, p. 136).[34]

Finally, the view is clearly expressed that deficit-financed public expenditure, by raising the overall level of income, generates increased revenues to balance it.[35] This was, of course, an essential point for clearing the ground of the obstacles raised by the supporters of the balanced-budget rule; it was argued, instead, that strict application of this rule might even cause destabilising effects. Therefore, the Stockholm School (particularly Myrdal, who prepared the Appendix to the *Report* on fiscal policy) promoted adoption of a twofold (current and capital) public budget,[36] where the balancing of the capital budget were conceived as just a long-term target. This position, it should be noted, accords with that of Keynes, whose proposals, however, came ten years later.

Similarities with Keynes can also be found in regard to supporting mass consumption. No priority is given to this route, first, because its effects on demand are difficult to assess insofar as they depend on the relative propensities to consume of those benefiting from income transfers and those charged with additional taxes[37] (being consumption expenditures, they should not be deficit financed); in addition, a greater stimulus to consumption could be generated by public works.

The work that was being carried on in Sweden certainly drew Kalecki's interest, since he spent some time there in 1936;[38] however, it is hard to find in Kalecki's writings and in those of the Swedish economists, evidence of exchanges[39] or, at least, of specific interest by one side in the research carried on by the other. Nevertheless, along with remarkable differences, there are affinities that deserve consideration. On a general level, they share awareness of the linkages between the institutional setting and the working of the economy, and the view that the capitalist market is far from the competitive standard, and that it is not possible to argue in terms of 'imperfections' but rather in terms of deeply rooted monopolistic features.[40] Specifically, there is a common conviction that economic analysis should aim at studying instability and unemployment jointly; nevertheless: (1) divergences can be found in the approach to price–output relationships; (2) Kalecki (also spurred on by Keynes) leans toward logically separating the question of unemployment from that of instability: from this standpoint, Myrdal represents perhaps a *trait-d'union* between the two approaches.

8 Kalecki and the 'Post-Keynesians'

The term 'post-Keynesian' originally indicated[1] the stream of thought linked to Keynes's closer disciples, which was chiefly concerned with the relationships among distribution, accumulation and steady-growth dynamics. More recently, other economists have been gathered under this label who, though interested in different topics, refer to a core of common propositions: on one hand, the rebuttal of the neo-classical approach to value and the conception of income distribution as a phenomenon ruled by circumstances which are outside the productive process; on the other, the introduction into the Keynesian matrix – featured, first of all, by the income multiplier and by the autonomy of some components of demand – of a number of specifications and integrations (especially concerning prices and distribution) which were foreign or, at least, not explicit to it. The widening of the criterion of classification, of course, amplified the range of approaches which can be termed 'post-Keynesian' – from disciples of Keynes and Kalecki to some neo-Marxist branches, from those referring to Sraffa to American institutionalists, and so on – and has led to a live debate even within the stream. This state of things renders the post-Keynesian approach a source of stimulating ideas and impulses but, at the same time, makes it difficult to set up a unique theoretical *corpus*, a new paradigm to match the neoclassical one.

However, things are somehow less intricate from our standpoint. It has been stated that post-Keynesian theory originates from a synthesis between Kalecki's thought (as regards the real sector) and that of Keynes, for the monetary part.[2] While the first statement will be investigated later, the second can be readily accepted,[3] which permits setting aside those contributions, especially those from the United States, which chiefly focus on monetary phenomena, uncertainty and instability. Accordingly, we will address our attention to the relationship among distribution, accumulation and the level (or the dynamics) of income, which represents the core and the original source of inspiration of post-Keynesian theory and, at the same time, the most suitable field for comparisons with Kalecki.

It is well known that the origin of the post-Keynesian approach to distribution was from the outset indicated by Kaldor (1956) in Keynes's apologue of the widow's cruse in the *Treatise* and, more generally, in the ideas outlined in Chapters X and XI of that book; once integrated with the principle of the income multiplier and with the extension to the long period of firms' autonomy to invest, these ideas would represent the basis of 'post-Keynesian' theory. Accordingly, the influence of both the *Treatise* and of the *General Theory* would be reflected in that approach: the introduction of the principle of income adjustment would allow moving the theory of profits from the uncertain ground of disequilibrium to the sounder one of equilibrium situations.[4] An additional indication, particularly evident throughout Joan Robinson's reasoning,[5] can be found directly in the *General Theory* (1936a, pp. 123–4), when the distributive effects of changes in investments (the supply of consumption goods being rigid) are analysed.

Coming to Kalecki, the short-period equilibrium of income (as represented by equation (4.1)) is a proper starting point for comparison with the post-Keynesian theory. The equation results from the synthesis of distinct theories of profits and prices but, it has been argued, can be generalised to embrace more than one variant, one of which represents the post-Keynesian theory of distribution: given real output, as in Kaldor (1956), the distributive shares are determined by *discretional* spending decisions of agents. While the theory of profits is common to the Kaleckian and the post-Keynesian cases, differences arise with regard to the circumstances to which this theory is addressed and the variables it explains: when productive capacity is underemployed and, therefore, prices are determined by constant mark-ups, the theory of profits is a part of a theory explaining the level of real output, while in full-employment conditions, when prices are market-clearing, it becomes a part of a theory of distribution.[6]

Considerations made so far refer to equilibria at a given moment, i.e., to the short period, which represents the field where major affinities with Kalecki can be found. However, the short period is conceived by a part of the post-Keynesians (*grosso modo* by its historical group) as just the starting point of an analysis which has to be fully developed within the frame of dynamics and the long period.[7] Kalecki differs from the post-Keynesians (so specified) on how to approach long-period analysis and, indeed, there is no complete accord even among the latter; divergences spring from different visions of reality, as well as from different ways of conceiving the long period.

According to the post-Keynesians the boundary between the short and the long period is not the time horizon as such, but the nature of the situations considered; long-period analysis must aim at highlighting tendencies (or, at least, aspects) which cannot be grasped by short-period analysis, without inferring, however, that these aspects should necessarily materialise over time. Hence the emphasis on the *conditions* under which price and accumulation decisions are reconciled over the long run, as well as the notion of equilibrium as just a virtual situation which is consistent with the given conditions, without necessarily entailing it as also the concluding stage of the process of adjustment.[8] As a consequence, long-period equilibrium and the trend are conceived as autononous aspects which can be analysed independently of short-period equilibria and the economic fluctuations.

From this common basis different streams depart concerning the singling out of *stylised* facts which, 'beyond the details', would come to surface from the long-run dynamics of the capitalist society, and whether to focus the analysis on these facts or on more concrete situations. From this point onward, divergences take place within the post-Keynesian approach, concerning both the view of the tendencies of the economy and the methods employed.

Within the stylised facts, Kaldor points out the tendency towards full-employment steady-state growth; consistently, he strives to pass from a stage of analysis where the conditions for dynamic equilibrium are merely assumed to one where they spring as the conclusion of the theory; that is, from the statement of conditions to their conversion into actual tendencies of the economy. Joan Robinson argues instead the lack of actual tendencies towards full employment and even the impossibility of carrying on analyses framed in terms of *convergence* towards long-period equilibria; this view leads Joan Robinson to focus on the determinants of short-period equilibria and to deal with dynamics outside the steady-state method.

Kalecki criticises the steady-growth approach for both its conception of the capitalist process and for its methodology. As to the first, Kalecki's remarks[9] move from refuting the conviction which, according to him, this stream would be based on, i.e., that beyond cyclical fluctuations the capitalist economy would express inner tendencies towards a steadily ascending trend; this conviction, according to Kalecki, would rely on the idea that the conditions for dynamic equilibrium are such as to be self-contained and self-perpetuating. On the contrary, he objects:

> the system cannot break the *impasse* of fluctuations around a static position unless economic growth is generated by the impact of semi-exogenous factors such as the effect of innovation upon investment. It is only in such a case that cyclical fluctuations do occur around the ascending trend line (1962b, p. 134).[10]

In addition, the possibility for a steady trend to occur depends on the condition that the impact of the 'development factors' rises proportionately with the stock of capital – a condition which cannot be seen as automatically satisfied.[11]

Kalecki's negative appraisal cannot be shared in general, as he appears to mistake the mere statement of the conditions for dynamic equilibrium for that of their actual realisation, or to believe that the interest in this situation necessarily means tacit acknowledgement of its likelihood. This criticism may be correct in relation to Kaldor but cannot be legitimately raised against the post-Keynesian theory *en bloc*.

However, beyond these aspects, disagreement also emerges as to the way of conceiving long-period analysis. According to Kalecki the long period is not, even on the methodological ground, an autonomous entity but a mere series of short-run situations, so that the trend is just the resultant of short-term fluctuations of income; it follows that long-period analysis shows only the direction of the movement. On the contrary, post-Keynesians approach fluctuations as deviations of the actual rate of growth from a predetermined path of equilibrium growth.

A major area of agreement between Kalecki and the post-Keynesians can be found in the short-period analysis; in this area, the contributions of a large group of scholars (referring ideally to the *Journal of Post-Keynesian economics*) can be regarded fundamentally as revisions and developments of the Kaleckian theory of aggregate income.[12] The central idea on which this approach focuses is the inter-relationship between income distribution and the level of activity, and the Kaleckian ingredients consist chiefly (1) in the hypotheses concerning the propensities to save, (2) in the non-competitive features of markets, (3) in the mark-up pricing over L-shaped cost curves, and (4) in the emphasis placed on the twofold relation between investments and profits. Further specifications, according to cases, are then introduced in this Kaleckian framework, such as disaggregation in sectors (eventually considering different pricing criteria[13]), the dependence of distributive shares on the level of activity as well, the specification of hypotheses as regards mark-ups (for instance, by giving the rate of profit the role of key variable), more complex assumptions about spending behaviours, greater attention to financial aspects, and so on.

A final point worth consideration – concerning mainly the steady-growth models – is about the relationships among investments, prices and financial choices. The possibility, within the Kaleckian framework, for a joint determination of these variables comes from the fact that both price and investment decisions are controlled by firms, as well as from the fact that the maintenance of a certain equilibrium among financial sources is a vital necessity for them. This route – suggested by Kaldor (1966) and developed by Wood (1975) and Eichner (1976) – assigns to price policy a central role in the long-run strategy of firms, insofar as it may bring to reconciliation the need for equilibrium growth (i.e., equilibrium between demand and capacity) with the safeguard of the firms' financial equilibrium.

We have already observed that all the blocks of this new approach to the theory of price can be traced *separately* in the Kaleckian scheme, and that putting them together is a solution that can be pursued.[14] The question may be raised, however, whether Kalecki did not follow this route for it would have led him to conclusions contrasting with the idea that capitalism is perpetually subject to the threat of overaccumulation, i.e., to the conclusion that makes this approach a proper support for steady-growth models.

Acknowledging the possibility for firms to control both the flow of internal means and the debt ratio (i.e., the ratio of external to internal saving) means attributing to them as a whole the ability to govern the creation of overall saving *in relation to* their investment decisions. As a consequence, whatever the volume of investments they decide, firms on the whole would be able to attain both financial equilibrium and adequate demand. Except for the possibility of discrepancies between *ex ante* and *ex post* values (i.e., between decisions and results), this solution fits the steady-growth models well.[15]

In the Kaleckian framework, however, this approach would lead to different conclusions for the same reasons which bring the authors to refute the dynamic equilibrium theory: according to Kalecki investments raise capacity more than demand, since the growth in national income pushes the rentiers' propensity to save upward. Consequently, the ability of firms to govern the flow of overall savings does not eliminate that contradiction at its root but merely defers it – amplified – over time.[16]

Notes and References

1 General Aspects

1. In this regard, see Keynes (1934, p. 489).
2. It would be incorrect to define as Keynesian the perhaps most significant policies of the 1930s. As for the Swedish line we will see later; according to Roosevelt's New Deal, recovery was to be stimulated hand in hand with the reform and under the aegis of the state, namely, by the introduction of institutions of industrial democracy and economic regulation. Keynes agreed to the basic inspiration for this programme, but objected to the appropriateness of launching it at that moment because of the contradictory effects it might have had on the state of confidence of the business world (see Keynes, 1933d, pp. 290–1). As for the expansion of the German economy after Hitler's takeover, it was led by policies which – even if intended for civil purposes (in the period 1933–6) – responded to the precepts of a war economy rather than to those of Keynesian economics.
3. The concern for concrete problems, along with scepticism for market automatism, were a constant in the research of Keynes, Kalecki and the Swedish economists, who always followed the dual path of interpreting the economic mechanism and pointing out rules and tools for governing it. Thus, while Keynes lent his prestige to support Lloyd George's public works programme, Myrdal and Ohlin supplied the elements in support of the Swedish government's expansionary policy. Kalecki, in turn, was an attentive observer of experiments in employment policy, in the different versions carried out through the rearmament of Nazi Germany, the American New Deal, and the egalitarian policy of the Blum government in France.
4. The arguments Pigou advanced in 1912 and then in 1933 (Pigou, 1912, 1933, but already anticipated in the inaugural lecture at Cambridge in 1908) would be taken up again without substantial additions in Keynes (1929).
5. See Joan Robinson (Introduction to Kalecki, 1969, pp. 11–12). In this regard, it is significant that the first major work by Kalecki (1933) was unanimously interpreted at the time as a contribution to the theory of the business cycle rather than to a theory of underemployment equilibrium (see Tinbergen, 1935 and Frisch and Holme, 1935). Among the authors who were first to point out the originality of Kalecki's ideas, see Lange (1939), A.E. Robinson (1947), Klein (1947b and 1951), and J. Robinson (1964).
6. Ohlin's works which are potentially interesting for the Keynesian debate start as early as 1927. However, by the author's own admission, 'output as a *central variable* was not introduced into the core of the theory of money until the latter part of 1932 and the whole of 1933' (Ohlin, 1977, p. 153): the first of the two dates refers to the draft of an article which was later published as *Till fragan om penningteoriens upplagning* (Ohlin, 1933).

7. The *General Theory*, being centred on macroeconomic aspects, did not mean that everything was right at the microeconomic level, but more simply that – within the range of problems to be faced – unemployment was the most important (see Keynes's letter to Hicks dated 21 June 1935); on the other hand, the short-period approach of the analysis justified leaving out structural aspects. Finally, the attack on traditional theory might have seemed even more insidious if it had been conducted on the same ground of this theory.
8. Not by chance did the main exponents of the 'Keynesian right' – both the theorists of the neoclassical synthesis (with the notably exception of Patinkin and those of the neo-Walrasian line) – ignore Kalecki entirely, except for very marginal aspects of his thought (for example, Leijonhufvud, 1968, cites him only for his criticism of the Pigou effect).
9. In this regard see Schumpeter: 'the whole period between 1919 and 1936 was then spent in attempts, first unsuccessful, then increasingly successful, at implementing the particular vision of the economic process of our time that was fixed in Keynes's mind by 1919 at latest' (1954a, p. 42).
10. See Eichner (1979a) with regard to the integration, from which the post-Keynesian approach would spring, of a *real* perspective drawn from Kalecki with a *monetary* perspective due to Keynes.
11. See Ohlin (1937), Keynes (1937a).
12. See in particular the *Scandinavian Journal of Economics* (1978) and the *History of Political Economy* (1978 and 1981).
13. It is too easy to argue, after fifty years of discussion, that the *General Theory* is an emblematic representation of the difficulty of getting away from old ideas.
14. Let us not dwell on whether or not Keynes succeeded in demonstrating this proposition; what matters here is that it was (what appears undoubtedly) an integral part of his scheme.
15. 'there is no reason to suppose that positions of long-period equilibrium have an inherent tendency or likelihood to be positions of optimum output. A long-period position of optimum output is a *special case* corresponding to a special kind of policy on the part of monetary authority' (Keynes, *CW*, XXIX, p. 55).
16. In this sense see the second of the Harris Lectures given by Keynes in Chicago in 1931 (*CW*, XIII, p.356). Similarly, see the case of the 'banana plantation' in the *Treatise* (1930a, p. 160). Here a process of recession in demand and production, primed by a 'saving campaign', is described, where the possibility for a new equilibrium between savings and investments to occur at a lower income is outlined. The potential inherent in this concept, however, was not grasped by Keynes, who was interested in demonstrating how, as a result of the fall in income (due to the 'increasing poverty'), the process of recession gives rise to forces able to interrupt and reverse it, and not in the possibility of unemployment equilibrium in itself.

    Joan Robinson regretted that Keynes had overlooked this point: 'He completely overlooks the significance of this discovery, and throws it out in the most casual way without pausing to remark that he has proved that output may be in equilibrium at any number of different levels, and while there is a natural tendency towards equilibrium between savings and investment (in a very long run), there is no natural tendency towards full employment of the factors of production' (1933b, p. 56). It should be emphasised that this article was published as early as 1933, proving that Keynes's theory had already taken almost definitive form and significance in this regard.

17. It is well known that the ultimate meaning of Say's law is that aggregate demand cannot restrain production. However, it should be allowed that persons of good sense, who nevertheless accepted this principle, were also ready to acknowledge that it could not work *symmetrically* in the upward and in the downward direction; indeed, since the population has to live there would at least be a level – determined by the demand for subsistence – below which production could not descend. This amounts to recognising the existence of an autonomous component of demand (albeit restricted) together with another component depending *one-to-one* on income (as in Say's law); it follows that when production drops to the level of the first component, an equilibrium determined by demand occurs. The upset of the causal nexus between demand and production, however, is a *particular case*, as such incapable of invalidating Say's law in so far as it applies in general.
18. According to Kalecki the share of profits will be constant or increasing with national income, depending on the hypotheses he advances from time to time concerning the conditions of production and the degree of competition.
19. The quotation, drawn from (Kalecki 1933a, p. 12), suggests a fix-price model (the increase in profit per unit of output is due to the reduced impact of fixed costs as production rises), which is consistent with the author's later position; in the original test, however (1933b, p. 79), the adjustment occurs through joint variations in prices and quantities.
20. In this regard see Osiatynski (1989).
21. As Kaldor put it: 'The difference between Keynes and Kalecki was mainly that the former was a deviationist from Marshall whereas the second was a deviationist from Marx' (Kaldor, 1989, p. 8).
22. Consequently: 'an increase in the rate of interest, as a remedy for the state of affairs arising out of a prolonged period of abnormally heavy new investment, belongs to the species of remedy which cures the disease by killing the patient' (Keynes, 1936a, p. 323).
23. See for example (Keynes, 1934, pp. 490–1).
24. 'Practically I only differ from these schools of thought (those involving underconsumption) in thinking that they may lay a little too much emphasis on increased consumption at a time when there is still much social advantage to be obtained from increased investment' (1936a, p. 325). Keynes reached this point of view earlier (as proved in 1934, pp. 490–1).
25. See Keynes (1937d).
26. 'But if, on the other hand, persuaded and guided by the spirit of the age and such enlightenment as there is, it permits – as I believe it may – a gradual evolution in our attitude towards accumulation, so that it shall be appropriate to the circumstances of a stationary or declining population, we shall be able, perhaps to get the best of both worlds – to maintain the liberties and independence of our present system, whilst its more significant

faults gradually suffer euthanasia as the diminishing importance of capital accumulation and the rewards attaching to it fall into their proper position in the social scheme' (1937d, pp. 132–3).

27. 'Will this be a benefit? If one believes at all in the real values of life, the prospect at least opens up the possibility of benefit. Yet I think with dread of the readjustment of the habits and instincts of the ordinary man, bred into him for countless generations, which he may be asked to discard within a few decades' (1930b, p. 327).
28. In this sense, see the concluding notes of the *General Theory*.
29. See Kalecki (1954, p. 159).
30. Unlike Keynes's hypothesis, this asymmetry cannot be reabsorbed through changes in income distribution, since prices – 'set' by the degree of monopoly – are rigid as regards variations in the level of production.
31. See Kalecki (1945, pp. 87–8).
32. See Kalecki (1944, pp. 50–1).
33. See Kalecki (1945, p. 90).
34. Several phases can be distinguished with regard to Keynes's economic policy proposals, in which he shows great adaptability to situations and constraints that arise every time, together with firm continuity with his basic ideas.

    There is a first phase (1925–1931) dominated by the concern for the consequences of the return to the Gold Standard, which was followed by a second, covering the 1930s, whose dominant theme was recovery. The third one is the 'canonical' phase, i.e., it relates to the usual Keynesian pattern of an economy working below its potential, without taking benefit from the available policy instruments; this is the context most widely developed by Keynes and is therefore the one we are chiefly concerned with. Finally, there is a last phase – which, Keynes argues, will succeed the others – 'when investment demand is so far saturated that it cannot be brought up to the indicated level of savings [of full employment] without embarking upon wastful and unnecessary enterprises' (*CW*, XXVII, p. 321); here economic policies will require measures that go beyond the economy and be such to lead to the transition towards a 'reformed capitalism'.
35. 'The sustained enjoyment of prosperity requires as its condition that as near as possible the right proportion of the national resources, neither too much nor too little, should be devoted to active investment ... The proportion will be just right if it is the same as the proportion of their incomes which the community is disposed to save when the national resources of equipment and labour are being fully employed' (Keynes, 1937c, p. 386).
36. 'The long-term rate of interest must be kept *continuously* as near as possible to what we believe to be the long-term optimum. It is not suitable to be used as a short-term weapon' (Keynes, 1937c, p. 389).
37. It is worth remembering that, according to Keynes, public spending should be carried on subject to a tendential balanced budget; more precisely, for capital expenditure the principle is that equilibrium should be assured as a long-period target, whilst for current expenditure the rule is more strict; in such a case the budget should be currently balanced, exceptions being admitted as an *ultima ratio*, when it proves to be impossible to attain the desired level of employment by manoeuvring the capital budget only (see

CW, XXVII, p. 352). The 'fiscal crisis' of the state, which marks today a main point of misinterpreted Keynesian policies, is therefore quite foreign to the genuine Keynesian outlook.

38. In accord with Keynes's rising scepticism, this need seems to have been increasingly felt as time passed. Thus, while in the *General Theory* he confined himself to pointing out the matter in rather broad terms, in 1943 he quantified that need for Great Britain as between two-thirds and three-quarters of overall investments (see *CW*, XXVII, p.352).
39. In this sense, see Kalecki (1962a, p. 399).
40. 'This [the high level of employment] explains the fact that in the United States there is no significant opposition to armaments or the cold war; that the anti-capitalist undercurrent which characterized the New Deal period has slackened; and that the trade unions are part and parcel of the armament – imperialist set-up. Workers in the United States are not duller and trade unions leaders are not more reactionary 'by nature' than in other capitalist countries. Rather, the political situation in the United States is simply, in accordance with the precepts of historical materialism, the unavoidable consequence of economic developments and of characteristics of the superstructure of monopoly capitalism in its advanced stage' (Kalecki, 1956, pp. 96–7).
41. It should be noted that on these themes Kalecki departs from his usually prudent tone. This change can be explained in various ways: in general, by the fact that his view of capitalism changed over time (following a parabola), and when he came to express the above opinions (the fifties) his disillusion as to the possibility of reforming capitalism was at its height; specifically, by his deep aversion for American capitalism (to which the cited passages mainly refer), in which he saw reflected the trend of all market economies. Finally, the period in question coincides with the cold war and with his return to Poland. This polemical mood led him to set forth rather uncautious statements, such as the one according to which the American masses' disaffection from capitalism would be enhanced by the fact that 'the growth rate of the USA lags behind that of the socialist countries' (1962a, p. 401).
42. Indicative of the distance dividing Keynes from Kalecki is the conviction that policies in support of demand would have beneficial consequences for peace, rendering the struggle to conquer market outlets less urgent (see, in this regard, Keynes, 1936a, pp. 378–9).
43. 'It is of the essence of state planning to do those things which in the nature of the case lie outside the scope of the individual... It does not aim at superseding the individual within the field of operations appropriate to the individual, or of transforming the wage system, or of abolishing the profit motive. Its object is to take hold of the central controls and to govern them with deliberate foresight and thus modify and condition the environment within which the individual freely operates with and against other individual' (Keynes, 1932, p. 88).
44. See Keynes (1936a, pp. 378–9).
45. Keynes's most representative writings as far as the criticism to *laissez-faire* is concerned, are: 'Am I a liberal?' (1925a), 'The economic consequences of Mr. Churchill' (1925b). 'A short view on Russia' (1925c), *The End of the Laissez-faire* (1926), 'State planning' (1932), 'National self-sufficiency' (1933c).

46. See, in particular, Keynes's famous attack on the metaphysical premises of the *laissez-faire* doctrine in (1926, pp. 284–8).
47. In this sense see, for example, Keynes (1937c, p. 385).
48. See, in this regard, Keynes's correspondence reported in Kahn (1978, pp. 555–7). Wage control is made even more necessary by the fact that full employment was destined to raise conflict since, in spite of the growing power of unions, the decreasing productivity associated with it imposed a decline in real wages. This pessimistic view was attenuated in 'Relative movements of real wages and employment' (Keynes, 1939), in which Keynes argues (p. 401) that the case of constant productivity (suggested by 'Bowley's law') would smooth the conflict and further weaken the objections to expansionary policies.
49. 'One of the most important functions of fascism, as typified by the Nazi system, was to remove capitalist objections to full employment ... The dislike of Government spending, whether on public investment or consumption, is overcome by concentrating Government expenditure on armaments. Finally, "discipline in the factories" and "political stability" under full employment are maintained by the "new order", which ranges from the suppression of the trade unions to the concentration camp. Political pressure replaces the economic pressure of unemployment' (Kalecki, 1943a, p. 352).
50. The thesis of the economic–political cycle, as outlined by Kalecki, does not seem to offer a satisfactory interpretative model, at least not a general model. In order to accomplish the task called for by capitalists, the crises must presumably be severe and prolonged; this case, though fitting the events of the period in which Kalecki conceived this theory, is instead exactly the opposite of what occurred in the fifties and in the sixties. Indeed, according to that scheme, this new situation should lead to the conclusion that capitalists are not interested in the purposes Kalecki assigned to them, or that they have been forced to a much more pregnant compromise than the one inherent in the political cycle.
51. Kalecki finds confirmation of the thesis of the political business cycle in the deliberate interruption of the American recovery after the New Deal when, during the second half of 1937, the economy was brought to recession.
52. Even Keynes is aware that the preservation of political freedom would in the long run be compromised by the persistence of economic anarchy, Fascism and Bolshevism, he remarks (1925a, p. 304), represent political degenerations devised to put an end to anarchy; in contrast with these solutions he upholds the possibility of promoting the transition 'to a regime which deliberately aims at controlling and directing economic forces in the interest of social justice and social stability' (1925a, p. 305).
53. See, in particular, Kalecki (1961, 1967a).
54. In this regard see n. 40, above.
55. The omission from the reprints of (1943a) – notably in (1971b) – of the part concerning the reform of capitalism as a means for overcoming its limits is significant of this change of opinion.
56. In this sense see Vicarelli (1983, pp. 166–7) who, in relation to Keynes, writes: 'The logical model which he presents ... makes it possible to identify those forces which, at a given point in time, that is independently of the passage of time, determine income and employment. The operation of these forces may be formalised in a mathematical model, the determinacy of which confirms the logical nature of the process of induction. The

solution of this model can be called "equilibrium". It is clear however that what we are dealing with here is a "virtual equilibrium" in which all the magnitudes appear as *ex-ante* values and in which expectations are an exogenous variable. The comparison with the effective values of the magnitudes in question, and the verification of whether or not the expectations are fulfilled, imply a different level of analysis to which Keynes had no intention of devoting himself'.

Only one notation should be added to Vicarelli's reasoning, for it may seem that the fact that the model offers solutions of equilibrium or disequilibrium might be a matter of secondary importance. From a strictly formal point of view either case derives, evidently, from stating equilibrium conditions or not; the difference between the two cases – important for the significance of Keynesian unemployment – is that equilibrium alone does not present endogenous stimuli towards change. In this sense, consider the following passage from the *General Theory*:

> It follows that, although expectation may change so frequently that the actual level of employment has never had time to reach the long-period employment corresponding to the existent state of expectation, nevertheless every state of expectation has its definite corresponding level of long-period employment (1936a, p. 48).

57. 'It is clear that the present phenomena are also a basis for investment decisions, which, however, will be relevant for the formation of investment output only in future, and so on' (Kalecki, 1937b, p. 81). Incidentally it is worth noting how this point is similar to Keynes's, when he argues that 'The *realized* results are only relevant in so far as they influence the ensuing expectations in the next production period' (*CW*, XIV, p.179).

The lack of a clear distinction in Keynes between investment decisions and their effects was grasped early by Kalecki in his review (1936) of the *General Theory*, in which he remarked that the mingling of the two aspects mars Keynes's theory of investment and ends up by weakening the mechanism of income adjustment. If a clear-cut distinction is not traced between the two aspects, he argued, the process following a variation of investment does not lead to a new equilibrium since it reflects back on expectations: 'Keynes takes as given the state of expectations of returns, and from this he derives a certain definite level of investment, overlooking the effects that investments will in turn have on expectations' (Kalecki, 1936, p. 231).

Kalecki, therefore, seems to conceive Keynesian equilibrium as a situation towards which the system tends, at least in logical terms – an interpretation which does not appear justified. Nor would Kalecki's solution entail a real advance on this same level, being limited to replacing Keynes's hypothesis of a constant state of expectations with that of decisions of investment that are unchanging over the current period. However (and this is the most interesting point since it helps to clarify the concept of equilibrium Kalecki has in mind), the first step to make, he suggested, is to free the Keynesian scheme from the confusion between decisions and results. The additional step is to complete it by introducing dialectics between the two aspects, which is the mainspring of change: 'the solution of the problem of investment decisions, of *ex-ante* investment' must be the starting point of an analysis aiming to explain how plans are reformulated once compared to facts; in this way 'the level of investment in the dynamic process ... is subject to continuous change; but at every level of investment, employment and production will be determined along the lines of the first part of Keynes's theory' (1936, pp. 231–2).

58. A different and more complex matter is the tendency of equilibrium to occur, i.e., considering it as a state which the system is bound to approach. Obviously, such a convergence can take place only if factors defining equilibrium keep steady, where 'steadiness' can be conceived in chronological or in logical terms – i.e., as constancy *during* the process of adjustment or as constancy *relative* to the process itself (the first case involves the second, not the other way round). In the first case, we are concerned with a process of adjustment which has a time dimension; in the second the nature of the process is logical. In the former case equilibrium will be attained, while in the latter that might not occur since the position itself may shift *exogenously*, thus preventing the gravitation from being fulfilled. Needless to say, the steadiness of factors defining the equilibrium relative to the process of adjustment is a minimum vital condition for looking at this as a centre of gravity: admitting that the process of gravitation is able to shift the centre of gravity – i.e., that equilibrium can be changed by positions external to it – would contradict the very nature of *dominant* forces, insofar as it would entail that variables defined as independent are affected by others defined as dependent.

    It does not seem correct to attribute to Keynes or to Kalecki the idea that equilibrium represents a situation toward which the system actually converges over time. In this case two unlikely compatible conditions would have to be reconciled, i.e., the period of adjustment must be long enough to allow the multiplier process to be accomplished and, at the same time, sufficiently short to justify the constancy of the state of expectations (Keynes) or the immutability of investment decisions (Kalecki), in spite of changes occurring in the level of income.

    Difficulties would also be met in conceiving this process as just a logical tendency: even if the hypothesis of constant incentive to invest were maintained, the fact remains that the adjustment of income towards the equilibrium would cause the rate of interest to vary (money supply being given), and consequently affect investments. Therefore, the position of equilibrium would be changed by the process of adjustment towards it.

59. See Kalecki (1939a). Kalecki seems to give less importance to the effects of divergences between *ex ante* and *ex post* situations; this does not mean that these situations coincide but that, as a spur to change, the *dual* nature of investments is more important than unexpected changes in inventories or orders.

60. 'An increment of employment is liable, however, to raise the schedule of liquidity preference ... Thus the position of equilibrium will be influenced by these *repercussions* ... hence the extreme complexity of the actual course of events. Nevertheless, these seem to be the factors which it is useful and convenient to isolate ... The above is the summary of the General Theory' (1936a, pp. 248–9, emphasis added).

61. This approach is later abandoned (Kalecki, 1968c) with the unification of the two aspects, since:

> the long-run trend is but a slowly changing component of a chain of short-period situations; it has no independent entity, and the two basic relations mentioned above [Kalecki refers to the relationship which binds national income to investments and to the one – opposed – which makes the latter depend on the level and rate of change of economic activity] should be formulated in such a way as to yield the trend cum business-cycle phenomenon (1968c, p. 165).

According to Kalecki, this change in analysis is made even more appropriate since 'By this separation of short-period and long-run influences I missed certain repercussions of technical progress which affect the dynamic process as a whole' (1968c, p.166).

62. Kalecki (1968c, p. 183). And again: 'This is, indeed, very different from the approach of purely "mechanistic" theories (based frequently on such fallacious *a priori* assumptions as a constant degree of long-run utilization of equipment)' (1968c, p.183).
63. See respectively Kalecki (1954, Chapter 15 and 1938a).
64. In this regard, see Sebastiani (1983).
65. See Kalecki (1968c, p. 165).
66. Keynes's use of the long period as a methodological device is particularly apparent in Chapter XVII of the *General Theory*, where the treatment of the own-rates of interest is worked out (see Sebastiani, 1992).
67. Indeed, this task is rather insidious, being based on selections of writings (not always otherwise available in western languages) often made by Kalecki himself. It follows that the study of the development of his thought over time has to be founded on texts which have been adjusted in respect of their original formulations – i.e., texts that have passed through the filter of the author's own retrospective reinterpretation, with a view to making them coherent with his more recent positions; in this way, the elements of continuity are inevitably strengthened.
68. In Kalecki's reasoning about income distribution, a short-period (microeconomic) theory has often been distinguished from a long-period (macroeconomic) one (see J. Robinson, 1965, p. 99 and Feiwel, 1975, p. 89); accordingly, the feeling has been encouraged that they were alternative, or complementary theories over different time spans. This distinction appears unfounded, since both theories concur in the determination of income at a given time, each one with a specific task: the microeconomic approach, departing from a theory of price, explains the structure of distribution; the macroeconomic one, logically subsequent, is in itself a theory of effective demand, in which the distributive aspects (the determination of the level of profits) derive from the equilibrium condition of income.
69. Let us assume two social classes: capitalists (profit earners) and wage earners; moreover, the public sector and foreign trade are neglected, so that consumptions and private investments are the only components of aggregate demand.

2 The Theory of Pricing and Distribution

1. Consider the works of J. Robinson (1933a) and Chamberlin (1933).
2. See Hall and Hitch (1939) and Sweezy (1939).
3. See, in particular, Rothschild (1947), Steindl (1952), Bain (1956), Sylos Labini (1961), as 'pioneers' on the subject.
4. For an extensive treatment of this subject, see Kriesler (1987).
5. The question of prices, approached with reticence even in the original version (1933b), was completely left out in subsequent versions, circulated in English and therefore better known (1933a). This omission appears meaningful since the lack in the latter of explicit references to the problem of prices suggests that the model of determination of income presupposes fixed prices, i.e., prices whose definition is outside the logic determining the level of activity. In this regard the textual comparison of certain parts of the two version is significant: compare in particular (1933b, p. 79) with (1933a, p. 12), where the part of the adjustment process originally running through changes in prices is completely omitted in the latter version.
6. Kalecki's exposition is rather muddled. For instance, he speaks of *real* magnitudes as though he meant *physical* magnitudes, which would imply the existence of a unique product; this hypothesis is overruled, instead, by introducing the distinction between consumer and investment goods. We will present Kalecki's reasoning below, keeping in mind what appears to be his basic meaning, namely, that what determines profits and real income of the community are the *real* spending decisions of capitalists even if everything inevitably runs through the mediation of prices. We will mainly follow the original version (1933b), both for its completeness and as reflecting Kalecki's former view.
7. More precisely the relationship hypothesised by Kalecki is: P/K P (P/Y) (Y/K), with Y/K the rate of activity (1933b, p. 98)
8. Kalecki (1933b, pp. 98–9).
9. A vague indication is offered by Kalecki when he distinguishes between the prices of consumer goods and the prices of capital goods. As to the former he argues only that, given the spending habits of the two classes, they 'are directly linked to the distribution of social income between capitalists and workers' (1933b, p. 102). The prices of capital goods, instead, reflect the way in which overall profits are divided between the two sectors and, in equilibrium, must be set at such a level as to render the profit rates in the two sectors uniform (1933b, p. 102). As we can see, Kalecki's argument does not go beyond the statement of equilibrium conditions.
10. Abstracting from fixed costs (as occurs in the original version), we have:

$$\frac{P}{Y} = \frac{pX - APCX}{pX} = 1 - \frac{APC}{p} \qquad (2.5)$$

with APC variable average cost and P gross profit (i.e., inclusive of depreciation and interest). Equation (2.5) expresses the profit margin of individual firms or sectors; for the economic system as a whole, instead, since $APC = w/a$ (neglecting foreign trade), (2.5) is tantamount to (1.5) and indicates the share of profits. Staying on the microeconomic level, the condition of maximisation of profit requires that marginal cost (MC) and marginal return (R') coincide; therefore (with e the elasticity of demand) we have:

$$\frac{P}{Y} = 1 - \frac{APC}{MC/(1-1/e)} \qquad (2.6a)$$

as the general case and, in perfect competition:

$$\frac{P}{Y} = 1 - \frac{APC}{MC} \qquad (2.6b)$$

whereby the conclusion can be drawn (abstracting from the course of elasticity in equation (2.6a)) that the profit margin increases with output, since – with normal U cost curves – the ratio *APC/MC* decreases along the relevant stretch of marginal costs. It ensues from Kalecki's definition and from (2.6a) that marginal firms are those bearing – for each level of production – a higher ratio *APC/MC* and a higher price elasticity of demand.

11. Kalecki's view about the shape of firms' costs and supply functions is rather obscure. We have assumed above the usual form for them (initially decreasing and then rising), the difference between marginal and non-marginal firms being that the former have (quantities produced being equal) higher average and marginal costs than the latter, and a higher *APC/MC* ratio. In that case, *both* groups of firms undergo a breakdown in activity and in profits during a recession, though the second suffer smaller losses than the first; in the extreme case, the marginal firms might be forced to leave the market if prices fall below their average costs.

However, there is a passage in Kalecki's 1933 essay which might justify a different interpretation:

> With a fall in capacity utilization, competition sharpens through reductions in gross profit margins, shifting the fall in utilization to marginal plants. These plants, however, will not be completely closed if the fall in total demand is less than their previous supplies (1933b, p. 99).

From that statement one could infer that the fall in overall demand and prices affects the production of the marginal firms *only*, while no loss is suffered, as far as output is concerned, by non-marginal firms. This would require that the latter firms carry on their production along the very upper (vertical) stretch of marginal cost curves, since under that hypothesis only a fall in prices would reduce the margins without affecting the level of production.

However, this case seems neither plausible nor corresponding to what Kalecki appears to have in mind. In fact, it would imply identifying non-marginal firms with those which – in any circumstances – fully utilize capacity, so that the variations in the overall level of activity would affect the marginal firms exclusively, which would enter or leave the market according to the phase of the business cycle. This eventuality does not correspond with what Kalecki holds in other parts of the essay; moreover, it is in contrast with the short-period framework of the analysis and it is unnecessary for supporting Kalecki's thesis.

The interpretation (see Chilosi, 1979) according to which Kalecki would have had in mind L-shaped functions of average and marginal costs, with marginal firms running along the horizontal stretch and non-marginal firms along the vertical one appears even less plausible. Indeed, in perfect competition the demand for each firm is perfectly elastic and the equilibrium price is equal to the marginal cost. It follows that – for marginal firms – the demand function and the marginal costs function (both being horizontal) must flatten the one on the other; this seems to be the sense of Chilosi's argument (1979, p. 17) that the marginal costs curve *must* be horizontal *in order that* the reduction in the margins may force the marginal firms to *leave* the market. However:

(a) in the short period such an equilibrium can happen only by chance;

(b) in the horizontal stretch the price also equals the variable cost, so that the gross margin is, by hypothesis, nil and the net margin is negative;

(c) 'equilibrium' can take place only in correspondence with the angle formed by the marginal costs curve, since the firms would have no reason for stopping production at a lower level; this would mean that both marginal firms and the others operate at maximum capacity, i.e., that (say) the general equilibrium of the firms is necessarily associated with full employment of capacity. Chilosi's view could be acceptable in relation to imperfect competition, but in this case it would not be necessary to postulate the constancy of marginal and average costs.

For the above interpretation to hold, Kalecki would have to have had in mind – *for competition* – a marginalist explanation of prices, for example one based on mark-up. This, too, seems implausible, since:

(a) it would be a theory unsuited for explaining prices under free competitions (even more so considering the state of economics at that time);

(b) in subsequent works Kalecki refers to the marginalist scheme when dealing with the problem of prices in competitive markets;

(c) no mention of preceding works is made by Kalecki when (in 1939a) he explicitly put forward the hypothesis of an L-shaped supply function.

12. 'We assume that, throughout the entire cycle, cartels maintain a constant profit margin' (1939b, p. 107).

13. Precisely, with a given structure of average and marginal costs, as the overall level of activity changes, the demand functions for each firm should shift (by changing in inclination and height) in such a way that profits continue to be maximised for those particular quantities at which the corresponding prices (given the average cost relative to those same quantities) leave the profit margin unaltered; in terms of equation (2.6a), the relative changes in *APC* and *MC*, induced by variations in the level of activity, should be neutralised by changes in *e*.

14. It should be added that the invariance of the distributive shares also requires, alternatively:

(a) that all the firms have the same margin;

(b) that changes in production be proportionately distributed among the firms so as to leave their importance (the incidence of their margin on the profit share) unaltered.

15. Two reasons lead Kalecki to consider the share of income from *manual* labour instead of that from *total* labour (see 1938a, p. 97): first, 'the relative share of *manual labour* in national income is more suitable for theoretical analysis'; second, 'the statistics of national income include in the salaries the incomes of directors, managers, ect., which should rather be placed under the heading of profits'. This second reason was reversed in the revised version (1939a), where Kalecki concedes that 'from the social point of

view' the share of labour as a whole would be more interesting (p. 13); the reductive choice, however, is still confirmed there because of its greater analytical suitability.

16. See Bowley, 'Wages and Income in the U.K. since 1860'; Clark, 'National Income and Outlay'; King, 'The National Income and its Purchasing Power, 1908–1928'; Kuznets, 'National Income and Capital Formation, 1919–1935'. 'Bowley's Law' inspired Keynes's (1939) article in which he reconsidered the hypothesis of decreasing returns on which the inverse relationship between real wages and the level of employment (accepted throughout the *General Theory*) is based (in this regard see Chapter 1, n. 48 above).
17. See Lerner (1934).
18. As has been rightly noted (Bauer, 1941; Andrews, 1949; Sylos Labini, 1961), this definition of the degree of monopoly is unsatisfactory since the covering of fixed costs would also appear as 'monopolistic exploitation'.
19. This point is much more clearly argued in (1939a) version than in (1938a), which confirms the conclusion upheld in the preceding section. Quoting from (1939a):

    > The prevailing type of average wage–cost curve seems to have the following shape. It is more or less horizontal up to a point corresponding to the 'practical capacity' of the plant, but slopes sharply upwards beyond it. This point is seldom reached – factories, e.g., only exceptionally work in more than two shifts (p. 20).

    It is worth comparing the above statement with the corresponding, vaguer, one of the earlier version of the essay:

    > In most industries the average cost of manual labour falls slowly, remains constant, or rises slowly until full employment if two shifts of six days a week is reached (1938a, p. 101).

20. Equation (2.8) is drawn from (2.7) in a manner which need not be reported here in details (see Kalecki, 1938a, p. 106). Since at the microeconomic level (where (2.7) is situated) the marginal cost includes, in addition to the cost of labour, also that of raw materials, the subsequent passage to the macroeconomic level (the definition of the share of profits) either requires assuming that the cost of materials is balanced out within the economy as a whole, breaking up into profits and wages (as hypothezid in (1.5)), or alternatively (as occurs in (2.8)), it also requires taking into consideration the profits accruing to the production of inputs, the incidence of which – given the degree of monopoly – is measured by T/Y.
21. A further question Kalecki considers (the one that inspired his article) is the stability proved by the share of wages in national income; this is due, according to Kalecki, to counterbalancing tendencies the degree of monopoly and the 'rate of turnover' would be subject to. During the course of the business cycle, he argues, changes in the degree of monopoly inversely affect T/Y (Kalecki, 1938a, pp. 106–9); in the long run, on the other hand, the secular tendency for the degree of monopoly to rise, as industrial concentration intensifies, has been historically offset by the decline in prices of raw materials to manufactured products (1938a, p. 109).

22. In particular see Bauer (1941), Lange (1941), Kaldor (1956), Nuti (1970).
23. Our translation from Botta (1974). For a similar criticism see Bauer (1941).
24. 'A world in which the degree of monopoly determines the distribution of the national income, in a world far removed from the pattern of free competition. Monopoly appears to be deeply rooted in the nature of the capitalist system: free competition, as an assumption, may be useful in the first stage of certain investigations, but as a description of the normal state of capitalist economy it is merely a myth' (Kalecki, 1939a, pp. 40–1).
25. In this sense see Kalecki (1938a, p. 105; 1939a, p. 27).
26. In case of profit maximisation ($MC = R'$), note that $m = 1/e$, with e elasticity of demand.
27. Considering that:

$$e = \frac{dX}{dp}\frac{P}{X}$$

substituting in (2.7), we have, in equilibrium:

$$p = MC + \frac{dp}{dX}X \qquad (2.9)$$

from which it is possible to conclude that the constancy of p and of MC requires that variations of X be compensated for by changes in the inclination of the function.
28. Of course, the meaning of the constancy of the degree of monopoly is not that the relationship between prices and costs is unchangeable but that its changes are due to decisions taken discretionally instead of being a definite function of variations in the level of activity.
29. In this sense see in particular Kaldor (1956, p. 225). It should be pointed out that, as far as the elasticity of demand is concerned, the object of Kaldor's criticism is the (1938a) article, whereas the accusation of tautology is raised against Kalecki's reasoning in (1954); we will discuss this criticism when examining that work.
30. The reason why (according to Harrod, 1936, pp. 86–7) the degree of market imperfection varies during the course of the business cycle lies in the greater or lesser accuracy with the public makes its purchasing choices according to the more or less favourable economic situation.
31. Kalecki therefore concludes that 'It can be stated on the basis of data quoted above that the influence of these factors in raising the degree of monopoly during the slump is stronger than that of the diminishing imperfection of the market' (1939a, pp. 35–6).
32. See what Kaldor (1934, pp. 59–61) calls the *imagined demand curve*, as the guide for producers in non-competitive markets.
33. The fact that operators are aware they lack knowledge of the market does not invalidate this behaviour, which is the only one consistent with the principle of maximisation, *given* the informations available.
34. After examining the determination of long-period equilibrium under perfect competition, by making use of the usual U-shaped cost curves, Kalecki observes: 'This is quite in accordance with the prevailing long-run theory of distribution ... Such is not the case with the peculiar shape of marginal-cost

curves assumed ... and if we admit, instead of free competition, a certain given degree of monopoly' (1938a, p. 104).

The definition of long-period equilibrium in non-competitive contexts is rather elaborate, and Kalecki proceeds by making successive approximations.

At a first stage, plants are assumed as given (with short-period L-shaped cost curves), together with a given degree of monopoly and a given level of price; since margin (*p-APC*) has also to cover fixed costs, it follows that the net profit per unit of output, and even more so the rate of profit, depend on the firm's level of activity. Kalecki then defines as the *normal* use of plants that which allows the firms to earn *normal* profits ('i.e., the rate of profit at which the industry in question neither expands nor contracts' (1938a, p. 103)). This is already a position of long-period equilibrium since it implies intersectoral mobility, even though not all the implications of the long period have yet been developed. This occurs in the second stage of the analysis, in which the possibility of choosing among different types of plants and the substitution among factors are taken into consideration. In this case, 'the long-run equilibrium is represented by the normal use of such type of equipment that – with a given degree of monopoly – it is impossible to earn profits higher than normal in employing plants of a different type' (1938a, p. 105).

In other terms, the core of Kalecki's reasoning appears to be that, given profit margins, prices are proportional to unit prime costs, which are constant for each type of equipment; on the other hand, plants of different efficiency give rise to different unit costs and to proportionally different prices. Given the demand function for each firm, the quantity it can sell will be greater the more efficient its equipment is, and therefore the net profit per unit of product and the rate of profit will be higher (for the sake of simplicity, we are not considering any possible relationship between efficiency and the price of capital goods). Long-period equilibrium will therefore be reached when all the firms, driven to seek higher profits, have adopted plants of such a type that it will be impossible to increase profits further. (We shall examine the weakness of this reasoning later – section 2.5, in particular n. 76).

35. For example, variations in capital intensity, due to technical progress or to changes in the interest rate, give rise to changes in fixed costs and therefore cannot but lead firms to adjust margins and prices in the long run.

36. This seems to be what Kalecki has in mind when he remarks that 'a change in the rate of interest or technical progress affects the size of enterprises which is essential for the degree of monopoly ... In that way such changes influence the distribution of income, but this is not in contradiction with our results because it is the channel of the degree of monopoly [that is, through a 'discretional' channel] through which this influence makes itself felt' (1939a, pp. 105–116).

37. Assuming the degree of imperfection of the market as given, that is to say, the elasticity of demand for the product of the *i*th firm being a definite function of the ratio of its price to the average price of the industry ($\overline{p}$):

$$e_i = E_i(p_i / \overline{p}), \qquad E_i' > 0 \qquad (2.10)$$

Kalecki derives the equilibrium condition of the firm in 'pure' imperfect competition as:

$$p_i = \frac{MC_i}{1 - \frac{1}{E_i(p_i / \overline{p})}} \qquad (2.11)$$

In equation (2.11) the price set by the *i*th firm is a function of its marginal cost and of the average price of the industry, the incidence of which, in turn, depends on the degree of imperfection of the market (i.e., on the characteristics of function E_i); by considering the average price of the industry among factors determining firms' pricing decisions, Kalecki is anticipating here what will become a constant in his subsequent formulations. Assuming these magnitudes as given and MC_i as constant up to full capacity, Kalecki infers that the supply function of the firm also is shaped as an overturned L (this conclusion, however, is subject to the conditions mentioned in n. 27). From the individual enterprise Kalecki goes on to consider the industry as a whole, and argues that its supply function has a similar shape.

38. In this case equation (2.11) becomes:

$$p_i \frac{a_i MC_i}{1 - \frac{1}{E_i(p_i / \overline{p})}} \qquad (2.12)$$

with $a_i > 1$, degree of oligopoly of the *i*th firm. It is clear that the degree of *oligopoly* and that of *monopoly* (defined according to Lerner) are different; the latter is positive even if the former is nil – i.e., if $a_i = 1$ (this is the case of (2.11)). The inclusion of elasticity in (2.12) may suggest that the firm knows precisely the pattern of its demand function and therefore it may seem at odds with the nature of the oligopolistic market. Kalecki realises this point, and specifies that the firm has only a vague idea of the price elasticity of demand and that, accordingly, its behaviour is guided by an estimate (E_i^*) of this function; however, he adds, 'if the shape of E_i^* changes only in a manner parallel to that of E_i this does not introduce any substantial changes in the above discussion' (1938a, p. 98).

39. As is well known, the writings of Hall and Hitch, and Sweezy, who raised this point, date from 1939.

40. Equation (2.1) does not thus accord with the hypothesis of a kinked demand curve, since the elasticity (on which the price depends) cannot be measured in correspondence with the price.

41. Here, too, MC_i is constant up to full employment of capacity, but Kalecki argues this hypothesis differently. He notes that normally the entrepreneur does not know precisely the shape of both his marginal and average costs, and takes price decisions on the basis of 'a crude notion such as the average cost of manual labour and raw materials at 'normal' output' (1940a, p. 98); the constancy of marginal and prime costs is therefore *assumed* by the firms, since precise elements about their actual trend are lacking.

42. Kalecki believes that the degree of market imperfection is stable as it is subject to opposing forces: on the one hand, buyers' greater or lesser shrewdness according to the phases of the trade cycle and, on the other, variations in transport costs. Even less importance is given to a third cause of price variation, the changes in the incidence of 'prime selling costs' on prices (1940a, p. 99); for this reason this variable, which appears in the original price equation, has been omitted here.

43. 'A fall in the prices of prime factors causes, with a given output, a proportionate fall in prices and consequently in profit margins (in which are included overheads) per unit of output. And a fall in output causes *ceteris paribus* a proportionate fall in profits if the supply curve is horizontal, and more than proportionately if it is increasing' (Kalecki, 1940a, p. 101).
44. Similarly, Kalecki (1942b).
45. With *APC* (as usual with the L from) being a raw approximation of the marginal cost.
46. Within a partial framework, if marginal cost decreases, the maximising firm cuts the price moving along its demand function, with consequent changes in elasticity; if, however, the other firms in the industry also reduce prices, then all the individual demand functions move downward; finally, if prices change in the same proportion (so that $(p_i/\bar{p}$ remains constant), the demand functions must shift in such a way as to leave the elasticity unaltered at the new prices (see 1943b, p. 10n.).
47. Moreover, the weight of each firm within the industry is to be unchanged.
48. See, for example, Chilosi (1979, p. 26).
49. As it generally known, this dual criterion, which draws from the classical – Ricardian tradition, was later taken up by the 'post-Keynesian' approach: in this regard, see in particular Sylos Labini (1961), Kaldor (1976), Burbridge (1979), Hark (1980), Asimakopoulos (1980). Specifically, Kalecki distinguishes (1954, p. 11) between finished goods and raw materials (including foodstuffs).
50. For example, Asimakopulos (1980, p. 166).
51. For example, nothing excludes (in the little space Kalecki devotes to the subject) that the supply of certain goods might be *artificially* rationed for the purpose of keeping the price at the desired level.
52. Naturally, what happens in the primary sector is not unimportant for the analysis of prices of manufactured goods, since demand-determined changes in prices of raw materials affect industrial prices; nevertheless, since these impulses work through the channel of costs, the study of industrial prices can be isolated from that of primary goods without losing generality (see 1954, p. 11).
53. 'In view of the uncertainties faced in the process of price fixing it will not be assumed that the firm attempts to maximise its profits in any precise sort of manner' (1954, p. 12).
54. This is one of the aspects Kalecki notes in underlining the peculiarity of his formulation with respect to that of the so-called *full cost* theory (1954, p. 18), i.e., the explicit dependency of the margin on the prices set by competitors; the second element of differentiation is the idea that the margin does not necessarily change as a result of changes in overheads in relation to prime costs.
55. 'The firm must make sure that the price does not become too high in relation to prices of other firms, for this would drastically reduce sales, and that the price does not become too low in relation to its average prime cost, for this would drastically reduce the profit margin. Thus, when the price p is determined by the firm in relation to unit prime cost u, care is taken that the ratio of p to the weighted average price of all firms, $\bar{p}$, does not become too high' (1954, p. 12).

56. 'Propositions based on implicit definitions of this kind make of course no assertion about reality and possess no explanatory value. Unless the 'degree of monopoly' can be defined in terms of market relationships of some kinds ... and an attempt is made to demonstrate how these market relationships determine the relation between prices and costs, the theory does not provide a hypothesis which could be affirmed or refuted. There is no need, of course, to follow Kalecki in the attempt to lend spurious precision to the doctrine through implicit theorising – a vice which afflicts all theories which we grouped together as 'neo-classical' in varying degrees' (1956, p. 225).

    Even if this type of criticism were founded in relation to Kalecki's reasoning in (1938a), it would be unjustified in relation to what he argues in (1954); and it is surprising that Kaldor does not acknowledge on Kalecki's behalf at least what he asserts in the passage immediately following the one just cited, i.e., that his theses have some explicative content, however scanty it may be: 'Fundamentally, the proposition that the distribution of income between wages and profits depends on market structures, on the strength or weakness of the forces of competition, is not a tautological one; it asserts *something* about reality (which may in principle proved false) even if that 'something' cannot be given a logically precise formulation' (1956, p. 225).
57. Kalecki speaks of trade union influence on the *degree of monopoly* instead of mentioning the *ratio p/u*, as would be more correct; indeed, the strength of a trade union does not weaken the degree of monopoly as such (understood as the firms' power within the market of products) but simply gets the firms not to use it as they could. The confusion Kalecki encounters confirms his reluctance to distinguish between the concept of the degree of monopoly *as the relationship* between prices and costs and the concept of the degree of monopoly *as a cause* of this relationship.
58. (1954, p. 18) Kalecki returns to this point in (1971a).
59. See (1938a).
60. This thrust is made stronger by the fact that the incidence of overheads on unit of output changes according to the phases of the cycle.
61. See also Kalecki (1943b, p. 9). As we have see, in (1938a) the threat of potential competitors is more palpable and constitutes an integral part of the equilibrium condition of the industry.
62. This point will be returned to later (section 2.5).
63. Even leaving aside the explicative shortcomings, Kalecki's reasoning is still not very convincing. The statement according to which $m/(1-n)$ is an index of the degree of monopoly since, as derived from (2.13), assuming $p=\bar{p}$:

$$\frac{p}{u}=\frac{m}{1-n}, \quad n<1 \qquad (2.14)$$

    is not always true (in this regard see Asimakopulos, 1975, p. 317). Indeed, if the two parameters are set independently (otherwise it would be worth unifying them into one) then, for each given m, the value $n = 0$ should indicate the situation where the firm fixes the price independently of its competitors (i.e., monopoly or price leadership); on the contrary, $m = 0$ and $n = 1$ should indicate a state of competition or subalternation in pricing, that is to say, absence of degree of monopoly: in the first case equation (2.14) is not an indicator of the degree of monopoly on the lines suggested by

Kalecki, while in the second it offers no meaningful results. Finally the condition $n < 1$ applies only to the industry as a whole (in relation to which it has been derived) and not to single firms too.

64. In (1971a) Kalecki restates (2.13) as:

$$p = u(1 + f(\bar{p}/p)), \qquad f' > 0 \tag{2.15}$$

where the parameters of (2.13) are unified in function f.

This formulation was strongly criticised (see Asimakopulos, 1975, p. 318) for being: (a) simply wrong, since – u and $\bar{p}$ being given for each firm – it would follow that $f' < 0$; (b) tautological.

The first criticism is, in our opinion, unfounded, as can be easily deduced by assuming, for example, $f = a$, i.e., by assuming a linear relationship; in this case (2.15) becomes:

$$p(p-u) = au\bar{p}$$

in which, given u, price p increases for a and $\bar{p}$. It should also be considered that the meaning of p in the denominator of the average price (2.15) is that of the price *currently* applied by the firm when making a *new* price decision, while the price p to the left of (2.15) represents the *outcome* of this decision – i.e., the programmed price. Kalecki's statement that 'f is an increasing function: the lower is p in relation to $\bar{p}$ the higher will be fixed the mark-up' (Kalecki, 1971a, p. 160) is to be understood in this sense. As for the explicative failing, no more elements support this accusation as regards (2.15) than (2.13), which instead is 'absolved' by Asimakopoulos. Indeed, it is precisely here that we find the most disappointing aspect of the entire question: that after seventeen years – between (1954) and (1971a) – Kalecki proposed nothing more than the old formulation, with all its weaknesses, and this in spite of the criticism and the many indications offered by the economic literature in the meantime.

65. $\bar{m}$ represents the average of m, weighted on the basis of total prime costs of each firm; $\bar{n}$ and $\bar{u}$ are instead averages of the variables relative to each firm, weighted on the basis of their output (Kalecki, 1954, p. 16n.).

66. See Chilosi (1979, p. 27).

67. 'Let us denote the "new" unit prime costs by u_1, u_2, etc., and the "old" prices by p'_1, p'_2, etc. The weighted average of these prices is $\bar{p}'$. To this correspond new prices p_1'', p_2'', etc., equal to $mu_1 + n\bar{p}$, $mu_2 + n\bar{p}'$, etc. This leads in turn to a new average price, $\bar{p}''$, and so on, the process finally converging toward a new value of $\bar{p}$ given by the formula (2.17). This convergence of the process depends on the condition $n < 1$. Indeed, from equation (2.16):

$$\bar{p}'' = m\bar{u} + n\bar{p}'$$

and for the new final $\bar{p}$:

$$\bar{p} = m\bar{u} + n\bar{p}$$

Subtracting the latter equation from the former, we obtain:

$$\bar{p}'' - \bar{p} = n(\bar{p}' - \bar{p}) \tag{2.18}$$

which shows that the deviation from the final value $\bar{p}$ diminishes in geometric progression, given $n < 1$' (Kalecki, 1954, p. 15).

68. The removal of $\overline{u}$ from (2.18) requires this to have an identical value in the equations from which (2.18) is derived, i.e., in the equations of the average price relative to the *different* stages of the process of adjustment towards the new equilibrium; as we have seen, this hypothesis is not correct since this process also runs through changes in the average cost $\overline{u}$. The validity of Kalecki's conclusions therefore depends on the behaviour of $\overline{u}$ in the various stages of the process.

With $\overline{p}^i$ and $\overline{u}^i$ being the price and average cost at the ith stage of the adjustment process, and $\overline{p}$ and $\overline{u}$ their 'equilibrium' values, equation (2.18) can be generalised:

$$\overline{p}^i - \overline{p} = m\left[\sum_{k=1}^{i} d\, n^k(\overline{u}^{i-k} - \overline{u})\right] + n^{i-1}(\overline{p}^1 - \overline{p}) \qquad (2.19)$$

from which we are derive that the addition of convergence of $\overline{p}^i$' towards $\overline{p}$ is that $(\overline{u}^{i-k} - \overline{u})$ tends to zero.

69. In this case changes of $(\overline{p}/\overline{u})$ – which represent an approximate measure of the distribution of income in the industry (approximate because $\overline{u}$ includes the cost of materials purchased outside and $(\overline{p}-\overline{u})$ has also to cover overheads) – reflect variations in the degree of monopoly *only*: 'The ratio of average price to average prime cost is equal to the ratio of aggregate proceeds of industry to aggregate prime costs of industry. It follows that the ratio of proceeds to prime costs is stable, increases or diminishes depending on what happens to the degree of monopoly' (1954, p. 16).

70. From (2.20) and (2.21) we have:

$$k = \frac{M + W + P + C_c}{M + W}$$

from which:

$$(k-1)(M+W) = P + C_c.$$

By adding W to both members of the preceding equation and putting $(P + C_c + W = Y_i)$ we have (2.22).

71. In this regard, Kalecki (1954, p. 28).

72. The generalisation of (2.23) to the entire manufacturing sector modifies the meaning of j since, except for raw materials, consumer materials are now produced within the sector so that their value leads back to the price of raw materials, the wage costs and the degree of monopoly in the preceding stages of production. Thus 'roughly speaking, j', which equals the ratio of unit costs of materials to unit wage costs, is determined by the ratio of prices of primary products to unit wage costs and by the degree of monopoly in manufacturing' (1954, p. 29). For the indication of the conditions the above is subject to, see (1954, p. 29n.).

73. A final point to consider concerns the behaviour of the share of total income from *hired labour* in the overall gross income of the private sector. Kalecki gives limited attention to this theme and confines it to its short-period aspects, since 'the application of the theory of income distribution to the analysis of long-run changes in the relative share of wages and salaries in income would be difficult because of the growing importance of salaries in

the sum of overheads and profits as a result of increasing concentration of business' (1954, p. 39). The stability of the salaries (which are substantially constant costs over the short period) renders labour income less sensitive to short-term conjunctural thrusts than total income of private sector. V being the first and Y being the second, we have (see 1954, pp. 39-40):

$$V = aY + B \tag{2.24}$$

with $a < 1$, and B which is a positive constant over the short period but which is subject to changes in the long period. It follows from (2.24) that:

$$\frac{V}{Y} = a + \frac{B}{Y} \tag{2.25}$$

hence the conclusion that – a and B being constant – the share of salaries and wages in the private sector's income shows a trend opposite to the short-run variations of private income.

74. For a criticism of the ambiguity of the definition of industry in a context of monopolistic competition, see Davidson (1959, pp. 53–4).
75. See Riach (1971), in this regard.
76. It is worth considering the type of adjustment envisaged by Kalecki. Replying to criticism raised by Whitman (1941) – according to which there is a contradiction between the hypothesis of a given degree of monopoly (given margin in the various sectors) and the condition of long-period equilibrium (uniform rates profit) – Kalecki (1942b, p. 123) objects that compatibility between the two conditions is assured by changes in the degree of exploitation of plants. Thus, if with the given degree of monopoly the rate of profit of industry A is greater than that of industry B, the firms will move towards the former industry till the rise in the K/Y lowers their rate of profit to the level of industry B. The levelling out of the rates of profit in the long period, therefore, does not take place through changes in margins but through changes in the degree of utilisation of plants. (A similar point of view was stated in 1938a – see n. 34 above – but on that occasion the levelling out of profit rates, margins being constant, was assumed to come about as an effect of changes in K/Y also determined by shifts in techniques.) Now, while it is likely that firms keep margins constant when *short-period* fluctuations of output occur, this is no longer reasonable when changes in the utilisation of plants turn out to be permanent, owing to the entry of new competitors. If Kalecki's hypothesis of behaviour were correct – though disavowed by Kalecki himself when assuming the degree of monopoly to be a function of the risk of entry by new firms (1938a) – then, in order to safeguard margins, businessmen would be ready to undergo reductions in both the level and the rate of profit, as well as in the market shares.
77. On this point Kalecki is here more cautious than in (1938a), explicitly admitting that the long-period factors affect the degree of monopoly. However, the indication of these factors is scanty, being confined to technical progress after all; this, Kalecki argues (1954, pp. 19–20), gives rise to contrasting effects on the degree of monopoly (p/u) and on the rate of profit. On the basis of historical series related to the United States economy between 1875 and 1927, Kalecki concludes that the degree of monopoly (p/u) is rather steady, except in periods marked by deep structural changes – more or less directly induced by technological progress (such as the

formation of large industrial concentrations (1979–1889) and the 'commercial revolution' (1923–1929) – in which it showed a decisive tendency to rise. As for the effects on the rate of profit, Kalecki concludes they are negative since the capital-intensive pattern of technical progress is not countered by the growth in *p/u*, so that profits are compressed by the rise in overheads. Naturally, this tendency might be countered by efforts to defend profit, but according to Kalecki there is no proof of this.

78. See section 4.1.2.
79. 'As neoclassical economists assume as a starting point this last market form [pure competition], Kalecki's criticism is centred on its subtitution by imperfect competition' (Messori, 1977, p. 72). Therefore, 'the only substantial and original difference between the two types of analysis would come down to a different point of departure, derived more or less directly from experience. In this case, i.e., the degree of monopoly would be nothing more than the "measure" (empirical) of the non competitive form of market, which has replaced the competitive form, that it is a more adequate expression of the real world' (p. 73, our translation).
80. Our translation.
81. The U-shape of cost functions is not strictly necessary for the marginalist theory of price, once pure competition falls. However, the substitution of these curves for L-shaped ones would also bring about the rebuttal of their *theoretical foundations* – namely, substitutability among factors – which would be fatal for the theory of distribution based on marginal productivity.
82. Kalecki writes (as early as 1939): 'The sphere where increasing marginal costs prevail is agriculture, where an increment in yield requires a disproportionate outlay of fertilisers and labour. The position is altogether different in industry. If, for instance, in a given establishment two shifts rather than one are worked, the cost of raw materials and labour will increase more or less proportionately. Only the third shift may involve some technical problems. It is therefore reasonable to assume that in an industrial enterprise the curve of the marginal cost is horizontal over a rather long range of output and starts rising only when full capacity is approached' (1969, p. 50)

3 The Theory of Effective Demand

1. In this regard, see Kalecki's Introduction to (1971b): 'It is interesting to notice that the theory of effective demand, already clearly formulated in the first papers, remains unchanged in all the relevant writings, as do my views on the distribution of national income' (p. viii).
2. The mainsprings of the trade cycle are singled out in the productive nature of investment, which marks the limits and the inner contradiction of accumulation of capital; these aspects will be dealt with in Part II, Chapter 5.
3. In particular, Kalecki (1939a, 1943b, 1954, 1971b).
4. 'What is the proper meaning of this equation? Does it mean that profits in a certain period determine capitalists' consumption and investment, or the other way round? The answer to this question depends on which of these quantities is directly subject to the decisions of capitalists. Now, it is clear that they may decide to consume and to invest more in a certain short period than in the preceding period, but they cannot decide to earn more. It is

therefore their investment and consumption decisions which determine profits, and not the other way round' (Kalecki, 1942a, p. 259). In the same vein, see Kalecki (1954, p. 46)

5. In this regard see in particular (1971b, p. 12), already quoted in Chapter 1. See also the concept of 'quasi-equilibrium' outlined in (1934b, p. 215)
6. Joan Robinson remarks that the Kaleckian analysis of the relationships between investment and saving is made easier than Keynes's by its assumptions concerning the spending habits of social classes. Apart from their general significance, these hypotheses would help emphasise the spreading of the impulses prompted by changes in investments by clarifying how these are transmitted among productive sectors: 'Kahn, at the 'circus' where we discussed the *Treatise* in 1931, explained the problem of saving and investment by imagining a cordon round the capital-good industries and then studying the trade between them and the consumption-good industries; he was struggling to rediscover Marx's schema. Kalecki began at that point' (J. Robinson, 1964, p. 96). As will be seen later, Robinson's interpretation of Kalecki's route is not entirely convincing.
7. In the *Essays* (1939a, pp. 52–3), from the following equations:

$$Y = W + y, \quad \text{with } y \text{ income of 'non-wage earners'} \tag{3.1}$$

$$W = C_w \tag{3.2}$$

$$y = C_y + I \tag{3.3}$$

$$C_y = cy \tag{3.4}$$

$$W/Y = a. \tag{3.5}$$

Kalecki draws the equilibrium condition:

$$Y = \frac{I + C_y}{1 - a} \tag{3.6}$$

from which, considering (3.4), we obtain:

$$Y = \frac{I}{(1-a)(1-c)} \tag{3.7}$$

the similarity of which with 'our' (1.6) is evident. It should be noted that for simplicity we have given (3.4) a linear form, while Kalecki only assumes $C_y = f(y)$ (1939a, p. 62). Among 'non wage-earners', Kalecki includes those receiving salaries and doles, interests and dividends, as well as small entrepreneurs and joint stock companies (1939a, p. 59). Accordingly, lacking specifications about relative changes of profits and of other incomes, the preceding equations do not permit deriving a theory of profits, which actually remains unexpressed in the *Essays*.

This point is dealt with in (1954, pp. 59–60) by adding to a scheme similar to the above the equation:

$$V = aY + B$$

with $V = W + R$, where R means salaries and Y the gross income of the private sector, which for simplicity we approximate to the gross national income (the difference between the two, Kalecki notes (1939a, p. 60), consists in salaries of public employees and indirect taxes). It has already been observed (Chapter 2, n. 73) that, owing to the characteristics of the preceding equation (where a and B are constants), the share of wages and salaries in national income decreases when the latter rises, while the share of profits increases.

8. In this regard, see Kaldor (1958, p. 28).
9. Again: 'In the capitalist system, however, the price–cost relationship ... is maintained and profits fall by the same amount as the investment plus capitalists' consumption through the reduction in output and employment. It is indeed paradoxical that, while the apologists of capitalism usually consider the 'price mechanism' to be the great advantage of the capitalist system, price flexibility proves to be a characteristic feature of the socialist economy' (1954, pp. 62–3).

   Even passing over the last, rather daring statement, the comparison between the mechanisms of saving – investment adjustment in capitalist and in socialist economies, as formulated by Kalecki, does not seem appropriate because of the diversity of the conditions hypothesised in the two cases. It is evident that the background in which the process of adjustment for the socialist economy is placed is the long period, since otherwise it would have to be admitted that there is – even with full employment of labour – a *current* excess of productive capacity in the consumer goods sector as well as a *prospective* excess in the capital goods sector, which struggles with the rationality that (Kalecki claims) inspires a planned system (nor should it be thought that the hypothesis that capital consists of parts of a meccano set applies in this case only). The superiority of the socialist mechanism of adjustment is then substantially redimensioned, being reduced to the principle that the production of investment goods (in keeping with the example) should not be allowed to drop until employment opportunities have been created in the sectors planned for expansion; or, in other words, that in a planned system investments can, by definition, be planned. Putting things in this way, the conclusion ensues that the maintenance of full employment does not rest on the thaumaturgic capacity of the socialist price system but on the political control of investment, i.e., on full employment being an objective.
10. The criterion for classifying agents varies; sometimes Kalecki group workers *tout-court* in one category and capitalists in another – as in (1954) – while at other times (1939a) only manual workers (the wage earner) are included in one and all the other earners in the other. The main difference between the two cases is the different placement of salary earners; this point is rather important since – salaries being substantially unchanging with respect to output – their inclusion in the first category would make the share of labour variable in relation to overall income. A further element worthy of attention is the distinction, among profit earners, of capitalists–entrepreneurs from rentiers (Kalecki does not take into account Pasinetti's point (1962) that saving by wage earners implies that they, too, are in a position to gain profits). This distinction, outlined in (1954, p. 159) but not in (1939a), is important to the theory of investment for the opposite consequences that saving by the two classes of profits earners would have on investment: positive, as far as entrepreneurial saving is concerned, negative for saving taking place outside the firms (see 1954, p. 159).

11. Kalecki often takes the hypotheses concerning spending habits to the extreme of nil propensity to save by workers, so that the consumption functions are:

$$C_w = W \tag{3.8}$$

$$C_p = A + c_p P \tag{3.9}$$

where c_p 'is a rather small fraction and A is a certain slowly changing magnitude dependent on the past economic and social developments ..., which therefore will be considered ... a slowly changing function of time' (Kalecki, 1968c, pp. 167–8).

Equation (3.9) often appears with a time-lag, so that capitalists' consumption is delayed with respect to changes in profits; according to Kalecki, this lag is due, on the one hand, to the savings accumulated by this class (freeing it from strict dependence of consumption on new profits) and, on the other, to the fact that a part of the profits is distribited as dividends and interest, and therefore becomes spendable income with a certain delay compared to the moment of their creation.

12. A different problem, of course, is whether this view of capitalism is correct or not. In our opinion this extremely negative characterisation is excessive in the same way as that – on the opposite side – put forward by *laissez-faire*; both tend to lump everything together, overlooking the fact that capitalistic societies represent such a composite reality that it is simplistic to pretend to use interpretative schemes valid for all.

13. Pasinetti (1962) argues along this line (though with greater flexibility), by abandoning the identification of profit earners with capitalists and including workers among the first. By so doing, profit loses, strictly speaking, its class feature, and the real nature of the conflict becomes clearer; the contrast is between those who control the process of production and accumulation and those who are actually excluded from it, rather than between profits and wages as such; this is after all the meaning of the maintenance, in spite of the above considerations, of the key role of capitalists' propensity to save and investment decisions.

14. As Lange (though being one of the most alert appraisers of Kalecki) puts it in his review of the *Essays*: 'In his zeal for concrete statistical results Mr. Kalecki shows a boldness in his handling of statistical material which sometimes takes the breath away from the statistically more cautious readers' (1941, p. 285).

15. According to what is indicated in sections 1.2.1 and 4.2.2.

16. 'Our analysis shows ... that long-run development is not inherent in the capitalist economy. Thus specific "development factors" are required to sustain a long-run upward movement' (1954, p. 161). And again: 'Harrod observes rightly that his exhibits the basic "antinomy" of the system; he think that "antinomy" leads to fluctuation around the trend line. I believe that the antinomy of the capitalist economy is in fact more far reaching: the system cannot break the *impasse* of fluctuations around a static position unless economic growth is generated by the impact of semi-exogenous factors such as the effect of innovations upon investment. It is only in such a case that cyclical fluctuations occur around the ascending trend line' (1962b, p. 134)

17. Kalecki distinguishes the 'developments in technology' from 'innovations in the sense of gradual adjustment of equipment to the current state of technology [which] are assumed to be part and parcel of "ordinary" investment' (1954, p. 158); in the first case innovations (or inventions – the term being used indifferently) fall within the semi-exogenous factors of investment, in the second they are instead normal elements of the investment activities.

    Among the development factors Kalecki also mentioned rentiers' saving, as well as changes in the capitalists–entrepreneurs' (as distinct from rentiers') propensity to consume and the growth of population; to these the 'external markets' are added, including the market created by public expenditure. Apart from the latter, 'the existence of current savings outside firms, which we shall call "rentiers' savings", tend to depress investment and thus to detract from long-run development' (1954, p. 158). As for changes in the propensity to consume from entrepreneurs' profits, their effect follows the principle that everything which contributes to increasing effective demand (in case of an upward change) favours investments by raising expected profitability; in this case, however, the effect is contrasted by the negative impact of the reduced flow of saving by firms. Finally, as regards the consequences of population growth, Kalecki does not believe definite conclusions possible because the population increase, though potentially stimulating, is in itself insufficient to ensure support to investments (1954, pp. 159–61) (compared with Keynes's position, section 3.2.3).
18. 'The effect of innovations is not exogenous in character in the strict sense, since they are inherent in the normal functioning of the capitalist system. There is no doubt, however, that the influence of changes in profits, national income, the stock of capital equipment, etc., upon the stream of inventions is very complex and subject to long time-lag' (Kalecki, 1962b, p. 147).
19. In this regard, see Kalecki (1967b, pp. 150–1); see also (1968c). For an interpretation that emphasises these aspects of Kalecki's thought, see Steindl (1981).
20. We shall return to these aspects later (section 3.2.3).
21. 'The smaller is the own capital of an entrepreneur investing the amount k the greater the risk he incurs. For his possible losses bear a greater proportion to his wealth and – since the amount of credits considered by his creditors as "normal" is a certain proportion to his own capital – the danger of "illiquidity" is greater too' (Kalecki, 1937a, p. 443).
22. 'The access of a firm to the capital market, or in other words the amount of rentier capital he may hope to obtain, is determined to a large extent by the amount of its entrepreneurial capital. It would be impossible for a firm to borrow capital above a certain level determined by the amount of its entrepreneurial capital' (Kalecki, 1954, p. 91).
23. In the *General Theory* (pp. 144–5) Keynes hints at the 'entrepreneur's or borrower's risk' which is linked, however, not to the form of financing as such, but to the risk involved in the prospective yields of investment; thus if an entrepreneur 'is venturing his own money, this is the only risk which is relevant' (1936a, p. 144). In addition, there is the 'lender's risk', which allows the lender to claim higher interests, so that credit-financed investments are more costly than those which are self-financed.

Consequently, according to Keynes, owners of capital only enjoy sparing the portion of interest corresponding to the lender's risk; for the rest, the different channels of financing are equivalent. Kalecki's standpoint, therefore, is much more radical in considering self-financing – both subjectively and objectively – an obligatory choice.

24. In this regard, for example, see D'Antonio (1978).
25. 'As it is the long-term rate that is relevant to the determination of investment ..., it can hardly be considered an important element in the mechanism of the business cycle ... [since] ... for reasons discussed above, [it] does not show marked cyclical fluctuations' (Kalecki, 1954, p. 88).
26. We will return to this subject later when dealing with monetary theory (section 3.3).
27. The most important stages of Kalecki's reflection are illustrated in (1933, 1937a, 1939a, 1943b and 1954).
28. 'Three stages should be distingiushed in the investment activity: (1) investment orders, i.e. all types of orders for investment goods for the sake of reproduction and expansion of the capital equipment, the volume of which per unit of time will be denoted by *I*; (2) production of investment goods *A* which, according to the above, is equal to the gross accumulation; (3) deliveries of finished equipment per unit of time *D*' (1933a, p. 2).

   Denoting *h* the 'period of construction' of capital goods, among the above variables the following relationship is set:

$$D_t = A_{(t-h/2)} = I_{(t-h)} \tag{3.11}$$

   The dynamics of investments originate from this three-stage articulation of investment activity and from the contradictory effects it exerts on the incentive to invest.

29. To be precise, investment orders are initially made dependent on the expected *net* profitability $(p/k)_n$ (p. 6):

$$\left(\frac{P}{K}\right)_n = \frac{p - bk - ik - iyk}{k} = \frac{p}{k} - b - i(1+y) \tag{3.12}$$

   where *p*, expected gross profit; *k*, fixed capital; *b*, depreciation rate; *i*, interest rate; *y*, ratio of circulating to fixed capital. Having assumed that coefficients *b* and *y* are constants during the business cycle, Kalecki concludes that – given their value – investment is a function of expected gross profitability and of the interest rate. The implausibility should be noted here of the hypothesis that the ratio of circulating to fixed capital remains unchanged during the business cycle, since the first follows the fluctuation in production while the second does not.

30. 'The demand for money in circulation increases during the upswing, falls during the downswing. The rise and fall in the rate of interest follow suit. This is the basis for our assumption that the rate of interest *i* is an increasing function of the gross profitability *P/K* (which is only a crude approximation)' (Kalecki, 1933a, p. 14).
31. 1933a, p. 7. Kalecki remarks that 'it is not the investment orders *I* that should be considered a function of *P/K* and *i*, but rather the ratio of *I* to the volume of capital equipment *K*, i.e. *I/K*' (1933a, p. 6). the hypothesis that made it possible to exclude the rate of interest from (3.10) clearly implies interpreting this equation as an aggregate function of investments.

32. The fact that expected profitability changes *as a consequence* of the accomplishement of investment orders does not represent a limitational factor as far as *decisions* to invest are concerned, since it is an effect of the behaviour of investors as a whole and, as such, is perceivable *ex post* only.
33. The existence of some contraint, however, implicitly emerges from the sign of the derivative of (3.10), i.e., from the fact that a *growing* gap between gross profitability and the interest rate is required as a condition for increasing investments (in this regard, see Kalecki, 1933a, p. 7).
34. Being $s_w = 0$, the equilibrium level of profits is defined by:

$$P = \frac{B^{\bullet} + A}{s_p} \qquad (3.12a)$$

with $B^{\bullet}$ autonomous consumption of capitalists, A gross accmulation, s_p marginal propensity to save from profits.
35. An evident slip can be found in equation (3.14), since it implies that I (which represents the total *gross* investment) may also be negative, which occurs for $(B^{\bullet} + A)/K < n/m$.
36. Kalecki considers here a static system, where investments fluctuate around the level necessary to offset depreciation, and the capital stock, at the end of each cycle, returns to what it was at the beginning: 'An increase in investment orders calls forth an increase in the production of investment goods which is equal to the gross accumulation. This is turn causes a further increase in investment activity, as indicated by equation (3.14). However, after an interval of time h has elapsed from the time when investment orders have exceeded the level of replacement requirements, the volume of capital equipment starts to increase. Initially this restrains the rate at which investment activity is increasing, and at a later stage causes a declined in investment orders. In particular it is impossible to stabilise investment activity at a level exceeding the replacement requirements' (Kalecki, 1933a, p. 9). For a more complete and elegant formalisation of the business cycle see the original English version of the essay (Kalecki, 1935b, pp. 4–6).
37. According to Kalecki's interpretation, the shape of the Keynesian function of investment is based primarily on the growing price of capital goods.
38. See (1937a, pp. 441–2). See also (1954, p. 91): 'Dis-economies of large scale ... seem to be rather unrealistic. [This argument] has no technological basis because, although every plant has an optimum size, it is still possible to have two, three, or more plants. The argument with respect to difficulties of management arising out of large-scale enterprises also seems doubtful since adequate measures of decentralisation can always be introduced to meet this problem'.
In section 3.2.4 to this chapter we will return to the relationships between the Kaleckian theory of investment and marginalist analysis.
39. In this regard, see Kalecki's acknowledgement in (1939a, p. 99n.).
40. See Chilosi (1979 and 1982) and Denicolò and Matteuzzi (1985) in this regard. Note that the point raised by Breit is similar to that considered by Keynes, as recalled in n. 23 above.

41. The reference to Breit's thesis is evident here: 'If, however, the entrepreneur is not cautious in his investment activity it is the creditor who imposed on his calculation the burden of increasing risk charging the successive portions of credits above a certain amount with rising rate of interest' (Kalecki, 1937a, p. 442).

42. Kalecki's reasoning partially recalls a Keynesian outlook; the equilibrium condition of investments is (see 1937a, p. 441).

$$\frac{dp}{dI} = i + o \qquad (3.15)$$

where *dp/di* is the expected profit rate (or *Emi*) from the investment of an additional unit capital (*dI*), while *i* and *o* stay, respectively, for the interest rate and the marginal risk. For the reason already cited, Kalecki departs from the Keynesian approach by denying that investors are able – individually – to foresee the fall in *Emi as an effect* of their own programmes, and by assuming instead *Emi* as a given for each of them. Since the interest rate, too, is a variable independent of the decisions of single investors, it follows that the determination of the amount invested rests on the shape of marginal risk, as illustrated by Figure 3.1.

Figure 3.1

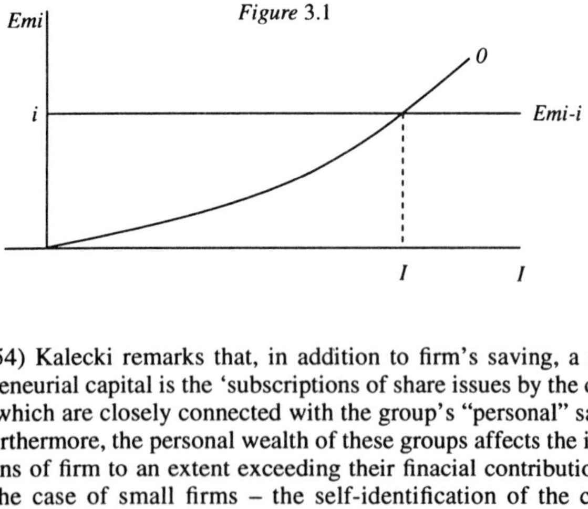

43. In (1954) Kalecki remarks that, in addition to firm's saving, a source for entrepreneurial capital is the 'subscriptions of share issues by the controlling group which are closely connected with the group's "personal" savings' (p. 94). Furthermore, the personal wealth of these groups affects the investment decisions of firm to an extent exceeding their finacial contribution, since – as in the case of small firms – the self-identification of the controlling groups with the firms leads them to see their own wealth as an element of risk compensation.

On the other hand, Kalecki is sceptical about the possibility of relying on the stock market in general. When the objection is raised (Buchanan and Calkins, 1938) that investments financed through new share issues do not involve increased risk and as such are theoretically exempt from the limitation the other sources of financing are subject to, he replies that the forced narrowness of this channel is such that the scope of the general principle cannot be invalidated. Indeed, he argues, the stock market for a firm is limited:

(a) by the public's propensity 'to distribute their risks by holding a variety of shares' (1954, p. 93) (Kalecki does not seem to realise that this limit does not hold *in general*, but only (1) for issues made by single firms in isolation and, eventually, (2) for large issues by industrial giants);
(b) by the expediency of not granting new shareholders prospective dividends that are overly high compared to the rate of interest, which narrows the market for new issues (1939a, p. 101);
(c) symmetrically, by the necessity not to increase the above spread beyond certain values, which would become inevitable when attempting to 'force' the market (1939a, p. 101);
(d) by the controlling groups' concern that their leadership might be undermined by releasing large issues (1954, pp. 93–4). In this regard see also (Kalecki, 1938c).

44. See (1937a, pp. 447). There are ambiguities and contradictions in Kalecki's argument, which spring from the diversity of factors affecting risk. These factors are represented in (1937a, p. 443) by:
(a) the extent of losses, which is a function of the ratio of investment decisions to a firm's own capital;
(b) the danger of illiquidity, which depends instead on the debt ratio;
Of course, the two risks are not independent of each other since illiquidity sharpens the danger of losses which, in turn, makes access to credit more difficult; this complication aside, however, it is obvious that if investment coincides with the flow of internal saving, the first type of risk rises with the amount invested while the second decreases; the risk of illiquidity becomes even greater if (as Kalecki presumes) firms, keeping the debt ratio constant, carry out investments exceeding their savings.

45. Looking at Figure 3.1, for each given value of d, changes in the flow of saving s give rise to shifts in the marginal risk function; changes in v affect instead the function (*Emi-i*), hence reverberating on d (we will return to this subject in section 4.1).

46. Firms' commitments consist of 'the past investment constituting its capital equipment (K), plus investment orders in execution ($I^{\bullet}$), or recently given (I), minus private capital of the firm (C) ... inclusive of amortisation' (1939a, pp. 105–6). Commitments (D) are then defined by:

$$D = (K + I^{\bullet} + I) - C. \qquad (3.17)$$

47. Finally, it is assumed that investments are only in fixed capital.

48. See (1939a, pp. 120–30). The completion of investment orders gives rise to additional savings, through the income multiplier, such as $I^{\bullet} = S$; since savings are added entirely to firms' capital (and only firms save), it follow that $(K + I^{\bullet} - C)$ in (3.17) is constant and that the only source of variation of the commitments is represented by unfulfilled orders I.

49. In this sense, see Kalecki (1939a, pp. 132–3). The relationship so derived is weakened by its microeconomic defects. Only at the aggregate level do capitalists' savings balance realised investment, while there will probably be investors 'in surplus' and others 'in deficit', i.e., some investors increasing their commitment and others going the opposite way. The possibility of isolating the aggregate relationship between investment decisions and risk

from the influence of commitments requires assuming that the conditions of the two categories of entrepreneurs, when their commitments change, balance each other.

50. The role of firms' savings is not considered here (the hypothesis should be recalled that only firm save). At the microeconomic level, investors in deficit (for whom $S < I^\bullet$) will be discouraged, while those in surplus will be encouraged. For the same reason, at the macroeconomic level, variations in savings *due* to variations in investments $I^\bullet$ do not affect the incentive to invest, since they do not alter the level of commitments (on the contrary, they act in such a way as to keep it constant). A different case is when a firm's saving rises because of its growing *propensity* to save (for instance, by increasing the retention rate on profits): investment decisions will now be encouraged by the fact that the increased savings are added to the firm's capital without being matched *immediately* by a rise in commitments. However, this positive effect on investments is countered by reduced expenditure on the part of consumers.

51. It is worth noting that, contrary to what Kalecki held in (1933a, 1933b), the distinction is drawn here between the short-term and long-term interest rate, and the reason for its exclusion from the investment function differs.

52. This relationship rests on the hypothesis that, on the one hand, profits are an increasing function of the national income and that, on the other, the expected rate of profit is appraised taking into account the realised one.

53. 'There are good reasons to believe that the curve representing the function f is S-shaped. For when things are improving, entrepreneurs become more optimistic about their future, and the rate of investment decisions increases strongly; but after a certain point doubts begin to arise as to the stability of this development, optimism ceases to keep pace with the boom, and the rate of investment decisions tends to increase less rapidly. In the slump a symmetrical development is likely to occur' (Kalecki, 1939a, p. 135).

54. This way of arguing may appear in contrast with Kalecki's bias for the demand side, but it is only an apparent contradiction. The hypothesised relationship springs from two other underlying relations: the first, between firms' savings and investments, which has a casual nature; the second, between overall savings and entrepreneurial savings, which emerges only indirectly owning to the alleged constancy of the distributive shares and the propensity to save. The negative consequences for demand of an increase in external saving are taken into consideration in a different way, i.e., through their impact on profit expectations.

55. Also in (1943b) and in (1954) Kalecki continues to exclude the long-term interest rate as a relevant factor for investment fluctuations; for this reason, explicit reference to it has been left out of equation (3.21).

56. For coefficient d, which incorporates the trend factors, see the next paragraph.

57. Kalecki's assertion (1954, p. 97) according to which dP and dK 'determine conjointly changes in the rate of profit', and by this may lead (3.21) back to the framework of increasing risk, is rightly criticised by Chilosi (1979, p. 37), who remarks that these variations 'cannot indicate as such the variation occurred in the profit rate without being confronted with their respective levels'.

58. 'The appearance of new inventions has a similar effect in the sphere of investment activity as a rise in current profits; the repercussions of the "spreading" of inventions by replacing old by modern equipment may be compared with those of a fall in current profits' (Kalecki, 1943b, p. 89); see also (1954, p. 158).
59. See Kalecki (1943b, pp. 89–91).
60. This is a point that should be made against Steindl's thesis, according to which (1966, p. 431) Kalecki put forward a substantially endogenous theory of trend, since the effect of the innovations is a consequence of the process of accumulation carried out in the past and thus – even though delayed – of investment decisions.
61. In this regard, see Kalecki (1954, pp. 159, 161).
62. For an extensive treatment of these subjects see Sawyer (1985); see also Sawyer (1989).
63. The change in Kalecki's approach concerns the joint study of the business cycle and of the trend; however the latter is not made endogenous, and keeps relying on the influence of innovations. On this subject, see Sordi (1989).
64. Besides firms' gross savings (which here return to represent the entire saving), investment decisions are made in relation to the spread between the gross profit rate (r) and the gross 'standard' or 'normal' rate of profit (r^*), the latter being defined as the reciprocal of the '"pay off period" during which the entrepreneurs expect "normally" to recover the capital invested' (1968c, p. 175). The gross rate of profit on new capital goods depends on the course of profits as the level of activity and technical progress change, the latter leading to the 'transfer' of profits from the old to the new, more productive, plants; in this way, technical progress enters into the determinants of the incentive to invest, but its influence is made a function of time, being promted by 'past economic, social and technological developments' (1968c, pp. 173–4). Since 'it is clear that the higher – *ceteris paribus* – the level of investment, the lower is the rate of profit it "fetches" (1968c, p. 169), investment will be pushed to the point where the gross rate of profit, as it decreases, coincides with the 'normal' one.

    Kalecki's arguments are sketchy in many ways. First of all, he lacks a *standard* to evaluate the 'normality' of the profit rate, his definition of it as reciprocal of the 'normal' period of depreciation being tantamount to deferring the problem. Furthermore, the decrease in r is simply assumed as a hypothesis: even though the underlying cause of this (i.e., that profits tendentially do not keep step with investments) accords with Kalecki's general view, it operates *ex post*, and therefore does not explain the investment decisions.
65. 'This is, indeed, very different from the approach of purely "mechanistic" theories (based frequently on such fallacious *a priori* assumptions as a constant degree of long-run utilisation of equipment), but seems to me much closer to the realities of the process of development. To my mind future inquiry into the problems of growth should be directed not towards doing without semi-autonomous magnitudes ... but rather towards treating also the coefficients used in our equations ... as slowly changing variables rooted in past development of the system' (1968c).

66. As regards the post-Keynesian approach, see Part II, Chapter 8.
67. See Keynes (1936a, p. 254).
68. For a quite different way of handling the question see Keynes (1930b).
69. According to Keynes the determinants of the accumulation of capital in the long period are the growth in population, in the standard of living (i.e., the average level of consumption) and in capital intensity ('capital technique'), that is to say, the average period of production (1937d, p. 126).
70. These aspects have been dealt with in section 1.2.3.
71. The debt to Kalecki is widely recognised, for example, by Steindl (see in particular the Introduction to the 2nd edition of (1952)), and by Baran and Sweezy (1966).
72. The central idea of this approach is that with the advent of monopoly capitalism, competition shifts from prices to innovations, so that decreases in the cost of production brought about by technological changes do not convert into price reductions but into increased surplus and profits. This results in a constant growth of resources available for investment, which however are not worth being invested because of the weak propensity to consume: 'Twist and turn as one will, there is no way to avoid the conclusion that monopoly capitalism is a self-contradictory system. It tends to generate ever more surplus, yet it fails to provide the consumption and investment outlets required for the absorption of a rising surplus and hence for the smooth working of the system. Since surplus which cannot be absorbed will nor be produced, it follows that the *normal* state of the monopoly capitalist economy is stagnation' (Baran and Sweezy, 1966, p. 113).
73. In this regard, see Steindl (1952, pp. 133–4).
74. Steindl 1952 (p. 133).
75. See Steindl (1966, 1981).
76. 'The proposed marriage of exogenous and endogenous causes of the trend leaves ample room for the role of history while at the same time admitting that the impulses coming from outside are seized and moulded by the inherent mechanism of the economic dynamics which acts through the multiplier and the distribution of income, through the accumulation of retained profits and utilisation of capital equipment' (Steindl, 1981, p. 46).
77. For an interesting comparison between Kalecki and Steindl see Boitani (1984).
78. It will be remembered that in this essay *Emi* is supposed independent of the volume of programmed investment since each curve which represents it is associated with a given method of production and since market imperfection cannot be assessed *ex ante* (1937a, p. 443); therefore, constant returns to scale occur.
79. And again: 'The classical thesis of the low rate of interest causing the use of more capitalistic method of production was often applied not only for the long run equilibrium position but also for entrepreneurs' planning in "disequilibrium". This interpretation is of course wrong and as we have shown above, if we neglect imperfect competition and introduce the principle of increasing risk the fall of the rate of interest has no *immediate* effect on the method of production applied in the plans of entrepreneurs' (1937a, p. 445, emphasis added).

Kalecki thus avoids countering marginalist theory and prefers sharing the ground with it. The question arises, however, whether this way of arguing is correct, that is to say, whether these two approaches are compatible and, as such, able to live together, each one in its own field of application. For this purpose we will follow Kalecki in his attempt to complete the marginalist process of adjustment.

In the context of the traditional theory – i.e., constant returns to scale and no constraints affecting investment decisions *ex ante* – a drop in the interest rate 'must create a tendency to plan investment of infinite size and with indefinite method of production [since] every method applied on infinite scale gives8 an infinite profit' (1937a, pp. 444–5). In other terms, as *every method* becomes potentially profitable to an infinite extent, then a decrease in the interest rate will act solely on the scale of production. This, however, is only the first phase of the process of adjustment; once extensive investments have been realised and the output increased, the price level starts falling 'and this makes again possible the restoration of the long run equilibrium in which the marginal productivity equations are satisfied' (1937a, p. 445).

The precise working of this second phase remains unexplained however; it is evident that changes must occur in methods of production but neither the how nor the why are specified. The most reliable hypothesis is that during the realisation of extensive investments – once market imperfection begins to be perceived – entrepreneurs come to realise that prices are dropping, so that – while the marginal productivity of capital *still* exceeds the interest rate – they change strategy and turn to rationalising investments. In this way equality is restored between marginal productivity of capital and the interest rate through declines both in prices and in physical productivity.

Kalecki's argument appears in contrast with the reasoning underlying marginalism. According to the latter, the elasticity of substitution among factors *directly* comes from the maximising behaviour of investors, and it is the means whereby they pursue the objective of profit. In Kalecki's interpretation (an interpretation necessary for demonstrating continuity between the two approaches), substitution among factors is a route that firms choose *residually*, only after excluding the other possibility.

One need not say that the conciliatory tone used in the text by Kalecki does not fit well with his denial that elasticity of substitution among productive factors, even in the long run, may have some influence on income distribution.

80. 'In fact the actual conditions are probably represented by something intermediate between these two alternatives [those of the excerpt cited above], because the imperfection of the market for products limits to some extent the planned output and the imperfection of the capital market limits the available capital. Thus the reduction of the rate of interest would, in theory, tend to induce more capital intensive investment, but by no means to such an extent as is frequently assumed. In practice even this influence is doubtful' (1944, p. 51).
81. For example, see Eichner (1979a, pp. 7–8, 1979b, p. 40).

82. Joan Robinson recalls that 'this was the point [the fact that the availability of financial resources must precede investment while saving follows] over which Keynes stumbled when we showed him the *Econometrica* [Kalecki's] article' (1977, p. 192). It was precisely along these lines of argument, the distinction between finance and savings, that the discussion on the theory of interest in the *General Theory* would be focused – as reported in the *Economist Journal* and the *Quarterly Journal of Economics* – between Keynes (1937a), on the one hand, and Ohlin (1937), Hicks (1936) and Robertson (1936) on the other.
83. For Keynes's position, see in particular (1937a, p. 212).
84. 'The third theme of the Keynesian revolution – that the rate of interest is a monetary phenomenon – which raised so much controversy for us, seems to have come quite naturally to Kalecki. This also was probably due to his immunity from orthodox teaching, in which (even today) there is a strong tendency to confuse the rate of interest with the rate of profit' (J. Robinson, Introduction to Kalecki, 1969, p. xi).
85. Consider, for example, the exclusion of monetary writings in (1971b) which, in Kalecki's mind, was to include his most important contributions.
86. This outlook is fully in line with his Marxist background.
87. In the Keynesian scheme, portfolio equilibrium is attained mainly by virtue of changes in the conditions of the financial market, these changes being brought about by agents reacting to disequilibrium. As in the theory of investment, Kalecki considers instead the role of the *internal* conditions of agents, too, and this – by emphasising the *ex ante* aspects – allows a better analysis of financial choices. Note that this aspect was dealt with earlier by Hicks (1935, pp. 54–5).
88. The hypothesis whereby Kalecki argues that investment 'finances' itself is that only capitalists save.
89. When placing the order (*I*) the investor must find corresponding finance which freezes an equal amount of funds ('*investment reserves*'); since the use of these funds and their flow back into the banking system as realised profits occur gradually as investments are accomplished (*A*), the overall demand for 'investment reserves' increases by (*I-A*) per unit of time, that is to say, by the difference between the amount of the orders, which commits a corresponding fund, and that of deliveries, which permits their unfreezing. Therefore 'the effective expenditure *A* "finances itself", i.e. it soon returns to the banks in the form of realised profits. On the other hand, the increment in investment reserves (*I-A*) must be created by credit inflation' (Kalecki, 1933b, p. 81).

    The subject is taken up again in more detail in (1939a, pp. 108–10), assuming that investment is financed '*en bloc*' by bank advances – through an '*investment finance fund*' (hereafter *Iff*), a concept (Kalecki points out) equivalent to Keynes's 'finance' – at the beginning of the period of construction (*h*). Since *Iff* gradually diminishes as construction proceeds – being fully spent at the end of the period – then the 'average period of turnover' is *h*/2, and *I*(*h*/2) is the average stock of *Iff*. Since investment, as it is realised, creates an equal amount of saving which is accumulated in deposit accounts – '*intermediate savings fund*' (*Isf*) – for the latter, too, the average turnover will be *h*/2. Therefore *Iff* = *Isf* = *I* (*h*/2) is the average demand for finance.

90. Except for the version published in *Econometrica* (1935b).
91. See, in this regard, n. 30 above.
92. To the 'lender's confidence', as Kalecki states referring to Keynes (1937b, p. 87).
93. 'The short-term rate of interest is the remuneration for forgoing the convenience of holding cash in its pure form. When holding money is compared with holding short bills, the only difference is that the bill is not directly usable for settling transactions and that it yields interest. When, however, holding money and holding a bond is compared, the risk of a fall in the price of the bond also has to be taken into consideration' (Kalecki, 1954, p. 74).
94. Except for a brief anticipation (Kalecki, 1941a), the determination of the short-term rate is dealt with in (1943b) and then, without substantial changes, in (1954).
95. In this regard see also (Kalecki, 1943b, p. 32). The reference to 'transactions' in the passage cited above calls for brief reflection; a conventional interpretation of the term might lead us to conclude that there is no room in Kalecki's thought for money *as an asset*, and that the only reason for the interest rate to depend on the demand for money is the greater or lesser propensity to pay for the advantage of carrying out exchanges smoothly. In practice, the boundary between the one and the other hypothesis of demand for money is loose, since this is in any case made with a view to *more or less definite* prospects of future transactions; it is therefore the meaning given to this concept – i.e., the object, motivations and the time-lag between demand for cash and transactions, as well as the 'degree of concreteness' of expected future exchanges – that makes it possible or not to single out a demand for money as an asset from the transaction demand for money. In short, the very difference between the two cases lies in the *discretionary nature* of choices concerning liquidity; a high degree of freedom in this regard is the requisite on which liquidity preference as such rests, a conception which is poles apart from the mechanistic approach of the quantity theory. There seems to be no doubt that Kalecki embraced this *latu sensu* concept of liquidity preference.
96. See, in this regard (Kalecki, 1943b, p. 33).
97. To be more precise, Kalecki was initially (1940b) concerned with connections between short-term and long-term rates, and later (1943b) with the explanation of the first.
98. Kalecki's reasoning refers to two representative assets, one short-term ('bill of exchange') and the other long-term ('Consol') (see 1954, p. 80).
99. This relationship between short-term and the long-term rates is not shared by Kahn (1954), who joins it with his criticism of Hicks (see Hicks, 1946). According to Kahn, Kalecki's reasoning rests on the hypothesis that a person 'need take it for granted that if he decides at the moment on bills, he needs to renew the bills when they mature. He may have it in mind that when the bills mature he may decide to put the proceeds into bonds. All that he is concerned with is what will happen during the lifetime of the *bills*' (Kahn, 1954, p. 75).

    Kahn's interpretation of Kalecki's viewpoint does not appear correct. The premise from which Kalecki moves is that the purpose of the investor is to commit his capital for a relatively 'long' period – a span of time in any case exceeding that of bills; consistently, at the time of his initial decision he must evaluate the relative advantages of different forms of investment in order to cover *that span* of time, that is to say, the purchase of a long-term asset once and for all, or the periodic renewal of a short-term one. The fact that the latter possibility is considered by the operator when investing his sums does not necessarily mean that he then feels bound to follow it to the end. If this were so, no problem of choice would exist; instead, the acquisition of short-term assets means precisely the will to be in a position of reconsidering choices periodically.

100. Term g (usually much less than one) reflects, on the one hand, the probability that the maximum estimated depreciation may really occur and, on the other, the length of the investment (in this regard, see Kalecki, 1954, p. 81).

101. Equations (3.25) and (3.26) are unduly restrictive, since they consider only the case of price falls. This choice may be perhaps explained by virtue of the exclusion of speculative motives, which make the public more sensitive to the fear of declines in prices than to the hope for rises. However, it is one thing to overlook 'organised' speculation and another to completely disregard the fact that operators may even take into account the possibility of an increase in prices. The equations above can indeed be easily generalised by simply substituting the expected values *in general* to those expected as maximums or minimums; in this case the coefficient u can also assume negative values.

102. 'This "increasing risk" is accounted for by a higher g. Thus, *ceteris paribus*, if the amount of long-term assets relative to all liquid attets held by the public rises, g tends to increase' (Kalecki, 1954, p. 82).

103. This occurs since, in (3.27), $(1 + g/r_{max}) > 1$.

104. In this regard, see Kalecki (1944, p. 48 n.).

105. In this case the supply function presents an intermediate stroke between the horizontal and the vertical ones.

106. Although his point of view in this regard is, in general, quite complex – see on this Moore (1984) – Keynes in the *General Theory* moves within the framework of a given money supply, as shown particularly in Chapter XVII, where the stickness of the interest is ascribed to the 'essential property of money' not being able to be produced at the public's request. This frees Keynes's theory of interest from the limits we have brought out for Kalecki, but weakens the idea of autonomy of investments.

107. The endogenous or non-endogenous nature of the money supply is one of the main points of controversy the broad array of post-Keynesians raise against monetarists. The argument is highly important for interpreting the correlation – brought out by statistical data – between the trend of the money supply and that of the national money income: according to the monetarists this correlation confirms the leading importance of monetary policy (even if limited to the short period or to the dynamics of prices), while for the others it demonstrates 'precisely the *opposite*, the variation in the stock of money being no more than a reflection of the change in the volume of money transactions' (Kaldor, 1980, p. 297). However – exception being made for Kaldor (for example 1981, 1982a and 1982b) and a few others – the consequences for the determination of the interest rate, which

logically originate from that point, are rarely derived; it is interesting to note that this problem was raised by the Radcliffe Report (1959).

108. Except for the possibility, already mentioned – but which Kalecki does not seem to consider very important – that this condition would imply a negative short-term interest rate.

4 A Synthesis

1. For the sake of simplicity we have kept Kalecki's 'slip', namely that wage earners do not share profits although they contribute to saving; we have also omitted the existence of autonomous consumption.
2. Strictly speaking, equation (4.2) implies a closed economy, which is a necessary condition for restraining variable costs to labour costs only; for simplicity we do not include imported inputs in the equation.
3. According to the principle of increasing risk the *ratio* of investment to the firm's own capital – then the ratio of investment to the internal flow of savings – is a function of expected net profitability. This dependence can also be expressed by putting the debt ratio (which, as inferred by (4.3), is the ratio of deficit-financed investment to self-financed investment) in relation to profitability; in this way, d is to be interpreted as the debt ratio *sustainable* for a given gap between expected profitability and the long-term rate of interest (subject to the condition that ($d \leq C/S_p$), where C is the maximum available credit for investments – a condition made even more plausible by the rise of interest rates as the situation considered is approached). Needless to say, term v in (3.16) can be discarded, being taken into account in equation (4.4).
4. In this sense, see Kalecki (1937a, p. 440). The most frequent way of approaching this aspect in Kaleckian-inspired models (see, for instance, Asimakopulos, 1975, 1977a and 1977b) and in post-Keynesians models (see J.Robinson, 1962), is to assume that investment decisions, conceived as a function of the expected rate of profit, are made in real terms; this reasoning appears in contrast with the strict application of the principle of increasing risk.
5. Money demand and supply are expressed in nominal terms, and how they are affected by changes in prices is taken into account through their impact on T.
6. This case requires that prices be set taking into account an estimated value of a, for instance that corresponding to the normal (or expected) level of output (Kalecki points out that a characteristic feature of his approach, separating it from full cost pricing, is that the 'degree of monopoly' does not necessarily change with unit overheads). Alternatively (though it would take us away from Kalecki's reasoning), $a=f(X)$ could be included in equation (4.2), so that prices and output would be determined contextually.
7. In this regard see Kalecki (1954, p. 47; 1968b; 1971a).
8. Precisely, equation (4.11a) is expressed as follows:

$$C_w = \frac{\dfrac{w}{p_w}\left(\dfrac{I_x}{a_i} + I_x \dfrac{p_i}{p_k}\dfrac{1}{a_k}\left(\dfrac{1-s_p}{s_p}\right)\right)}{1-\dfrac{w}{p_w a_w}} \tag{4.11b}$$

9. Equation (4.12) is a variant of the equation Kalecki derives from Marxian schemes of reproduction (1968b, p. 460).
10. See Kalecki (1968b, pp. 461–2). For a similar hypothesis see also Keynes (1936a, pp. 123–4) and, more generally, the post-Keynesians (particularly, J. Robinson (1962a). As we shall see, the mainspring of inflation according to Kalecki is the existence of bottlenecks in the production of wage goods.
11. Let us assume that profits are set in relation to fixed capital only and that no overheads (including depreciation) exist.
12. Of course, nothing ensures that the expected conditions will be fulfilled and, particularly, that the realised production will coincide with the production estimated in setting prices; since this kind of argument refers to results, it affects subsequent behaviour and not the sphere of decisions the model is concerned with.
13. In that case equation (4.2) must be replaced by:

$$p=\frac{w}{a}(1+q) \qquad (4.14)$$

14. The identification of profit earners with entrepreneurs, put forward at the beginning of section 4.1.1, also permits the assumption that their savings are entirely employed in their own firms, i.e., the assumption that *distributed* profits are wholly consumed. This is, of course, a highly unrealistic hypothesis, which can be removed by distinguishing between s_p (the retention rate) and s_c (capitalists' propensity to save, i.e., propensity to save out of distributed profits), and then putting:

$S_p = s_pP$, firms' saving
$S_c = s_cP(1-s_p)$, capitalists' saving.

15. The estimated trade-off between margin q and expected output ($\bar{X}$) can be generically expressed as:

$$q = zf(\bar{X}), \qquad f'<0 \qquad (4.16)$$

where $z>1$ is a magnitude subject to the firm's control, insofar as the firm can influence its demand function. When market conditions give the firm a sufficiently wide degree of freedom, then q may be directly determined by equation (4.15), while the financial requirements of investments (S_p) are considered as given; alternatively, given the constraint set by (4.16), equation (4.15) fixes the retention rate.
16. In other words, expected profitability affects investment by acting on both the firm's *external* (the evaluation of market perspectives) and *internal* conditions (the propensity to risk).
17. Finally, if the case of adaptability of money supply is considered, i will be replaced by M as unknown (subject to the condition that $M\leq\bar{M}$, the latter being the ceiling fixed by the monetary authorities). This change enables us to disregard the effect of the dependence of money demand from income (subject to $L\leq\bar{M}$).
18. In abstract terms, a 'general equilibrium' solution might be alternatively conceived by putting $\bar{X}=X$; it would, however, be a way of argument foreign to Kalecki's approach.
19. The political aspects of public policy were considered in Section 1.3.

20. The rebuttal of the marginalist postulate of an inverse relationship between real wages and employment is a constant point of reference in Kalecki's thought since its 'pre-Keynesian stage' (see, in particular, Kalecki, 1935d).
21. See, in this regard, (1939a; 1939b; 1954; 1971a).
22. 'This process may be presented by means of our scheme of three departments. According to our assumption the capitalists' consumption and investment do not change initially. Therefore there is no change either in the production of the department of the capitalists' consumer goods or in the department of investment goods. The same applies to the employment in both these departments as a result of which the effective demand for wage goods produced by the third department decreases in the proportion of the wage reduction. But as the marginal costs in this department decline in the same proportion as well, there will be no change in the production of the third department either. As a result production and employment in all three departments will remain for some time unchanged, while the prices equal to the marginal costs decrease in the same proportion as wages. In this situation, however, there is no reason for the capitalists to increase their consumption and investment, as the expected increase in profitability did not materialize' (Kalecki, 1939b, pp. 48–9).

    Kalecki continues by arguing that not only direct effects on employment are lacking, but that it would also be useless to rely on indirect effects as they are weak and contradictory. A decrease in money wages (1939b, p. 49) exerts contrasted consequences on the long-term rate of interest, and hence on investments:

    (a) positive, as it increases the economy's real liquidity (though weak owing to the length of the monetary circuit);
    (b) negative, since it raises firms' real indebtedness and pushes banks to lift rates in order to offset reduced confidence in firms' solvency (note Kalecki's application here of the principle of increasing risk to the supply conditions of loans, as according to Breit).

    When open economy is considered, the above conclusions are adjusted by Kalecki (1939b, pp. 56–8), since the fall in wages and prices gives rise to direct, though contradictory, effects on employment:

    (a) positive, insofar as it increases the competitiveness of domestic output;
    (b) negative, since it brings about a compression in real wages as the prices of imported goods do not decrease, thereby slowing down the reduction in the general level of prices.
23. In this sense see Kalecki (1939a, p. 83).
24. In this sense see Kalecki (1939b, p. 56).
25. According to Kalecki, the ability of trade unions to achieve real increases in wages is strictly related to the size of profit margins, that is to say, to the possibility for firms to meet workers' claims. In fact, firms would be made reluctant to transfer the cost of higher wages on prices:

    (a) by the expectation that restoration of the preceding mark-ups might give rise to a 'new round' of claims;
    (b) by the fear of missing competitiveness with other industries (since Kalecki adds, 'bargaining is proceeding by industries' (1971a, p. 161n.)).

    As to the first point, therefore, firms are dissuaded from lifting prices not so much because they believe that the erosion in purchasing power would lead to new demands (which would only be the consequence of firms acting *as a whole*, and as such could not be anticipated by each firm individually), but by the conviction that bargaining originates from the wish to benefit from the favourable conditions of the industry.

The second point is open to criticism. Competition among *industries* takes place not so much by means of goods as by means of capital, so that it is the fear of new entry which curbs firms from raising prices, rather than that of missing competitiveness to the benefit of rivals. Therefore: if wage increases occur in an industry only, the *restoration* of previous margins does not make it more profitable than it was before; if, instead, the rise in wages spreads over all industries, then all of them together will transfer it to prices without increasing the risk of new entry. Finally, the equation Kalecki refers to on this occasion (2.15) appears to conceive competition as a phenomenon internal to each industry. Consequently, it is necessary to assume that bargaining takes place at the single-firm level in order to validate Kalecki's conclusions about the effects of wage claims (on this theme see Jossa, 1989).

26. Kalecki points out (1971a, p. 164) that income redistribution from profits to wages can occur only with excess capacity; in the opposite case prices are demand-determined, so that it would no longer be possible to increase wages relative to prices. To this view Asimakopulos (1975, p. 330) objects that the greater power workers enjoy in full employment can modify distribution, provided that it succeeds in reducing capitalists' real expenditure.
27. 'A wage rise showing an increase in trade unions power leads – contrary to the precepts of classical economics – to an increase in employment. And conversely, a fall in wages showing a weakening in their bargaining power leads to a decline in employment. The weakness of trade unions in a depression manifested in permitting wage cuts contributes to deepening unemployment rather than to relieving it' (Kalecki, 1971a, p. 163).
28. Kalecki warns against the circumstance that trade union power rises during booms and falls in depressions, thereby sharpening the business cycle. In particular, it may exert inflationary pressures in full employment (we will return to this point later).
29. In this regard see Kalecki (1971a, p. 158).
30. Suppose that prices keep unchanged as wages vary.
31. It must be added that the average rate of profit should rise along with the employment of equipment because of the reduction in unit overheads.
32. Profits in the wage goods sector rise to the detriment of those in the other sectors (see Kalecki, 1971a, p. 157).
33. This case, however, would be in contrast with the hypotheses underlying consumption and investment functions.
34. As we shall see, the effects of wage variations are similar to those of profit taxation, and it is difficult to understand (unless on the basis of political considerations) why Kalecki did not raise against the former the same doubts he mentioned in relation to the latter.
35. The reasoning underlying Kalecki's thesis – as set out especially in (1945) – can be translated as follows. Let us say:

$$\dot{K}_k = \dot{L} + \dot{K}$$

where $\dot{L}$ and $\dot{K}$ are, respectively, the rate of growth of active population and that of the capital–labour ratio, which are both supposed given an constant. Following Kalecki's assumption that *K/Y* is constant and taking into account that $K/L \equiv (K/Y)\,(Y/L)$, we deduce that $\dot{k} = \dot{l}$, where $\dot{l}$ is the rate of growth of labour productivity. As a result, the rate of increase of equipment, which is necessary to create jobs in step with active population, is:

$$\dot{K}_k = \dot{L} + \dot{l}$$

On the demand side, Harrod's condition for steady growth is:

$$\dot{Y} = \frac{s}{v} = \dot{K}_d, \text{ with } s = I/Y \text{ and } v = K/Y = \text{constant}$$

As s tends to increase, $\dot{Y}$ and $\dot{K}_d$ will also rise, so that $\dot{K}_d > \dot{K}_k$.

36. This thesis must not be confused with the neoclassical solution of Harrod's instability, i.e., capital intensity rises as interest rate decreases. As we have already seen (see Section 3.2.4), according to Kalecki the thrust in this direction comes chiefly from new inventions (see 1944, p. 51), whereas the impulse exerted by the rate of interest is practically negligible; the lowering of the interest rate stimulates an increase in scale of production (in the case considered, it compensates for the reduced exploitation of plants) but does not lead to introducing more intensive techniques.
37. Similar conclusions are reached (Kalecki, 1945, p. 90) when supposing that technical progress makes capacity grow less than capital stock, so that (the degree of utilisation of plants being equal) the capital – output ratio increases. In this case the disequilibrium between $\dot{K}_d$ and $\dot{K}_k$ becomes less sharp and may even cease; however, the obstacles to the maintenance of full employment do not disappear, as a fall in the rate of profits occurs anyway.
38. See in this regard, Kalecki (1976).
39. This view can be explained by various considerations. First, the difficulty in governing foreign trade (especially given the restrictions in the 1930s), in contrast with the agility of public spending; second, the impossibility of reconciling measures aimed at creating surplus in the trade balance of all capitalist countries made this proposal inadequate as a *general* criterion for employment policy; finally, we must add Kalecki's reluctance to theorise 'imperialism' as a way out from unemployment, even more when he aims at presenting himself as a strategist of 'enlightened' capitalism.
40. Kalecki prefers increasing taxation of higher incomes and capital incomes to indebtedness as, he argues, the former reduces inequality without being a burden on the public budget. Precisely for that reason this method is bound to meet strong opposition, so that: 'One cannot, therefore, make any definite choice between the Budget deficit and the income tax method. Income tax may be pushed as far as practically possible, but after this has been done, one should not hesitate to have in addition such a Budget deficit as is still required to achieve and maintain full employment' (1944, p. 55).
41. In the same sense see (1944, pp. 57–8).
42. For Kalecki's analysis of the effects of taxation see particularly (1937c; 1944; 1945). For a clear analysis of Kalecki's theory of taxation see Matteuzzi (1982); see also Asimakopulos (1979).

43. See (1937c, pp. 40–1).
44. 'It is now easy to see that two conditions must be fulfilled in order that full employment be achieved by the imposition of a higher income tax: (1) Income tax on higher incomes must be fixed at such a level that its stimulus to effective demand, in conjunction with the level of private investment as specified above, produces full employment. (2) In order to maintain private investment at the specified level, either the rate of interest must be fixed sufficiently low, or rather – as this may be difficult – a sufficient part of the income tax must be put on a modified basis (or replaced by a capital tax)' (1944, p. 54).
45. 'The increase of the rate of capital taxation does not tend to lower the net profitability of investment ... or to raise the rate of interest. Indeed, if somebody borrows money and builds a factory, he does not increase his own capital by this action and does not pay a greater capital tax. And if he ventures his own means, he also pays the same tax as he would if he abstained form investment. Thus the net profitability of investment is unaffected by capital taxation' (1937c, p. 41). In this case, too, Kalecki's reasoning is overly superficial, for it is easy to object that when investors take a loan they expect to repay it and to become full owners of capital. The expectation of being taxed, even if in the far future, will therefore inevitably lower the incentive to invest; moreover, such a tax is bound to raise the propensity to consume, so that (though not being recessive) it fails to attain the purpose for which it was designed. Finally, Kalecki's underlying reasoning that the *relative* profitability of different types of capital is unaffected by a general capital tax rests implicitly on ruling out international mobility of capitals.
46. 'Capital taxation is perhaps the best way to stimulate business and reduce unemployment . It has all the merit of financing the State expenditure by borrowing, but is distinguished from borrowing by the advantage of the State not becoming indebted. It is difficult to believe, however, that capital taxation will ever be applied for this purpose on large scale; for it may seem to undermine the principle of private property, and therefore in this case, as in general, "any government which had both the power and the will to remedy the major defects of the capitalist system would have the will and the power to abolish it altogether" (1937c, p. 42 – the quotation from J. Robinson, 1936).
47. The outstanding works of Kalecki on this subject (originally published in the *Oxford Institute of Statistics Bulletin*) have been collected in AA.VV. (1947).
48. 'To prevent "inflation in general" one must deal with "inflations" on particular groups of commodities, and this may be done only by rationing ... Rationing should be sufficiently comprehensive to make impossible the "shifting" of inflation from one sector of the economy to another' (1941b, p. 162).
49. Kalecki disagrees with policies different from rationing, such as price controls or compulsory savings, as proposed by Keynes (1940). To the first he opposes it as being unfair, since it would cause 'haphazard distribution' (1941b, p. 163). Against the second he argues that it 'does not differ essentially from income taxation. For the working class the consolation offered by prospective post-war enjoyment of compulsory savings is of a

rather shadowy character. As to the well-to-do, on whom in the last version of Mr. Keynes' scheme falls the burden of compulsory savings, it is even less efficient than income tax in cutting their consumption: seeing compulsory savings accumulating on blocked account they are more likely to save less on a voluntary basis or to dissave than they would if taxed on the same extent' (1941c, p. 2).

50. If wages increase more than productivity and prices are to be kept stable, subsidies should be granted to firms being financed by income tax. As a result of the redistribution of income, effective demand will rise (leading to inflation) 'unless the new income tax is higher than is necessary to finance the subsidies alone; and to the extent of this excess the budget deficit will fall' (1944, p. 55).
51. From this standpoint Schumpeter's statement on Marx seems to fit Kalecki's theory as well: 'Most of the creation of the intellect or fancy pass away for good after a time that varies between an after-dinner hour and a generation. Some, however, do not. They suffer eclipses but they come back again, and they come back not as unrecognizable elements of a cultural inheritance, but in their individual garb and their personal scars which people may see and touch. These we may well call the great ones – it is no disadvantage of this definition that it links greatness to vitality. Taken in this sense, this is undoubtedly the word to apply to the message of Marx ... We need not believe that a great achievement must necessarily be a source of light or faultness in their fundamental design or detail. On the contrary we may believe it to be a power of darkness; we may think it fundamentally wrong or disagree with it on any number of particular points. In the case of the Marxian system, such an adverse judgment or even exact disproof, by its very failure to injure fatally, only serves to spring out the power of the structure' (1954b, p. 3).
52. However, it should be recalled in this regard the importance Kalecki gives to the dual character of investment, which marks a step forward compared to Keynesian-type short-period macroeconomic schemes.
53. However, Kalecki does not pay much attention to this aspect even when the economy is close to full employment; the rules Kalecki proposes for this case concern aggregate demand management and not the supply policy.

5 Kalecki and Marx

1. See Chapter 4, no. 51,
2. See for example Graziani (1982, p. 703).
3. In this regard see Brus (1977, p. 59). 'He [Kalecki] felt, for example, a strong distaste for the Marxian theory of value, which he considered metaphysical and (if I am not mistaken) never wanted to discuss'.
4. See Klein (1947a, p. 118).
5. It is widely agreed that with his schemes Marx was a forerunner of modern approaches to macroeconomics, from dynamic equilibrium theory to Leontief's input – output analysis. In this connection see Samuelson (1967, pp. 616–8) who, after defining Marx as 'a not-uninteresting precursor of Leontief's input – output', concedes that 'Marx's model of expanded reproduction is perhaps the first example of those golden-age paths of

compounded interest which Cassel, D.H. Robertson, von Neumann, Harrod, Domar, and all the rest have made so fashionable in modern economics'. Though the contributions of these authors were developed independently of Marx, nevertheless 'we all might well have benefited earlier from study of the Marxian tableaux' (1967, p. 617).

6. See J. Robinson (1949, 1951), Sweezy (1942), Klein (1947a) and Kaldor (1960).
7. Kalecki also shares this opinion. Marx, though 'deeply conscious of the impact of effective demand upon the dynamics of the capitalist system ... did not systematically scrutinise the process described by his reproduction schemes from the point of view of the contradictions inherent in capitalism as a result of the problem of effective demand' (Kalecki, 1968b, p. 465). Such a step, Kalecki adds (1968b, p. 465), was precluded by Marx's failure to develop a theory of the motivations of investment decisions or an explanation of the consequences of them on the level of output (in this regard, see also Kalecki, 1939a, p. 45).
8. On more than one occasion Marx seems to confirm that capitalists invest what they can save: 'One part of the surplus-value is consumed by capitalists as revenue, the other part is employed as capital, i.e., it is accumulated. With a given mass of surplus-value, then, the larger the one part, the smaller the other. Other things being equal, the ratio of these parts determine the magnitude of the accumulation' (*Capital*, vol.I, p. 738). Marx's emphasis on the *ceteris paribus* condition might give rise to doubts whether he was indeed convinced that the surplus value could be regarded as a datum, i.e., as an amount independent of capitalists' consumption and investment; but this seems to concern once again the field of realisation of the surplus value rather than that of its creation.
9. Marx suggests the idea of a 'characteristic cycle of modern industry ... which takes the form of a decennial cycle ... of periods of average activity, production at a high pressure, crisis, and stagnation, [which] depends on the constant formation, the greater or the less absorption, and the re-formation of the industrial reserve army or surplus population' (*Capital*, vol.I, p. 785). See also the following passage: 'The market expands more slowly than production; ... there comes a moment at which the market manifests itself as too narrow for production. This occurs at the end of the cycle. But it merely means: the market is glutted. Over-production is manifest' (Marx, 1969, vol.II, p. 524). On these themes see Sardoni (1987).
10. Marx considers two sectors: sector I, producing capital goods, and sector II, which produces consumption goods.
11. It should be recalled that Marx assumes that exchanges occur according to labour values.
12. Initially Marx (*Capital*, vol.II, p. 582) considers the share of surplus value that is accumulated by capitalists (in both sectors) as given. This hypothesis is soon abandoned for being incompatible with equilibrium, and the propensity of capitalists in sector II to invest is made an endogenously determined variable. This reasoning has been sharply criticised by Rosa Luxemburg (1951, pp. 108–9), since 'there is no rule in this accumulation and in this consumption [of capitalists of section II], both being only justified with the requirements of accumulation in section

I'. Hence Luxemburg's conclusion that Marx set up a 'a wholly arbitrary picture of the relations within the sector II'. See also Morishima (1973, p. 125): 'The unnatural adjustment of the rate of accumulation by capitalists of department II to the exogenously determined rate of accumulation in department I was invented by Marx merely as a *deus ex machina*'. It is perhaps worth noting that Marx's argument can be seen from two distinct angles: (1) that of the conditions under which *initially given* productions are fully realised (i.e., equilibrium at a given point in time); (2) that of the conditions for a *steady* equilibrium. With numerical examples, Marx came close to defining the conditions for the first case, but he did not specify the conditions for dynamic equilibrium. Nevertheless, his examples depicted a system tending towards an equilibrium path characterised by uniform rates of growth of the two sectors, steady rates of accumulation and fully realised production. From the viewpoint of Kaleckian (as well Keynesian) theory, the first characteristic (i.e., equilibrium at a given time) is more interesting.

13. See Klein (1947a, pp. 126–7) in this connection: 'Actually, Marx made the groundwork for a complete equations system to determine the level of income (effective demand) but did not build the complete system'. Again: 'However, imbedded in Marx's literary discussion and numerical examples, there are several hypothesis and assumptions that can be used to build a system of equations' (1947a, pp. 118–19).
14. In particular see J. Robinson (1956, 1962b).
15. The change in relative prices will necessarily alter the 'organic composition of capital', i.e., the ratio of constant to variable capital, both being expressed in terms of prices. Alternatively, given the price structure, one can imagine that the adjustment runs through changes in techniques, that is, changes in what Marx calls the 'technical composition of capital'. Marx, however, does not even consider this eventuality, since his analysis of the reproduction schemes is grounded in the hypothesis of given techniques.
16. 'Kahn, at the "circus" where we discussed the *Treatise* in 1931, explained the problem of saving and investment by imagining a cordon round the capital-good industries and then studying the trade between them and the consumption-goods industries; he was struggling to rediscover Marx's schema; Kalecki began at this point' (J. Robinson, 1965, p. 96). Similarly Lange (1963, p. 309n.): 'The model worked out by M. Kalecki is often wrongly reckoned with those based on Keynes's theory; in fact it is derived from Marxist theory of reproduction and accumulation'.
17. Debt is instead acknowledged to Aftalian and Tinbergen.
18. 'Imagine that following Marx's "schemes of reproduction" we subdivide the economy into three departments: department I producing investment goods, department II producing consumption goods for capitalists, and department III producing consumption goods for workers. The capitalists in department III, after having sold to workers the amount of consumption goods corresponding to their wages, will still have left a surplus of consumption goods which will be equivalent to their profits. These goods will be sold to the workers of department I and department II, and, as the workers do not save, it will be equal to their incomes. Thus, total profits will be equal to the sum of profits in department I, profits in department II, and wages in these two departments: or,

total profits will be equal to the value of production of these two departments – in other words, to the value of production of investment goods and consumption goods for capitalists. The production of department I and department II will also determine the production of department III if the distribution between profits and wages in all three departments is given. The production of department III will be pushed up to point where the profits earned out of that production will be equal to the wages of departments I and II. Or, to put it differently, employment and production of department III will be pushed up to the point where the surplus of this production over what the workers of this department buy with their wages is equal to the wages of departments I and II' (Kalecki, 1954, p. 47).

19. Given the share of wages in each sector's output, and with $P=I+C_k$, from the equilibrium condition of the expanded reproduction (restated as $P_3=W_1+W_2$, i.e., profits of the wage sector equal to the demand for wage goods of the other sectors), Kalecki derives the equation whereby the overall level of production is made to depend on capitalists' expenditure and on the share of wages:

$$Y = I + C_k + \frac{w_1 I + w_2 C_k}{1 - w_3} \tag{1.1}$$

where I and C_k are investment and capitalists' consumption; and with:

$$\frac{w_1 + w_2 C_k}{1 - w_3} = C_w$$

consumption of wage earners equals the wage bill ($W_1 + W_2 + W_3$).

20. On this point, see Sardoni (1989).

21. The circuit of money (*Capital*, vol.II, Chapter 1) starts with the capital advanced by capitalists (their own or credit) to purchase labour or means of production; once the product has been manufactured and sold, capital resumes its money form and (with the accrual of surplus value) returns to the hands of those who advanced it. The circuit of capital thus includes its transformation from financial capital into capital embodied in labour and the means of production, then into real assets and, finally, into accrued financial capital.

As for the adjustment of monetary circulation to the requirements of production, according to Marx this takes place by virtue of the behaviour of the capitalists themselves: 'In relation to the capitalist class as a whole, the proposition that it must itself cast into circulation the money needed to realize its surplus-value ... is not only far from paradoxical, it is in fact a necessary condition of the overall mechanism' (1968b, p. 497). The increase in monetary circulation, Marx continues, can take place in three ways: (1) through an increase in money velocity of circulation ('a more economic use of the quantity of money in circulation' (1968b, p. 419)); (2) through a drop in capitalists' liquidity preference ('the transformation of money from the hoard form into the circulating form' (1968b, p. 419)); (3) ('to the extent that all these means together are not enough') through an increase in money supply ('there must be an additional production of gold' (1968b, p. 420)).

22. See Kalecki (1967b, p. 151; 1968b, p. 465).

23. 'Innovations break the impasse of simple reproduction only to some extent and they do not warrant the utilization of resources in the sense of Tugan-Baranowski' (Kalecki, 1967b, p. 151).

24. Among the reasons inducing Kalecki to reject Luxemburg's thesis in its rigid form is that it is partially the fruit of an error, as Luxemburg identifies the driving factor of demand in the *volume* of exports towards non-capitalist markets, instead of in the *trade balance*: this mistake, according to Kalecki (1967b, p. 152), leads to an overestimate of the role played by external markets. Kalecki's criticism is correct on both theoretical and historical grounds, but in a perspective sense the thesis of the inevitability of general overproduction emerges strengthened by this correction; indeed, what hinders the development of capitalist economies *taken as a whole* is not their inability to increase the volume of exports but the irreconciliability of the need, common to all of them, to maintain an active (and increasing) balance of trade.

25. '*Over-production* is specifically conditioned by the general law of the production of capital: to produce to the limit set by the productive forces ... without any considerations for the actual limits of the market or the needs backed by the ability to pay' (Marx, 1969, p. 534–5).
And further: 'The world *over-production* in itself leads to error. So long as the most urgent needs of a large part of society are not satisfied, or *only* the most immediate needs are satisfied, there can of course be absolutely no talk of an *over-production of products* – in the sense that the amount of products is excessive in relation to the needs for them. On the contrary, it must be said that on the basis of capitalist production, there is constant *under-production* in this sense. The limits to production are set by the profits of the capitalists and in no way by the needs of the producers. But over-production of products and over-production of *commodities* are two entirely different things' (1969, p. 527). Finally: 'The sale of commodities, the realisation of ... the surplus-value, is restricted not by the consumer needs of society in general, but by the consumer needs of a society in which the greater majority are always poor and must remains poor' (*Capital*, vol.II, p. 391n.).

There is a passage in *Capital* (vol.II, pp. 486–7) where Marx attacks the 'ingenuous' version of underconsumption (expressly attributed to Rodbertus): 'It is a pure tautology to say that crises are provoked by a lack of effective demand or effective consumption. The capitalistic system does not recognize any forms of consumer other than those who can pay ... If attempt is made to give this tautology the semblance of a greater profundity, by the statement that the working class receives too small a portion of its own product, and that the evil would be remedied if it received a bigger share, i.e., if its wage rose, we need only to note that crises are always prepared by a period in which wages generally rise ... From the standpoint of these advocates of sound and 'simple' common sense, such periods should rather avert the crisis. It thus appears that capitalist production involves certain conditions independent of people's good or bad intentions'. It would, however, be a mistake to interpret this passage as a proof that the volume of consumption is not relevant as a cause of crises; it should instead be understood in the sense that any attempt to overcome realisation problems by modifying the distributive order generates reactions (a drop in investments) which convert into causes of crises.

26. In this regard, see section 4.2.2.
27. Marx, however, is aware of the impact of the 'disruption' and of the 'devaluation' of capital in prompting the recovery (see *Capital*, vol.III, pp. 355–7).
28. See Marx, *Capital*, vol.III, p. 350.
29. In this connection, see the criticism put forward by J. Robinson (1949).
30. Both Marx and Kalecki hold the view that real wages move according to the business cycle. In Marx wage bargaining seems to be carried out in real terms, and he argues that 'Taking them as a whole, the general movements of wages are exclusively regulated by the expansion and the contraction of the industrial reserve army, and this in turn corresponds to the periodic alternations of the industrial cycle' (*Capital*, vol.I, p. 790). For Kalecki, real wages show a similar course during the cycle, though bargaining is conducted in nominal terms; as we have seen, his reasoning is that the power of trade unions (which is subject to change in the course of the cycle) works in two directions: in obtaining nominal increases and in dissuading the firms from making good through prices increases.
31. Marx's position here has also been interpreted as a prefiguration of what is now called the post-Keynesian approach. Indeed, Steindl (1952, p. 237) suggests: 'In the Marxian long-run analysis the adjustment concerns the distribution of income between workers and capitalists ... this distribution of income in the long-run is adjusted in such a way as to provide just the necessary saving to finance the *given* trend rate of accumulation' (emphasis added; see also Wood 1975, pp. 11–12).
32. As we have seen, Kalecki rejects the marginalist theory of distribution.
33. A further example of this difficulty can be found in the debate on the compatibility of Sraffa's price system with Marxian theory.
34. Schumpeter (1954b, p. 21) suggests a reason for this attitude towards Marx's thought: 'For the friends [of Marx] he was so much more than a mere professional theorist that it would have seemed almost blasphemy to them to give too much prominence to this aspect of his work'.
35. See, for example, Hobsbawm (1982, p. 6) on Marx: 'Inasmuch as a system of ideas survives its author, it is no longer confined to the bounds of content or original intents. Within the sweeping bounds traced by the exegetic capacity of men, or even by human willingness to recognize a link with a well-loved or a favourite predecessor, that block of ideas is subject to an unforseeable extensive series of changes and practical and theoretical transformations'.
36. See Joan Robinson (1979a, p. 253): 'With the light that Sraffa has thrown on the theory of value and Kalecki on the process of realization of the surplus, we can develop a complete system, not of neo Marxism but of *intelligible* Marxism'. This exercise, she adds (1979, p. 252), is all the more legitimate since: 'Considering the political use that has been made of [Keynes's ideas as revised by 'bastard Keynesianism'], it is natural enough for Marxist to be suspicious of Keynes, but what is the objection to Michal Kalecki, who set out almost exactly the same analytical system as the *General Theory* on the basis of the schema of expanded reproduction in Volume II of *Capital*?'.

6 A Digression on Keynes's *Treatise*

1. Kaldor's acknowledgement, in the same essay (1956, p. 228n. and p. 230), of Kalecki's contribution to the theory of profit (see Chapter 8, n. 4) must be noted.
2. 'The fundamental problem of monetary theory is ... to exhibit the causal process by which the price level is determined, and the method of transition from one position of equilibrium to another' (Keynes, 1930a, p. 120). And again: 'A principal object of this treatise is to show that we have here the clue to the way in which the fluctuations of the price level actually come to pass, whether they are due to oscillations about a steady equilibrium level or to a transition from one equilibrium to another' (1930a, p. 137).
3. (1930a, p. 111).
4. (1930a, pp. 112–13).
5. 'We shall mean by savings the sum of the differences between the money incomes of individuals and their money expenditure on current consumption. Thus profits, not being part of the income of the community, are not part of its savings either – even when they are not spent on current consumption' (1930a, pp. 113–14).
6. Keynes points out (1930a, pp. 136–7) that the condition according to which in equilibrium profits are equal to zero applies to each industry as a whole and not to single firms; the essential point is that the individual position of the various firms as regards capital remuneration, as well as the course of prices of different goods, balance each other at the sectoral level. Since disparities among earnings lead, according to Keynes's assumptions, to adjustments in outputs and in prices, it should be inferred that profits and losses would *tendentially* compensate each other also at the level of single firms.
7. As Hicks (1967) rightly points out, the intricacy of Keynes's definitions should not lead us to forget that the scheme of social accounting which is today familiar, based on national income and expenditure, was not available in 1930.
8. 'If entrepreneurs choose to spend a portion of their profits on consumption ... the effect is to *increase* the profits on the sale of liquid consumption goods by an amount exactly equal to the amount of profits which have been thus expended ... Thus profits, as a source of capital increment for entrepreneurs, are a widow's cruse which remains undepleted however much of them may be devoted to riotous living. When, on the other hand, entrepreneurs are making losses, and seek to recoup these losses by curtailing their normal expenditure on consumption, i.e. by saving more, the cruse becomes a Danaid jar which can never be filled up; for the effect of this reduced expenditure is to inflict on the producers of consumption goods a loss of an equal amount' (1930a, p. 125). It is worth noting that there is no reference here to the mechanism of the multiplier, which is correct given the assumptions underlying Keynes's reasoning, i.e., that (1) real income is given, and (2) spending is not a function of money income.
9. With C' and I' as the value (at cost) of consumer and investment goods ($C' + I' = E$), we get:

$$C = C' + (I' - S).$$

Since p_c clears the market - i.e., $p_c = C/O_c$, with O_c as the quantity produced of consumer goods – by substituting we get equation (6.3).

10. (1930a, p. 12). Since C' is the remuneration of factors employed in the production of consumer goods (wages and normal profits), it should be concluded that Keynes assumes vertical integration in the production of raw materials and eventually (depending on whether normal profit is net or gross of depreciation) no deterioration of fixed capital.
11. In this connection see Hicks's (1935) acknowledgement.
12. (1930a, p. 128). As pointed out by Vicarelli (1977, p. 79), Keynes's arguing implies that the price of investment goods is closely bound to that of shares; according to Kahn (1978), by contrast, Keynes confuses one with the other.
13. This point is made very clear by the 'fundamental equations' (6.3–6.4), where output is given independently of divergences between investments and savings, that is, independently of demand.
14. Since the prices of the two commodities are determined separately, the general price level is deprived of the character of an autonomous analytical category, as it is in quantity theory, and demoted to the rank of a weighted average of prices of single goods, which is affected by changes in money circulation only through the effects exerted separately on each one; it follows that nothing ensures the neutrality of money with respect to relative prices (see Graziani, 1981b, pp. 217–8, on this point).

    Given: $p = (p_c O_c + p_i O_i)/O$, where $O = O_c + O_i$ are 'quantities of goods [measured] in such a way that a unit of each has the same cost of production at the base date' (1930a, pp. 121–2), we get: $p = (E + I\text{-}S)/0$, from which the 'second fundamental equation':

$$p = \frac{E}{O} + \frac{I - S}{O} \qquad (6.4)$$

15. According to Hayek (1931), this basis is missing entirely.
16. Again: 'Thus when the actual rate of entrepreneurs' remuneration exceeds (or falls short of) the normal as thus defined, so that profits are positive (or negative), entrepreneurs will ... seek to expand (or curtail) their scale of operations at the existing costs of production' (1930a, pp. 112–3).
17. Working through the supply, the mechanism of firms' response to disequilibrium (see n. 16) plays an essential role in restoring equilibrium. A subsidiary action is exerted by firms competing (when $I>S$) in the factors market in order to increase production, which causes the rates of factors' remuneration to rise. Changes in price level are therefore due to changes in both costs and in demand. Whenever these two causes of change do not interact with each other, then the disparity which arises between investments and savings (i.e., the occurrence of demand pressures on prices) gives rise to fluctuations around 'the long-period or equilibrium norm of the purchasing power of money' set by the cost of production (1930a, p. 137). In reality, this disturbing impulse encourages firms to change the rates of remuneration offered to factors, and therefore the cost of production, so that a new equilibrium will be attained at a price level different from the initial one (see *Treatise*, Chapters XVII–XVIII).

18. 'The normal supply price ... is that the expectation of which is sufficient and only just sufficient to make it worth while for people to set themselves to produce that aggregate amount' (Marshall, 1891, p. 310).
19. We shall not deal here with the controversial matter of whether, in Marshall's theory, the notion of long-period prices implies acceptance of the marginalist theory of distribution.
20. The competitive framework that accordingly emerges, however, contrasts with the presence of 'normal monopoly gains' included in the production cost.
21. This is true even if the above equilibrium conditions refer only to industries.
22. We do not share Graziani's position (1981a, pp. 102–3), who seems to miss the limits Keynes encounters confining himself to cases of disequilibrium: 'We can even accept the idea that, as regards equilibrium positions, Keynes accept the marginalist theory of distribution. But the more relevant question concerns income distribution *outside equilibrium*. In cases of disequilibrium ... income distribution thus become independent of any principle of productivity and depends only on the autonomous decisions of investors' (see also Graziani 1981b, pp. 219–20).
23. As it is well known, this point was raised by Robertson (1926) and even earlier by the Swedish School (starting with Wicksell, 1898).
24. See A.E. Robinson (1947), J. Robinson (1933b), Kahn (1978).
25. See Klein (1947b), Minsky (1975), Patinkin (1976), Moggridge (1976), Vicarelli (1977).
26. A different interpretation is put forward by Graziani (1981a, 1981b) and by Tonveronachi (1983), though in a somewhat subtle manner. According to Graziani (1981b, p. 224), Keynes's position in the *Treatise* can be summarised as follows: '(a) national income, as a rule, is smaller than would be permitted by available resources ...; (b) the actual level of income is determined by aggregate demand'. On these premises Keynes would have worked out (though not wholly aware of it) a new theory of national income, which deems that 'an increase or reduction of profits brings about increase or drop in production and income up to the point where, by very virtue of income changes, savings adjust to investments. At this point the economic system is once again in an equilibrium position: savings and investments are equal; monetary prices concide with costs of production, and are therefore stable; extra-profits, or losses, have disappeared' (Graziani, 1981a, p. 100).

    It is not possible to share this forward-oriented interpretation. Indeed, Keynes looks at unemployment as a manifestation of the *depression phase* of the cycle (see *Treatise*, pp. 252–5) and as a phenomenon of disequilibrium, not as a permanent phenomenon and even less as an equilibrium situation. This point is also confirmed by the passage in the *Treatise* already quoted (pp. 159–60), that is considered as the spearhead of Keynes's maturation towards the thematics of effective demand. It describes a recession in demand and production triggered by a 'savings campaign' and adumbrates the possibility that a new equilibrium between savings and investments is re-established at a lower income level. The potential inherent in this concept, however, was not perceived by Keynes, who at the time was interested only in showing that, by virtue of the re-equilibrating effect of income reduction (due to a 'growing poverty'), the recession contains its own potential for interrupting and inverting the trend; he was not, at the time, concerned with the existence of underemployment equilibria as such.

27. On this point see Tonveronachi (1983, p. 43): 'The scheme of the *Treatise* is essentially a periodic one, where the moment of decisions (*ex ante*) – in which both the levels of output and, given the rates of remuneration of factors, the prices of production and the factors incomes are established in relation to the results of the preceding period – is kept distinct from the market moment (*ex post*), when the demand for consumer and investment goods comes to face the outputs previously fixed. [Since prices are] market-clearing, the confrontation of demand and supply (the latter being equal to production) determines the market prices and the eventual coming into existence of profits and losses'. Hicks (1967) seems to move in the same perspective.
28. See Keynes (CW, XIII, pp. 339–42).
29. It is worth noting that fixed capital is included by Keynes among 'specialised factors'.
30. As Moggridge points out (1976, p. 76), while 'the formal logic of the theoretical segments of the book assumed a fixed "full employment" level of output in the economy ... nevertheless, in the actual non-formal discussions of the real world in the book, Keynes concerned himself with changes in both prices and output'.
31. In this connection see, for example, the *manifesto* of monetary theory as declared by Keynes in the opening of Chapter X.
32. The debt to Wicksell (though acknowledged with a certain reluctance) and to Robertson is evident throughout the *Treatise*. From Wicksell comes the frame of the credit cycle, as well as the idea that the non-automatic adjustment of investments to savings is caused by the disparity between savings and financial resources, due to the working of the banking system. The influence exerted by Robertson's book (1926) and by his discussions with Keynes – acknowledged in the Preface to the *Treatise* (p. xviii) – is well summarised by A.E Robinson (1947, p. 36): 'That book [Robertson's (1926)] was the first to bring home to us in Cambridge (I recognize that we may in important respects have been insular, isolated and behind the times) the essential distinction between the act of saving and the act of investment'.

7 The Stockholm School

1. See, in this regard, Myrdal's (1972) statement, quoted in section 1.3.
2. Again; 'In a process of expansion the upward movement of the price level and the upward movement of the volume of output are parts of the same mechanism: What we called "the economics of unused resources" would at the same time throw light on the development of the gross output and the movement of the price level. Am I right in saying that when reading British and American theoretical discussions later in the 1930s – after the *General Theory* – about variations in output as an essential "equilibrating" variable,

one often got the impression that this analysis was considered separately from the analysis of price level variations?' (1977, p. 153).

3. See Ohlin (1937, p. 57).
4. Lindhal (1930, translated in English as 1939) was only marginally concerned with the causes of change in output; though hints to possible unemployment equilibria can be found in that book as well as in immediately subsequent works, they were nevertheless given minor emphasis, being confined in notes and even omitted from the English edition.
5. In this regard, see Ohlin (1933, pp. 367, 374) and Myrdal (1939, Chapters IV–V).
6. Steiger (1976) points out that this view can be traced in Ohlin's writings as early as 1929. If this is correct, then Ohlin was at the time much ahead of Keynes, for in the same period Keynes and Henderson (1929) denied any basis for crowding-out, by ingenuously arguing that saving *exceeded* investment. On this aspect, by contrast, Kalecki's view agrees perfectly with that of Swedish economists.
7. It is quite evident here the similarity of Ohlin's reasoning to that argued by Keynes later in (1937a).
8. Out of the three conditions for monetary equilibrium, as stated by Wicksell – namely, the equality between the natural and the monetary rate of interest, the equality between savings and investments, and the constancy of price level – Myrdal maintains the second only, arguing (1939, pp. 38 ff) that the first is not correct and the third unnecessary.
9. Myrdal stresses the purely 'instrumental significance' of the notion of equilibrium, i.e., not being a representation of reality but a device for capturing it in its essential lines: 'The equilibrium relations, therefore, are studied at first only as important auxiliary instruments for the analysis of actual or hypothetical monetary and prices situations' (1939, p. 41).
10. The maintenance of monetary equilibrium does not rely on the constancy of the price level as such, but on that of the price structure, since changes in the latter would affect the profitability of investments and, in this way, their volume. Indeed, since, owing to 'the stickness of some prices, every primary change of some importance in the price system will disturb the parallelism within the complex of price relations ... a monetary policy aimed to preserve the equilibrium relations must, therefore, *adapt the flexible prices to the absolute level of the sticky ones*' (1939, pp. 134–5).
11. 'There is no reason why the planned investment plus the planned consumption should be equal to the expected total income for the society as a whole' (Ohlin, 1937, p. 237).
12. 'The advantage of a theory of underemployment equilibrium seems to lie chiefly on the pedagogical side. But, other more dynamic theoretical constructions can convey the same insight into the causal connections and perhaps, in a more realistic manner' (Ohlin, 1978, p. 144). The criticism Ohlin raises to Keynes derives from missing the meaning the latter gives to equilibrium: 'Keynes's very simple model rests on the simplifying assumption that the volume of investment will not be affected by the decline in output! He also seems to assume that the depression tendency will not bring about any essential decline in the rate of interest. In most cases these

assumptions are unrealistic, particularly the former. Wicksell's cumulative process with some further precisations is more realistic ... In the Stockholm theory we took account of a "feed-back" from changes in total output to changes in saving but also changes in investment and, *thereby*, in employment' (1978, pp. 144–5).

13. In this regard, see Patinkin (1978a, p. 416).
14. In this regard, see Myrdal (1939, p. 118). For his part, Ohlin (1937, p. 62) strongly criticises Keynes's consumption function, which he considers 'a little superficial' as it does not take into account consumers' income expectations: 'On what does this sum total of planned consumption depend? First of all on the consumer's income expectations. Not his expected income during the first coming period only, but on what he expects to earn over a long period in the future. If a man gets a temporary, well-paid job which gives him a much higher salary than he is used to and more than he can expect to earn later on, his standard consumption will obviously be much affected by considerations of this latter fact'.
15. This route could not be pursued by Keynes, as the dependence of consumption on current income would hinder the restoration of *ex post* equilibrium.
16. In (1934), which is available only in the original language, Myrdal's position on the process of income adjustment appears even more definite (in this sense, see Hansen, 1981, p. 259).
17. This passage is drawn from Steiger's citation in (1976, p. 351).
18. The most articulated criticisms have been raised by Landgren (1960) and Patinkin (1978a, 1978b, 1982).
19. In this sense, see Patinkin (1982, pp. 43–4); Patinkin's objections in the two essays of 1978 (cited above) are in the same direction.
20. See Patinkin (1978a, p. 415; 1982, p. 53).
21. Patinkin (1982, p. 52). Landgren's viewpoint is slightly different in holding that Ohlin alone would have broken with the Wicksellian tradition and anticipated (subject to the limitations below) the *General Theory*.
22. Patinkin (1982, p. 51).
23. Landgren (1960, p. 144).
24. As regards Myrdal, see what is referred to by Steiger (1978, p. 440n.). For Ohlin, see (1977, pp. 154–6), where he also suggests the opposite eventuality, that is, to have influenced the process of maturation of Keynes's idea through the 1929 correspondence on the question of war reparations.
25. The political and cultural influence that Keynes (and, more generally, the British liberal thought of the 1920s) might have exerted on the development of the 'new economics' in Sweden as well as on Swedish economic policy of the 1930s is a quite different matter; this thesis is upheld by Landgren but it is denied by the exponents of the Stockholm School, starting with Ohlin (1937).
26. It must be added that the multiplier process is described in Ohlin (1934) along with an accurate analysis of the effectiveness of different measures of demand support. However, the multiplier is conceived dynamically (together with the accelerator) on that occasion and not with a view to the restoration of equilibrium. This fact does not imply that Ohlin was unaware of the possibility of using the multiplier for that purpose, too; rather, he was

not interested in this aspect. This work, available only in Swedish, is reported by Brems (1978); anyway, a certain 'philo-Ohlinian extremism' which appears to permeate that article induces caution in fully embracing its thesis.

27. This interpretation, perhaps, has also been induced by Ohlin himself when, in opening his 1933 article, he notices that his purpose is to revise the monetary theory of the time (from Keynes to Cassel), which held that the factors of changes in the price level lay in the divergence between saving and investment. However, from that *minimal* programme came other results which went well beyond the scope of the contemporary theories of money.
28. See Ohlin (1933, pp. 370–2).
29. See Thomas (1937, pp. 136–7, 141).
30. In 1931 the first *Report on Unemployment* (drawn up by Hammarskjld) was produced by a Commission appointed by the Government in 1927 to analyse Swedish unemployment from 1860 to 1929. The second *Report* (also drawn up by Hammarskjold) – entitled *Measures Against Unemployment* – included as Appendices a number of studies carried out by Bagge, Johansson, Myrdal and Ohlin from 1931 and 1934, which represent the main source of the economic policy proposals put forward by the Stockholm School.
31. It must be recognised that the crisis was also less severe in Sweden than in other countries because the distributive structure was sufficiently equalised to make aggregate demand steady.
32. Ohlin (1934) appears to anticipate the notion of the liquidity trap, by arguing that there is a limit to the decrease in interest on bonds determined by the expectations of agents.
33. See Ohlin (1934).
34. Cited from Uhr (1977, p. 100). Similarly, Myrdal refused as 'static' the view according to which capital for financing new investments should be taken away from other enterprises; he argued instead that capital for industrial recovery does not exist as an accumulated stock, but is generated by the upward swing itself (1934, pp. 220ff., as mentioned by Thomas, 1937, p. 135). Finally, Ohlin only recognises the possibility for 'psychological' crowding-out, that is to say, the possibility for public investments to negatively affect business confidence (1933, as mentioned by Uhr, 1977, p. 108).
35. In this regard, see, for instance, Myrdal (1933).
36. This system had been introduced in Denmark as early as 1925.
37. See Thomas (1937, pp. 132–3).
38. As Patinkin reports (1982, p. 93), the fellowship programme Kalecki submitted to the Rockefeller Foundation (dated 28 February 1936) includes: 'Business cycle theory, particularly from standpoint of Wicksell's money theory. Will visit a number of Business Cycle Institutes in various European countries but will carry out the main part of his program in the Scandinavian countries (with Prof. G. Myrdal in Stockholm and Prof. R. Frisch in Oslo) and in England (Cambridge) under direction of Prof. J.M. Keynes'.
39. In (1937, p. 61) Ohlin writes that he is looking forward to receiving Kalecki's work on the principle of increasing risk, the essence of which he anticipates or reports.

40. As far as Swedish economists are concerned, this point is particularly emphasised by Myrdal.

8 Kalecki and the 'post-Keynesians'

1. See Kregel (1973).
2. See Eichner (1979a, pp. 7–8).
3. This second assertion is not entirely convincing, at least, since the endogeneity of credit and liquidity (which represent an important aspect of this approach) can be more clearly traced in Kalecki than in Keynes (at least in the *General Theory*).
4. As noted before, Kaldor also (1956, p. 228n.) recognises Kalecki's contribution in this direction: 'I should also like to mention here that I owe a great deal of stimulus to a paper by Kalecki, 'A Theory of Profits' (*Economic Journal*, June – September 1942) whose approach is in some sense reminiscent of the 'widow's cruse' of Keynes' *Treatise* even though Kalecki uses the technique, not for an explanation of the share of profits in output, but for showing why the *level* of output and its fluctuations is peculiarly dependent on entrepreneurial behaviour'. Then, after deriving profits as a function of investments and the capitalists' propensity to save, he adds: 'This is the assumption implicit in Keynes' parable about the widow's cruse – where a rise in entrepreneurial consumption raises their total profit by an *identical* amount – and of Mr. Kalecki's theory of profits which can be paraphrased by saying that "capitalists earn what they spend, and workers spend what they earn"' (1956, p. 230).
5. Especially in (1962).
6. For an ample treatment of this subject, see Sebastiani (1983).
7. Passing from short-period to long-period analysis is, according to Kaldor (1956), a necessary step since the process of adjustment between savings and investments through changes in distribution cannot be properly conceived (from the Keynesian standpoint) within a static or short-period situation without incurring the risk of rehabilitating Say's law, which states that the coordination among demands for different goods (given real income) is ensured by the flexibility of the price system. The compatibility with the theory of effective demand, according to Kaldor, can be restored by integrating the principle of income adjustment into a long-run theory, that is to say, into a model of full-employment growth of capacity, where the key variable is the share of investments in income and where the Keynesian spirit is perceptible in the independence of that share from the propensity to save: 'These two uses of the Multiplier principle [for determining the level of income and for determining the distribution of income] are not as incompatible as would appear at first sight: the Keynesian technique can be used for both purposes, provided the one is conceived as a short-run theory and the other as a long-run theory – or rather, the one is used in the framework of a static model, and the other in the framework of a dynamic growth model ... The interpretative value of the [latter] model ... depends on the "Keynesian" hypothesis that investment, or rather, the ratio of investment to output, can be treated as an independent variable, invariant with respect to changes in the two savings propensities' (Kaldor, 1956, pp. 228–9).

8. In this regard Joan Robinson (1965, p. 101): 'long-period equilibrium is not some date in the future; it is an imaginary state of affairs in which there are not incompatibilities in the existing situations, here and now'. See also Pasinetti (1962, p. 119): 'I should look ... at the analysis simply and more generally as a logical framework to answer interesting questions about what *ought* to happen if full employment is to be kept over time, more than a behavioural theory expressing what actually happens'.
9. See Kalecki (1954, p. 155).
10. It follows that the 'basic antinomy' of capitalism is not the one pointed out by Harrod which leads to fluctuations around the trend line, but the fact that the way out from the stationary state rests on the existence of external factors.
11. See Kalecki (1954, p. 156).
12. Among the many others, see for instance Aismakopulos (1975, 1977a, 1980, 1988) and Weintraub (1979, 1981, 1983).
13. Following the distinction suggested by Kalecki in (1954, p. 11).
14. See section 4.1.2.
15. This point can be verified by combining equation (4.3) with the Harrodian equation $g = s/v$, where:

$$s = s_r \frac{R}{Y} + s_p \frac{P}{Y}$$

with R, incomes other than profits, and s_r and s_p, propensities to save. Simplifying equation (4.1) for $F = O$, the conclusion can be drawn that, *in equilibrium* between savings and investments:

$$d = \frac{s_r}{s_p} \frac{R}{P} \tag{8.1}$$

The fulfilment of this condition is more casual than casual, since d is set by firms on the basis of the expected net profitability, while the structure of saving depends on income distribution and the propensities to save, unless a causal nexus (from left to right) is assumed, by allowing entrepreneurs to govern the overall savings of the economy through income distribution (R/P) and the retention rate (s_p). In this case the steady-growth equation becomes:

$$g = \frac{s_p \frac{P}{Y}(1+d)}{v} \tag{8.2}$$

in which the conditions for steady growth draw justification from the assumptions made as regards entrepreneurial behaviour: by regulating profit margins (P/Y) and s_p firms adjust the structure of savings to the desired debt ratio and, *in this way*, the average propensity to save to the share of investments in income. Alternatively, in a planned economy, F may be the variable to control.
16. Given d (equation (8.1)) the increase in s_r should be offset by a rise in the profit share, then in I/Y and in g; it follows that the depressionary effect of a rising income should be counterbalanced by speeding up the rate of growth – which (Kalecki would recognise) belongs to the paradoxes of capitalism.

Bibliography

AA. VV. (1947) *Studies in War Economics* (Oxford: Blackwell).

AA. VV. (1966) *Essays in Honour of Michal Kalecki* (London: Pergamon Press).

AA. VV. (1967) *The Economics of Full Employment* (New York: Kelley).

Andrews, P.W.S. (1949) *Manufacturing Business* (London: Macmillan).

Asimakopulos, A. (1975) 'A Kaleckian theory of income distribution', *Canadian Journal of Economics*, (August).

Asimakopulos, A. (1977a) 'Profits and investments: a Kaleckian approach', in Harcourt, G. (ed.), *The Microeconomic Foundations of Macroeconomics* (London: Macmillan).

Asimakopulos, A. (1977b) 'Post-Keynesian growth theory', in Weintraub, S. (ed.), *Modern Economic Thought* (Oxford: Blackwell).

Asimakopulos, A. (1979) 'Tax incidence', in Eichner, A. (ed.), *A Guide to Post-Keynesian Economics* (London: Macmillan).

Asimakopulos, A. (1980) 'Themes in the Post-Keynesian theory of income distribution', *Journal of Post-Keynesian Economics* (Winter).

Asimakopulos, A. (1988) *Investment, Employment and Income Distribution*, (Cambridge: Polity Press).

Bain, J. (1956) *Barriers to New Competition* (Cambridge, Mass.: Harvard University Press).

Baran, P. and Sweezy, P. (1966) *Monopoly Capitalism* (New York: Monthly Review Press).

Bauer, P.T. (1941) 'A note on monopoly', *Economica* (May).

Beveridge, W.H. (1944) *Full Employment in a Free Society* (London: Allen & Unwin).

Boitani, A. (1984) 'Oligopoly, investment and stagnation: some reflections on the models of Kalecki and Steindl', *Quaderni dell'Istituto di Studi Economici e Sociali* (Camerino: Università di Camerino).

Botta, F. (ed.), (1974) *Il dibattito su Sraffa* (Bari: De Donato).

Breit, M. (1935) 'Ein beitrag zur theorie der geld und kapitalmarkets', *Zeitschrift für Nationalökonomie*.

Brems, H. (1978) 'What was new in Ohlin's 1933–34 Macroeconomics?', *History of Political Economy* (Fall).

Brus, W. (1977) 'Kalecki's economics of socialism', *Oxford Bulletin of Economics and Statistics*, 39.

Buchanan, N.S. and Calkins, R.D. (1938) 'A comment on Mr. Kalecki's principle of increasing risk', *Economica* (November).

Burbridge, J. (1979) *A Two-Sectors Model of Inflation and Recession* (mimeo).

Caffé, F. (1979) 'Introduzione', in *L'economia della piena occupazione* (Torino: Rosemberg & Sellier).

Chamberlin, E. (1933) *The Theory of Monopolistic Competition* (Cambridge, Mass.: Harvard University Press).

Chilosi, A. (1979) *Kalecki* (Bologna: Il Mulino).
Chilosi, A. (1982) 'Breit, Kalecki and Hicks on the term structure of interest rates and the theory of investment', in Baranzini, M. (ed.), *Advances in Economic Theory* (Oxford: Blackwell).
D'Antonio, M. (1975) 'Introduzione' in *La crisi post-keynesiana* (Torino: Boringhieri).
D'Antonio, M. (1978) 'Kalecki e il marxismo', *Studi storici*, 1
D'Antonio, M. (1979) 'Il problema del controllo del mercato in Keynes e in Kalecki', in Telò, M. (ed.), *Crisi e piano* (Bari: De Donato).
Davidson, P. (1959) *Theories of Aggregate Income Distribution* (New Brunswick: Rutgers University Press).
Denicolò, V. and Matteuzzi, M. (1985) 'Introduzione', in Kalecki, M., *Saggi sulla teoria delle fluttuazioni economiche* (Torino: Rosemberg & Sellier).
Dobb, M. (1973) *Theories of Value and Distribution since Adam Smith* (Cambridge: Cambridge University Press).
Eatwell, J. (1979) *Theories of Value, Output and Employment* (London: Thames Polytechnic).
Eatwell, J. and Milgate, M. (eds.)(1983) *Keynes' Economics and the Theory of Value and Distribution* (London: Duckworth).
Eichner, A. (1976) *The Megacorp and Oligopoly* (Cambridge: Cambridge University Press).
Eichner, A. (ed.), (1979a) *A Guide to Post-Keynesian Economics* (London: Macmillan).
Eichner, A. (1979b) 'A Post-Keynesian short-period model', *Journal of Post-Keynesian Economics* (Summer).
Feiwel, G. (1975) *The Intellectual Capital of Michal Kalecki* (Knoxville: University of Tennessee Press).
Frisch, R. and Holme, H. (1935) 'The characteristic solutions of a mixed difference and differential equation occurring in economic dynamics', *Econometrica* (April).
Garegnani, P. (1979) *Valore e domanda effettiva* (Torino: Einaudi).
Garegnani, P. and Petri, F. (1982) 'Marxismo e teoria economica oggi', in AA. VV., *Storia del marxismo* (Torino: Einaudi).
Graziani, A. (1981a) *Teoria economica. Macroeconomia* (Napoli: ESI).
Graziani, A. (1981b) 'Keynes e il "Trattato della moneta", in Graziani, A., Jossa, B. and Imbriani, C. (eds.) *Studi di economia keynesiana* (Napoli: Liguori).
Graziani, A. (1982) 'L'analisi marxista e la struttura del capitalismo moderno', in AA. VV., *Storia del marxismo* (Torino: Einaudi).
Haavelmo, T. (1945) 'The multiplier effect of balanced budget', *Econometrica* (October).
Hall, R. and Hitch, G. (1939) 'Price theory and business behaviour', *Oxford Economic Papers* (May).
Hansen, B. (1981) 'Unemployment, Keynes and the Stockholm theory', *History of Political Economy* (Summer).
Hark, S. (1980) 'Primary products in a Kaleckian two-sectors model', *Australian Economic papers* (June).
Harrod, R. (1936) *The Trade Cycle* (Oxford: Clarendon Press).
Harrod, R. (1951) *The Life of J.M. Keynes* (London: Macmillan).
Hayek, F. (1931) 'Reflections on the pure theory of money of Mr. J.M. Keynes', *Economica* (August).

Hicks, J. (1935) 'A suggestion to simplify the theory of money', *Econometrica* (February); reprinted in Hicks, J. (1982).

Hicks, J. (1936) 'Mr. Keynes's Theory of Employment', *Economic Journal* (June).

Hicks, J. (1946) *Value and Capital* (Oxford: Oxford University Press).

Hicks, J. (1965) *Capital and Growth* (Oxford: Oxford University Press).

Hicks, J. (1967) 'A note on the *Treatise*', in Hicks, J., *Critical Essays on Monetary Theory* (Oxford: Oxford University Press).

Hicks, J. (1982) *Money, Interest and Wages. Collected Essays on Economics* (Oxford: Blackwell).

Hobsbawm, E.J. (1982) 'Il marxismo oggi: un bilancio aperto', in AA.VV., *Storia del marxismo* (Torino: Einaudi).

Jossa, B. (1989) 'Class struggle and income distribution in Kaleckian theory', in Sebastiani, M. (ed.), (1989).

Kahn, R. (1931) 'The relation of home investment to unemployment', *Economic Journal* (June).

Kahn, R. (1954) 'Some notes on liquidity preference', *Manchester School Review* (September); reprinted in Kahn, R. (1972).

Kahn, R. (1972) *Selected Essays on Employment and Growth* (Cambridge: Cambridge University Press).

Kahn, R. (1978) 'Some aspects of the development of Keynes' thought', *Journal of Economic Literature* (June).

Kaldor, N. (1934) 'Mrs. Robinson's *Economics of Imperfect Competition', Economica* (August); reprinted in Kaldor, N. (1960).

Kaldor, N. (1956) 'Alternative theories of distribution', *Review of Economic Studies*, 2; reprinted in Kaldor, N. (1960).

Kaldor, N. (1958) 'Capital accumulation and economic growth' (presented at the IEA Conference, Corfù); reprinted in Kaldor, N. (1978).

Kaldor, N. (1960) *Essays on Value and Distribution* (London: Duckworth).

Kaldor, N. (1966) 'Marginal productivity and macroeconomic theories of distribution', *Review of Economic Studies*, 4; reprinted in Kaldor, N. (1978).

Kaldor, N. (1976) 'Inflation and recession in the world economy', *Economic Journal* (December); reprinted in Kaldor, N. (1978).

Kaldor, N. (1978) *Further Essays on Economic Theory* (London: Duckworth).

Kaldor, N. (1980) 'Monetarism and the U.K. monetary policy', *Cambridge Journal of Economics* (December).

Kaldor, N. (1981) *Origins of New Monetarism* (Cardiff: University College).

Kaldor, N. (1982a) *The Scourge of Monetarism* (Oxford: Oxford University Press).

Kaldor, N. (1982b) *Limitations of the 'General Theory*' (Oxford: Oxford University Press).

Kaldor N. (1989) 'Personal recollections on Michal Kalecki', in Sebastiani, M. (ed.) (1989).

Kalecki, M. (1933a, 1933b) *Proba Teorii Koniunkturi* (An essay on the theory of the business cycle) (Warsaw); partially reprinted (as (1933a)) in Kalecki, M. (1971b, pp. 1–14); integrally reprinted (as (1933b)) in Kalecki, M. (1991, vol.I, pp. 65–108).

Kalecki, M. (1934a) 'On foreign trade and domestic export'; reprinted in Kalecki, M. (1971b).

Kalecki, M. (1934b) 'Three Systems'; reprinted in Kalecki, M. (1991, vol.I).

Kalecki, M. (1935a) 'Essai d'une théorie du mouvement ciclique del affaires', *Revue d'economie politique*, 2.

Kalecki, M. (1935b) 'A macrodynamic theory of business cycle', *Econometrica* (July).

Kalecki, M. (1935c) 'Stimulating the business upswing in nazi Germany'; reprinted in Kalecki, M. (1971b).

Kalecki, M. (1935d) 'The mechanism of business upswing'; reprinted in Kalecki, M. (1971b).

Kalecki, M. (1935e) 'The business upswing and the balance of payments'; reprinted in Kalecki, M. (1969).

Kalecki, M. (1936) 'Some remarks on Keynes's theory', *Ekonomista*, 3; reprinted in Kalecki, M. (1991, vol.I).

Kalecki, M. (1937a) 'The principle of increasing risk', *Economica* (November).

Kalecki, M. (1937b) 'A theory of business cycle', *Review of Economic Studies* (February).

Kalecki, M. (1937c) 'A theory of commodity, income and capital taxation', *Economic Journal* (September); reprinted in Kalecki, M. (1971b).

Kalecki, M. (1938a) 'The determinants of the distribution of national income', *Econometrica* (April).

Kalecki, M. (1938b) 'The lesson of the Blum experiment', *Economic Journal* (March).

Kalecki, M. (1938c) 'Mr. Kalecki's principle of increasing risk: a reply', *Economica* (November).

Kalecki, M. (1939a) *Essays on the Theory of Economic Fluctuations* (London: Allen & Unwin).

Kalecki, M. (1939b) 'Money and real wages', reprinted in Kalecki, M. (1969).

Kalecki, M. (1940a) 'The supply curve of an industry under imperfect competitive conditions', *Review of Economic Studies* (February).

Kalecki, M. (1940b) 'The short-term rate of interest and the long-term', *Oxford Economic Papers* (September).

Kalecki, M. (1941a) 'The short-term rate of interest and the velocity of cash circulation', *Review of Economics and Statistics* (May).

Kalecki, M. (1941b) 'What is inflation?', *Oxford Institute of Statistics Bulletin* (7 June).

Kalecki, M. (1941c) 'General rationing', *Oxford Institute of Statistics Bulletin* (11 January).

Kalecki, M. (1942a) 'A theory of profits', *Economic Journal* (June–September).

Kalecki, M. (1942b) 'Mr. Whitman on the concept of the "degree of monopoly"', *Economic Journal*, (April).

Kalecki, M. (1943a) 'Political aspects of full employment', *Political Quarterly*, 4; reprinted in Kalecki, M. (1991, vol.I).

Kalecki, M. (1943b) *Studies in Economic Dynamics* (Aberdeen: Aberdeen University Press).

Kalecki, M. (1944) 'Three ways to full employment', in AA.VV., *The Economics of Full Employment* (Oxford: Oxford University Press); reprinted in AA.VV. (1967).

Kalecki, M. (1945) 'Full employment by stimulating private investments?', *Oxford Economic Papers* (March).

Kalecki, M. (1950) 'A note on long-run unemployment', *Review of Economic Studies*, 1.
Kalecki, M. (1954) *The Theory of Economic Dynamics* (London: Allen & Unwin).
Kalecki, M. (1956) 'The economic situation in the U.S. as compared with the pre-war period'; reprinted in Kalecki, M. (1972b).
Kalecki, M. (1961) 'Economic aspects of West German rearmament'; reprinted in Kalecki, M. (1991, vol.II).
Kalecki, M. (1962a) 'The economic situation in the USA, 1956–1961', reprinted in Kalecki, M. (1991, vol.II).
Kalecki, M. (1962b) 'Observations on the theory of economic growth', *Economic Journal* (March).
Kalecki, M. (1965) 'Econometric models and historical materialism', in AA. VV., *Political Economy and Econometrics. Essays in Honour of Oscar Lange* (London: Pergamon Press).
Kalecki, M. (1967a) 'Vietnam and U.S. big business'; reprinted in Kalecki, M. (1972b).
Kalecki, M. (1967b) 'The problem of effective demand with Tugan-Baranowski and Rosa Luxemburg'; reprinted in Kalecki, M. (1971b).
Kalecki, M. (1968a) 'The determination of the rate of growth of a socialist economy under conditions of unlimited supply of labour', in AA. VV., *Essays on Planning and Economic Development* (Warsaw).
Kalecki, M. (1968b) 'The Marxian equations of reproduction and modern economics', *Social Sciences Information*, 6; reprinted in Kalecki, M. (1991, vol.II).
Kalecki, M. (1968c) 'Trend and business cycle reconsidered', *Economic Journal* (June); reprinted in Kalecki, M. (1971b).
Kalecki, M. (1969) *Studies in the Theory of Business Cycles (1933–1939)* (New York: A.McKelley).
Kalecki, M. (1971a) 'Class struggle and the distribution of income', *Kyklos*, 1; reprinted in Kalecki, M. (1971b).
Kalecki, M. (1971b) *Selected Essays on the Dynamics of the Capitalist Economy* (Cambridge: Cambridge University Press).
Kalecki, M. (1972a) *Selected Essays on the Economic Growth of the Socialist and Mixed Economy* (Cambridge: Cambridge University Press).
Kalecki, M. (1972b) *The Last Phase in the Transformation of Capitalism* (New York: Monthly Review Press).
Kalecki, M. (1976) *Essays on Developing Economies* (Hassocks: Harvester Press).
Kalecki, M. (1991) *Collected Works of Michal Kalecki (vols.I–II)* (edited by J.Osiatynski) (Oxford: Clarendon Press).
Keynes, J.M. (1972–1989) *The Collected Writings of John Maynard Keynes* (hereafter *CW*) (*vols.I–XXX*) (London: Macmillan).
Keynes, J.M. (1925a) 'Am I a liberal?', *Nation and Athenaeum* (8–15 August, August); reprinted in *CW*, vol. IX, pp. 295–306.
Keynes, J.M. (1925b) 'The economic consequences of Mr. Churchill', *Evening Standard*, (22, 24 July); reprinted in *CW*, vol. IX, pp. 207–30.
Keynes, J.M. (1925c) 'A short view on Russia', *Nation and Athenaeum*, (10, 17, 25 October); reprinted in *CW*, vol. IX, pp. 253–71.
Keynes, J.M. (1926) *The End of the Laissez-faire* (London: Hogarth Press); reprinted in *CW*, vol. IX, pp. 272–94.

Keynes, J.M. and Henderson, H. (1929) *Can Lloyd George Do It?* (London); partially reprinted in *CW*, vol. IX, pp. 86–125.

Keynes, J.M. (1930a) *A Treatise on Money* (London: Macmillan); reprinted as *CW*, vol. V.

Keynes, J.M. (1930b) 'Economic possibilities for our grandchildren', *Nation and Athenaeum* (11–18 October); reprinted in *CW*, vol. IX, pp. 321–34.

Keynes, J.M. (1931) 'An economic analysis of unemployment'; reprinted in *CW*, vol. XIII, pp. 343–67.

Keynes, J.M. (1932) 'State planning', (radiophonic speech, 14 March); reprinted in *CW*, vol. XXI, pp. 84–92.

Keynes, J.M. (1933a) 'The means to prosperity', *The Times*, (13–16 March); reprinted in *CW*, vol. IX, pp. 335–66.

Keynes, J.M. (1933b) 'Malthus', in *Essays in Bibliography* (London: Macmillan); reprinted in *CW*, vol. X, pp. 71–108.

Keynes, J.M. (1933c) 'National self-sufficiency', *The New Statesmen* (8–15 July); reprinted in CW, vol. XXI, pp. 233–46.

Keynes, J.M. (1933d) 'The "New Deal"', *The New York Times* (31 December); reprinted in *CW*, vol. XXI, pp. 289–96.

Keynes, J.M. (1934) 'Poverty in plenty: is the economic system self-adjusting?', *The Listener* (21 November); reprinted in *CW*, vol. XIII, pp. 485–92.

Keynes, J.M. (1936a) *The General Theory of Employment, Interest and Money* (London: Macmillan); reprinted as *CW*, vol. VII.

Keynes, J.M. (1936b) 'The general theory of employment', *Economic Journal* (February); reprinted in *CW*, vol. XIV, pp. 109–23.

Keynes, J.M. (1937a) 'Alternative theories of the rate of interest', *Economic Journal* (June); reprinted in *CW*, vol. XIV, pp. 201–15.

Keynes, J.M. (1937b) 'The ex-ante theory of interest rate', *Economic Journal* (December); reprinted in CW, vol. XIV, pp. 215–23.

Keynes, J.M. (1937c) 'How to avoid a slump', *The Times*, (12, 14 January); reprinted in *CW*, vol. XXI, pp. 384–95.

Keynes, J.M. (1937d) 'Some economic consequences of a declining population', *Eugenics Review* (April); reprinted in *CW*, vol. XIV, pp. 124–33.

Keynes, J.M. (1939) 'Relative movements of real wages and output', *Economic Journal* (March); reprinted in *CW*, vol. VII, pp. 394–412.

Keynes, J.M. (1940) 'How to pay for the war', *The Times* (14–15 February); reprinted in *CW*, vol. XXII, pp. 40–66.

Klein, L. (1947a) 'Theories of effective demand and employment', *Journal of Political Economy* (April).

Klein, L. (1947b) *The Keynesian Revolution* (London: Macmillan).

Klein, L. (1951) 'The life of J. M. Keynes', *Journal of Political Economy* (October.)

Kregel, J. (1973) *The Reconstruction of Political Economy* (London: Macmillan).

Kregel, J. (1976) 'Economic methodology in the face of uncertainty', *Economic Journal* (June).

Kregel, J. (1985) 'Deficit financing, economic policy and liquidity preference', in Vicarelli, F. (ed.) (1983).

Kriesler, P. (1987) *Kalecki's Microanalysis* (Cambridge: Cambridge University Press).

Landgren, K.G. (1960) *Den 'Nya Ekonomien' i Sverige* (Stockholm: Almqvist and Wiksell).

Lange, O. (1939) *The Neoclassical School of Economics* (Warsaw).

Lange, O. (1941) 'Review of Kalecki's "Essays in the Theory of Economic Fluctuations"', *Journal of Political Economy* (June).

Lange, O. (1963) *Political Economy* (vol.I) (London: Pergamon Press).

Leijonhufvud, A. (1968) *On Keynesian Economics and the Economics of Keynes* (Oxford: Oxford University Press).

Lerner, A. (1934) 'The concept of monopoly and the measurement of monopoly power', *Review of Economic Studies* (June).

Lindhal, E. (1930) *Penningpolitikens Medel* (The method of monetary policy) (Lund); reprinted in Lindhal, E. (1939).

Lindhal, E. (1932) 'Offentliga arbeten i depressionstider' (Public works in times of depression), *Proceedings of the Swedish Economic Society* (December).

Lindhal, E. (1939) *Studies in the Theory of Money and Capital* (London: Allen & Unwin).

Luxemburg, R. (1951) *The Accumulation of Capital* (London: Routledge & Kegan Paul).

Marshall, A. (1891) *Principles of Economics* (London: Macmillan).

Marx, K. (1969) *Theories of the Surplus Value* (London: Lawrence & Wishart).

Marx, K. (1977) *Capital* (vol.I) (New York: Vintage Books Editions).

Marx, K. (1981a) *Capital* (vol.II) (New York: Vintage Books Editions).

Marx, K. (1981b) *Capital* (vol. III) (New York: Penguin Books).

Matteuzzi, M. (1982) 'Note sulla teoria degli effetti delle imposte di M. Kalecki', *Studi economici*, 14.

Merton, R. (1961) 'Singleton and Multiples in Science', *Proceedings of the American Philosophical Society* (October); reprinted in Merton, R. (1973) *The Sociology of Science: Theoretical and Empirical Investigations* (Chicago: University of Chicago Press).

Messori, M. (1977) 'Kalecki e Keynes: un'analisi delle differenze', *Annali della Fondazione Einaudi*.

Milgate, M. (1982) *Capital and Employment* (London: Academic Press).

Minsky, H. (1975) *Keynes* (New York: Columbia University Press).

Moggridge, D. (1976) *Keynes* (Glasgow: Fontana Collins).

Morishima, M. (1973) *Marx's Economics. A Dual Theory of Value and Growth* (Cambridge: Cambridge University Press).

Moore, B. (1984) 'Keynes and the endogeneity of the money stock', *Studi economici*, 22.

Myrdal, G. (1934) *Finanspolitikens Ekonomista Verkningar* (The economic effects of fiscal policy) (Stockholm: Kungl. Boktryckeriet).

Myrdal, G. (1939) *Monetary Equilibrium* (London: Hodge & Co.) (enlarged version of 'Om Penningteoretisk Jamvikt', *Economisk Tidskrift* (1931)).

Myrdal, G. (1972) *Against the Stream*, (New York: Pantheon Books).

Nuti, D. (1970) 'Vulgar economics in the theory of income distribution', *De Economist*.

Ohlin, B. (1932) 'Prisstegringens Problem', *Det Ekonomiske Laget*.

Ohlin, B. (1933) 'Till fragan om penningteoriens Upplagning' (On the question of the construction of monetary theory) *Ekonomisk Tidskrift*, 2; printed in English as 'On the formulation of monetary theory', *History of Political Economy* (Fall).

Ohlin, B. (1934) *Penningpolitik, Offentliga Arbeten (etc.)* (Monetary policy, public works, subsidies and tariff policy as remedies for unemployment) (Stockholm: Kungl. Boktryckeriet).

Ohlin, B. (1937) 'Some notes on the Stockholm theory of savings and investment', *Economic Journal* (March).
Ohlin, B. (1950) *The Problem of Employment Stabilization* (Oxford: Oxford University Press).
Ohlin, B. (1977) 'Some comments on Keynesianism and the Swedish theory of expansion before 1935', in Patinkin, D. and Leith, J. (eds.) (1977).
Ohlin, B. (1978) 'Keynesian economics and the Stockholm School. A comment on Patinkin's paper', *Scandinavian Journal of Economics*, 2.
Osiatynski, J. (1989) 'A note on Kalecki's and Keynes's unemployment equilibrium', in Sebastiani, M. (ed.), (1992).
Pasinetti, L. (1962) 'Rate of profit and income distribution', *Review of Economic Studies* (October); reprinted in Pasinetti, L. (1974b).
Pasinetti, L. (1974a) 'The economics of effective demand'; in Pasinetti, L. (1974b).
Pasinetti, L. (1974b) *Growth and Income Distribution. Essays in Economic Theory* (Cambridge: Cambridge Unversity Press).
Patinkin, D. (1976) *Keynes' Monetary Thought: A Study of Its Development* (Durham: Duke University Press).
Patinkin, D. (1978a) 'Some observations on Ohlin's 1933 article', *History of Political Economy* (Fall).
Patinkin, D. (1978b) 'On the relations between Keynesian economics and the Stockholm School', *Scandinavian Journal of Economics*, 2.
Patinkin, D. (1982) *Anticipations of the General Theory?* (Oxford: Blackwell).
Patinkin, D. and Leith, J. (eds.) (1977) *Keynes, Cambridge and the General Theory* (London: Macmillan).
Pigou, A.C. (1912) *Wealth and Welfare* (London: Macmillan).
Pigou, A.C. (1933) *The Theory of Unemployment* (London: Macmillan).
Radcliffe Report (1959) *Report of the Committee on the Working of the Monetary System* (London).
Riach, P. (1971) 'Kalecki's degree of monopoly reconsidered', *Australian Economic Papers* (June).
Robertson, D. (1926) *Banking Policy and the Price Level* (London: King & Son).
Robertson, D. (1936) 'Review of Mr. Keynes *General Theory*', *Quarterly Journal of Economics* (November).
Robinson, A.E. (1947) 'J.M.Keynes (1893–1946)', *Economic Journal* (March).
Robinson, J. (1933a) *The Economics of Imperfect Competition* (London: Macmillan)
Robinson, J. (1933b) 'The theory of money and the analysis of output', *Review of Economic Studies* (October); reprinted in Robinson, J. (1951).
Robinson, J. (1936) 'Review of Harrod's *The Trade Cycle*', *Economic Journal* (December); reprinted in Robinson, J. (1951).
Robinson, J. (1941) 'Marx and Keynes', *Economic Journal* (June–September); reprinted in Robinson, J. (1951).
Robinson, J. (1949) *An Essay on Marxian Economics* (London: Macmillan).
Robinson, J. (1951) *Collected Papers* (vol.I) (Oxford: Blackwell).
Robinson, J. (1956) *The Accumulation of Capital* (Oxford: Macmillan).
Robinson, J. (1957) 'The theory of distribution', *Economie Appliqué.* (October–December); reprinted in Robinson, J. (1960b).
Robinson, J. (1960a) *Exercises in Economic Analysis* (London: Macmillan).
Robinson, J. (1960b) *Collected Papers* (vol. II) (Oxford: Blackwell).

Robinson, J. (1962a) '*The General Theory* after twenty-five years', *Economic Journal* (September); reprinted in Robinson, J. (1965).
Robinson, J. (1962b) 'A model of accumulation', in Robinson, J., *Essays in the Theory of Economic Growth* (London: Macmillan).
Robinson, J. (1964) 'Kalecki and Keynes', in AA. VV., *Essays in Honour of M. Kalecki* (Warsaw); reprinted in Robinson, J. (1965).
Robinson, J. (1965) *Collected Papers* (vol. III) (Oxford: Blackwell).
Robinson, J. (1969) 'A further note', *Review of Economic Studies* (April).
Robinson, J. (1977) 'Kalecki and the economics of capitalism', *Oxford Bulletin of Statistics*.
Robinson, J. (1978) 'Keynes and Ricardo', in Robinson, J. (1979b).
Robinson, J. (1979a) 'Who is a Marxist?', in Robinson, J. (1979b).
Robinson, J. (1979b) *Collected Papers* (vol. V) (Oxford: Blackwell).
Rothschild, K. (1947) 'Price theory and oligopoly', *Economic Journal* (September).
Samuelson, P. (1967) 'Marxian economics as economics', *American Economic Review* (May).
Sardoni, C. (1987) *Marx and Keynes on Economic Recessions* (Brighton: Wheatsheaf).
Sardoni, C. (1989) 'Some aspects of Kalecki's theory of profits: its relationships with Marx's schemes of reproduction', in Sebastiani M. (ed.), (1989).
Sawyer, M. (1985) *The Economics of Michal Kalecki* (London: Macmillan).
Sawyer, M. (1989) 'Kalecki's economics and explanations of economic crises', in Sebastiani, M. (ed.), (1989).
Schumpeter, J.A. (1954a) *History of Economic Analysis* (London: Allen & Unwin).
Schumpeter, J.A. (1954b) *Capitalism, Socialism, Democracy* (London: Allen & Unwin).
Sebastiani, M. (1983) 'Prezzi ed accumulazione di capitale nei modelli post-keynesiani', *Quaderni dell'Università di Camerino*.
Sebastiani, M. (1984) 'On the theory of profits in Keynes' Treatise', *Rivista di Politica Economica Selected Papers*, 18.
Sebastiani, M. (1985) *L'equilibrio di sottoccupazione nel pensiero di M.Kalecki*, (Roma: Nuova Italia Scientifica).
Sebastiani, M. (ed.), (1989) *Kalecki's Relevance Today* (London: Macmillan).
Sebastiani, M. (1991) 'Observations on Marx's and Kalecki's approaches to the theory of effective demand', in Caravale, G. (ed.), *Marx and Modern Economic Analysis* (Aldershot: Edward Elgar).
Sebastiani, M. (ed.), (1992) *The Notion of Equilibrium in the Keynesian Theory* (London: Macmillan).
Sordi, S. (1989) 'Some notes on the second version of Kalecki's business-cycle theory', in Sebastiani, M. (ed.), (1989).
Sraffa, P. (1925) 'Sulle relazioni fra costo e quantità prodotta', *Annali di economia*.
Sraffa, P. (1926) 'The laws of return under competitive conditions', *Economic Journal* (December).
Steiger, O. (1976) 'B.Ohlin and the origins of Keynesian revolution', *History of Political Economy* (Fall).
Steiger, O. (1978) 'Prelude to the theory of monetary economy: origins and significance of Ohlin's 1933 approach to monetary theory', *History of Political Economy* (Fall).

Steindl, J. (1952) *Maturity and Stagnation of American Capitalism* (Oxford: Oxford University Press); reprinted by Monthly Review Press, New York (1976).

Steindl, J. (1966) 'On maturity in capitalist economies', in AA. VV. (1966).

Steindl, J. (1981) 'Ideas and concepts for long run growth', *Banca Nazionale del Lavoro Quarterly Review* (March).

Sweezy, P., (1939) 'Demand under conditions of oligopoly', *Journal of Political Economy* (August).

Sweezy, P. (1942) *The Theory of Capitalist Development* (New York: Monthly Review Press).

Sylos Labini, P. (1961) *Oligopoly and Technical Progress*, trans (Cambridge, Mass.: Harvard University Press, 1969).

Thomas, B. (1937) *Monetary Policy and Crisis. A Study of Swedish Experience* (London: Routledge & Sons).

Tinbergen, J. (1935) 'Annual Survey: suggestions on quantitative business cycle theory', *Econometrica* (July).

Tonveronachi, M. (1983) *Keynes: dall'instabilità all'equilibrio di sottoccupazione* (Roma: Nuova Italia Scientifica).

Uhr, C.G. (1977) 'Economists and policymaking 1930–1936: Sweden's experience', *History of Political Economy* (Spring).

Vicarelli, F. (1977) *Keynes. The Instability of Capitalism* (trans, London: Macmillan, 1985).

Vicarelli, F. (ed.),(1983) *Keynes's Relevance Today* (trans, London: Macmillan, 1985).

Weintraub, S. (1979) 'Generalizing Kalecki and simplifying macroeconomics', *Journal of Post-Keynesian Economics* (Spring).

Weintraub, S. (1981) 'An eclectic theory of income shares', *Journal of Post-Keynesian Economics*, (Fall).

Weintraub, S. (1983) 'Una teoria macroeconomica della distribuzione per disperdere le nebbie dell'economia', *Moneta e Credito* (March).

Whitman, R.H. (1941) 'A note on the concept of degree of monopoly', *Economic Journal* (June–September).

Wicksell, K. (1898) *Monetary Interest and Price Level* (Stockholm).

Wood, A. (1975) *A Theory of Profits* (Cambridge: Cambridge University Press).

Index of Authors

Index of Subjects